THE POLYPHONY
OF JEWISH CULTURE

THE POLYPHONY
OF JEWISH CULTURE

Benjamin Harshav

Stanford University Press
Stanford, California

Stanford University Press
Stanford, California

Printed in the United States of America on acid-free, archival-quality paper

Library of Congress Cataloging-in-Publication Data
Harshav, Benjamin, 1928-
  The polyphony of Jewish culture / Benjamin Harshav.
    p. cm.
  Includes bibliographical references.
  ISBN 978-0-8047-5512-2 (cloth : alk. paper)
  1. Jews--Intellectual life--20th century. 2. Hebrew literature, Modern--History and criticism. 3. Yiddish poetry--20th century--History and criticism. 4. Jews--Identity.
I. Title.
DS113.H35 2007
305.892'4--dc22
                              2007005724

Chapter 9: From A. Sutzkever: *Selected Poetry and Prose by A. Sutzkever* [Barbara and Benjamin Harshav, trans.]. Introduction by Benjamin Harshav. © 1991 The Regents of the University of California, The University of California Press.

Chapter 5: From Benjamin Harshav, Preface and Introduction to *The Last Days of the Jerusalem of Lithuania*, © 2002. Reprinted with permission of Yale University Press.

Chapter 8: From Benjamin Harshav, "The Role of Language in Modern Art: On Texts and Subtexts in Chagall's Paintings." *Modernism/Modernity* 1:2 (1994), 51–87. © The Johns Hopkins University Press. Reprinted with permission of the Johns Hopkins University Press.

Designed by Bruce Lundquist
Typeset at Stanford University Press in 10/14 Minion

CONTENTS

Preface   vii

CULTURE AND HISTORY

1   Theses on the Historical Context of the Modern
    Jewish Revolution   3

2   Multilingualism   23

3   The Crisis of Jewish Identity: S.Y. Agnon's *Only Yesterday*   41

4   American Poetry in Yiddish and its Background   61

5   The Last Days of the Jerusalem of Lithuania   133

ART AND POETRY

6   On the Beginnings of Israeli Poetry and
    Yehuda Amichai's Quatrains: A Memoir   175

7   The Modern Hebrew Poem Itself:
    Nathan Alterman, Abba Kovner   187

8   The Role of Language in Chagall's Early Paintings   209

9   A. Sutzkever: Life and Poetry   253

10   Note on the Systems of Hebrew Versification: Bible to Present   271

Sources of the Chapters   287

PREFACE

Modern Jewish culture speaks with many voices.

Medieval Jewry was framed by its religion; there was an absolute boundary that defined a person either as a Jew or not. Being a Jew was a total framework, legal and mandatory. In the secular world Jewishness can be partial and voluntary. Many autonomous expressions, organizations and centers flourished in the modern age. Jews developed a new culture in Yiddish, in Hebrew, and in the languages of the global Diaspora. They built new institutions and wrote new types of texts in Russia, Poland, Germany, America, Argentina, Israel. Each movement, genre or ideological expression was a warm home for a group of adherents.

This book tries to reflect the polyphony of voices that make up together the totality of modern Jewish culture. The book grew out of a collection of essays written in English on various occasions. I tried to zoom-in on specific issues, understand the essential aspects of each phenomenon and mediate it to an English-reading audience. Indeed, several essays were first introductions to books. There is no attempt at being scholarly or comprehensive, just to cast a map of aspects and problems that touch the horizons of modern Jewish identity.

The framework is historical. It starts with the context of the Modern Jewish Revolution, which I developed in my earlier books, *The Meaning of Yiddish* and *Language in Time of Revolution*. I point out the unique situation in which the Jews found themselves in Eastern Europe in the nineteenth century, where they constituted—for the first time in history—an absolute majority on a polka-dotted map of hundreds of towns. And ends with the intensive life they conducted in the clutches of horror in the last days of Jerusalem of Lithuania. I try to make a case for seeing not one but two Holocausts: the physical annihilation of six million people (among fifty million who died in World War II) and the very different demise of a nation, a culture, a history.

I analyze the nature of multilingualism as a universal phenomenon and its place in the history of the Jews. I discuss the crisis of Jewish identity, the ambivalence between the Land of Israel and Diaspora, and between an orthodox and secular identity, as powerfully evoked in the key novel of that fundamentalist modernist S.Y. Agnon.

Several essays deal with Hebrew and Yiddish poetry, notably the flourishing of American poetry in the Yiddish language in the twentieth century. A long essay exposes the uses Marc Chagall made of the idioms of his first language, Yiddish, an example of language as a subtext in painting. And finally, a brief Note defines the basic forms of Hebrew verse from the Bible to modernism.

All essays were edited for this volume, yet substantially they remained as first written on various occasions. A list of the original sources of the articles is appended.

The interested reader will find further ideas in my published Hebrew writings and in the companion volume on literary theory, *Explorations on Poetics*.

ACKNOWLEDGMENTS

Most of the essays published here were provoked by the intelligent and beautiful translations made from several languages by my wife Barbara Harshav.

I thank the various publishers who encouraged my work and the assistants who helped me in the course of the years. The shape of the present manuscript gained a lot of time and precision by the work of Mary Schnabel from AccuSpeed in Hamden, CT.

CULTURE AND HISTORY

1 THESES ON THE HISTORICAL CONTEXT OF THE MODERN JEWISH REVOLUTION[1]

The new situation of the Jews in the world of the twentieth century came as a result of two big historical processes, unprecedented in Jewish history: a) the creation of a Jewish majority with its own language and national culture in a network of small towns over a vast territory in the Russian Empire in the nineteenth century; b) the modern Jewish revolution, which rejected the modes of existence and behavior of the small-town Jews and embraced the values and systems of European secular culture.

Needless to say, the Holocaust and the establishment of the state of Israel were events of momentous impact that shook the whole system, but the basic features of the transformations remained the same. Except that now the achievements of assimilated Jews centered not in Russia and Germany but in the U.S., and the internal culture shifted from Yiddish to Hebrew and from a national, trans-territorial community to a state, concomitantly.

The following theses aim at elucidating some basic concepts of a general model for the understanding of the transformations of the Jews in the modern age.[2]

---

1 Conference in Berlin, 2003. I thank my friends Menachem Brinker and Michael Brener for their valuable remarks on the draft of this paper.

2 In this paper, I am using statistical data from various sources. The figures mentioned are tentative and intended primarily to point out the nature of situations or tendencies.

1   THE MODERN JEWISH REVOLUTION

1.1   The modern Jewish Revolution brought about a total transformation of the Jews, their languages, conceptual worlds, professions, education, national institutions, and place in geography and in general history.[3] The negation of the old modes of existence was almost universal, but the new, positive answers—in theory as well as in reality—created a centrifugal movement in all directions, intrinsic as well as extrinsic.

1.2   In the intrinsic domain, the Modern Jewish Revolution consisted of three interlaced cultural movements: a) the foundation of a network of Jewish social and cultural institutions: schools, publishers, newspapers, libraries, trade unions, community governments (*kehilas*), as well as societies for promoting education, health, work and technology, Jewish art, Jewish theater, etc.; b) the emergence of a whole gamut of ideologies and political parties; and c) the flourishing of a polyphonic literature and textual culture in 2 + 1 languages: Yiddish, Hebrew, and the languages of state and culture, different from country to country. In many cases, several foreign languages were included: Russian and German (Dubnov) or Russian and French (Levinas). Dubnov wrote his multivolume history of the Jews in Russian, the history of Hasidism in Hebrew, and topical lectures in Yiddish. Martin Buber wrote his major works in German and later in Hebrew.

This three-pronged package amounted to nation-building—indeed, there was an unquestionable self-awareness of a Jewish nation—yet without power over a territory.

1.3   The whole cluster was then transplanted to places of immigration— and met with only temporary or partial success. Among other places, it was brought to Palestine by the founders of the Yishuv. Thus, the labor movement in Palestine founded not just trade unions but a newspaper, a publishing house, an educational network, health insurance, cultural clubs, and so on. Hebrew literature was said to be their "state on the road." The revived Hebrew language was expanded to cover all the new domains of life: education, agriculture, politics, science, military activities, and self-government. The language provided the lifeblood of the new nation.

1.4   The Jewish revolution was fueled by the intellectual and revolutionary fermentation in Russian society itself (in which many Jews played an im-

---

3   See my book *Language in Time of Revolution* (Stanford, CA: Stanford University Press, 1999).

portant role). But the internal self-image which prompted the changes was crystallized by modern Jewish literature and the ideological debates in periodicals, newspapers and at party-sponsored assemblies.

1.5   In the extrinsic direction, Jews mastered the languages of the majority countries and made indelible contributions to general culture, science, and society.

To be sure, the assimilation of Jews to the dominant language and culture had precedents throughout history. Yet it became a marked trend in the modern age since the assimilation of German Jewry in the eighteenth century—especially against the background of the East European Yiddish-speaking world.

1.6   The intrinsic move emerged first sporadically in the Haskalah (Enlightenment) of the eighteenth and nineteenth centuries, yet the new ideas were carried by only a few select individuals. It was only after the watershed year of 1882 that a full-fledged national culture crystallized. After that boundary, most of the new institutions emerged, including a multilingual modern Jewish literature, political parties, educational networks, and the state of Israel. Only after that watershed, millions of Jews—almost the whole nation—joined the process, assimilated to other languages (including Hebrew) and were involved in the transformation.

1.7   We must keep in mind that by 1900, about 6 percent of world Jewry were Sephardic or Oriental Jews, while the overwhelming majority were Ashkenazim. In the eighteenth and nineteenth centuries, the majority of world Jewry lived in Russia and in other areas formerly belonging to Poland (Silesia, Posen, Galicia). The new Jewish communities in Central and Western Europe, including most of the so-called "German" Jews, consisted largely of East-European immigrants or their descendants. It is only when those masses joined the trend that a general change in the historical situation of the Jews occurred.

2 JEWISH HISTORY AND THE HISTORY OF THE JEWS

2.1   We must distinguish between Jewish History and the History of the Jews.

Jewish History is the history of Jewish social, political, and cultural institutions and all texts and cultural products produced in Jewish languages or by or for Jewish societies in any language.

The History of the Jews is the history of all people who were considered "Jews" by themselves or by others, including persons of recent Jewish descent (religious or secular), whether participating in Jewish institutions exclusively, marginally, or not at all.

2.2   A related area is the thematization of the "Jew," i.e., the history of all external beliefs or actions directed toward the "Jews" as a distinct, recognizable social group endowed with several changing attributes—religious, national, genetic, or racial. This includes both positive and negative attitudes and actions, both anti-Semitism and support for the state of Israel. Strictly speaking, this area is part of general history, yet it is, of course, pertinent to both the history of the Jews and Jewish history proper.

2.3   The social entity labeled "Jews" cannot be defined by one essence or property, but by several shifting criteria—religious, historical, ethnic, cultural, linguistic, psychological, or biological/genetic. It designates a society, continuous in history, with changing dominant characteristics (in logical terms: a society that has a defined extension with shifting intensions). The label remains, even though the dominant trait and the mixture of traits vacillate and change. What was concomitant or peripheral in one context becomes dominant in another, and vice versa. The confusion of religion and nation, history and language, prophecy and culture—with the promotion of specific aspects in various contexts—has its firm foundations in the Bible.

Thus, today, not all religious Jews are Israelis; and not all Israelis are religious Jews. Not all Hebrew speakers are Zionists and not all Zionists are Hebrew speakers. Some Israeli religious Jews are consumers of Hebrew literature and theater and belong to the community of Hebrew culture, yet most are not; that community of culture includes mostly secular or atheist Jews. Most American Jews active in Jewish institutions are not consumers of a Hebrew or Yiddish community of culture. Children of religious Jews may become secular, while children of secular Jews may return to some form of religion or religious affiliation. Some American religious Jews are not considered religious Jews by the Israeli religious establishment. And some Americans of (partial) Jewish descent may invoke their Jewishness only when tested for some genetic disease. The same shifting definition can be observed on a diachronical scale, throughout history.

2.4   The shifting boundaries between Jewish history and the history of the Jews. We describe the Holocaust as the massacre of six million Jews and see it as a major event in Jewish history, but we do not usually include in our purview many of the same people when they were alive. A large part of the "Jews" slaughtered in the Holocaust were secular, assimilated to other languages, and did not use Jewish languages or participate in Jewish culture—or did so marginally—but acted and created as Russians, Poles, Germans, Frenchmen, Italians, Communists, physicists, novelists, psychoanalysts, etc. Their lives belong to the history of the respective nations and cultures, while their death is part of the history of the Jews.

2.5   Vestige Jewishness. We may discern two kinds of vestige Jewishness: religious and non-religious. In the census of 1897, almost 98% of the largest Jewish Diaspora in the world, the Russian Empire, declared Yiddish as their language. Two generations later, the situation totally reversed. Linguistically, in the twentieth century, most European Jews became assimilated to their respective nations and languages and did not consume Jewish culture or contribute to it. In the nineteen thirties, this included most of the three million Soviet Jews, most Jews of Germany, Hungary, France, Poland, England, Italy, etc.

In the self-styled bastion of Yiddish culture, Vilna, "the Jerusalem of Lithuania," there was a highly active library in the ghetto. As the librarian Herman Kruk[4] recorded, 80 percent of the books borrowed were in Polish with only 17 percent in Yiddish and a negligible number in Hebrew. And that in a city occupied by Poland for only one generation. Before the Holocaust, Jewish institutions in Poland, the world center of Jewish culture, were multifarious and vigorously active, but fast diminishing. In the largest Jewish community, Warsaw, with a third of a million Jews, there was not a single gymnasium in a Jewish language, and Vilna had one gymnasium in Hebrew and one in Yiddish.

2.6   Almost all Jews in the new centers—Moscow, Berlin, Tel Aviv, or New York—were children and grandchildren of immigrants (today also great-grandchildren). The saying in Berlin was "Ein echter Berliner ist aus Breslau" ("A true Berliner is from Breslau," the capital of Silesia). The Jewish cemetery in Weissensee in Berlin has some 115,000 graves, some of well-known German intellectuals or industrialists. Yet most of the parents buried there were born in one small town or another.

---

4   *The Last Days of the Jerusalem of Lithuania: Chronicles from the Vilna Ghetto and the Camps, 1939–1944,* by Herman Kruk. Edited and introduced by Benjamin Harshav; translated by Barbara Harshav, Yale University Press, 2002.

Hence, some bits and pieces of the "old home" culture survived in the transitional generations. Yet the dominant culture among them was in the new language, including Israeli Hebrew. In the U.S., the last wave of immigration was recent and there was, and still is, a plethora of Jewish activities, but these do not envelop the majority of the former "Jews." The creative contribution of assimilated Jews was not in the Jewish field: the first twenty psychoanalysts in Vienna were all Jews (most from Galicia), the Russian Formalists, the founding school of modern Poetics, were almost all Jews, and so were the members of the Frankfurt School of social criticism or the so-called "New York intellectuals" of the nineteen forties and fifties. Albert Einstein was a German physicist living in Switzerland; only with the ascent of the Nazis did he become overtly aware of his Jewish roots. The historian Peter Gay pointed out that Freud was a self-described "Godless Jew," but so were most "Jews" in this period.

2.7   True, some minimal religious link, however marginal, was observed by many of the European Jews. For example, in Poland, birth registrations were mandatory and could be done only in religious institutions, hence even secular Jews had to obtain rabbinical birth certificates, or convert. In Germany or Hungary most Jews prominent in the culture were Jews only genetically, though some went perhaps twice a year to the synagogue.

2.8   The major interbellum Polish poet Julian Tuwim identified himself as a Polish poet and intellectual and was rather disdainful of the typical "Polish Jew." Yet, while in exile in London during World War II, he wrote a famous essay, "We Polish Jews," declaring: "I am a Pole when the blood runs in my veins and a Jew when it runs out of my veins. . ." Typically, assimilated Jews have a "Tuwim complex." We can see the same in Western societies or in Russia today, where Jewish identity is largely based on solidarity with Jewish victimhood, Holocaust, or persecutions, or fear of those.

Many people of Jewish descent became aware of their Jewishness when some other Jews were in danger. Thus, the first Jewish organization in Germany emerged after the pogrom of Jews in Damascus in 1840, though culturally the two groups could not have been farther apart. The campaign "Let my people go!" conducted in the West to save Soviet Jewry in post-Stalin Russia brought about a wide awakening of "dormant Jews" both in Russia and in the West. Persecution of other Jews is the first catalyst of Jewish identity for "non-Jewish Jews" (to use Isaac Deutscher's term).

2.9   This one-sided identity also caused a slanted image of Jewish history. Although Jews had achieved considerable economic and social success in various diasporas and had also exhibited a great deal of internal creativity (including Hebrew and Yiddish poetry, medieval books of Hebrew grammar, Hasidism, and so on), the persecution-based identity of assimilated Jews endangered a distorted self-image, which often glossed over the periods and products of Jews flourishing in general society, their positive achievements and impact, as well as the culture created in internal, Jewish languages.

2.10   Jewish historiography tends to be retroactive and teleological, projecting present-day concerns on past situations, while the actual history of the Jews moved from the past into the past future. Hence, history was organized around questions such as: "How did some Jews in the past prepare or foreshadow the victory of Zionism?" or: "What were the early signs and antecedents of the Holocaust?" A truly historical perspective would ask instead: "What happened to the Jews of the nineteenth century, what did they do and where did they go in their own context?"

Historiography that is not a tool of contemporary politics will not start with foregone conclusions (to use Michael André Bernstein's apt term).

3   THREE BASIC MODELS OF JEWISH HISTORY

The history of the Jews can be described by three compelling models:

3.1   The Religious Model, which sees all Jewish history in light of a dichotomy: Promised Land vs. Diaspora or Exile. Zionism and Zionist historiography appropriated, secularized, and implemented this Religious/Zionist model. From this perspective, all periods and all Diasporas, under any political and demographic conditions, are essentially the same: "Exile" (*Goles, Galut, Gola*).

In Jewish folklore and popular perception, the exile from the Promised Land was conflated with the exile from paradise, i.e., it "Jewified" the human condition. Yet there was no wish to remedy that condition in actual history until Messiah comes. It was merely a matter for the imagination, a sign in the semiotics of culture, part of a fictional universe, a myth of identity, which was not intended to trigger any action. Thus, when Jews made a solemn wish, repeated every Passover: "Next year in Jerusalem," it was part of a ritual; they did not mean it literally. Like a dead metaphor, it was a "dead" perlocutionary expression, an image rather than an instruction for action. The Zionists were literalists, they revived the literal meanings of the same texts and required "hagshama," a realization of the "dead" metaphor or "dead" collocation.

3.2   The Dubnovian Model, which perceives Jewish history as a history of wandering centers of a "World Nation." (The key concept, "Am Olam" means both the eternal people and the people of the whole world, unattached in time and space.) Jewish cultural history can be described as a dialogue between two major centers, changing places in geography: Babylon and Eretz Israel, Sepharad and Ashkenaz, Russia and Germany, Eastern Europe and America—with smaller centers in the periphery, which may take over in times of upheaval.

In the light of this model, there are two major centers of Jewish existence and culture today: Israel and the U.S.A. (with several minor centers in Russia, France, England, Canada, Argentina, etc.). These two interdependent centers are very different from each other in their Jewish nature, culture, and ideologies. Only blindness (or first-model ideology) can overlook this fact. It makes no sense to see American Jewry (or any other Jewish community) as an inferior, "Exile" existence.

In the perspective of Jewish history, Israel, too, can be subsumed under the general Dubnovian model, as yet another historical center. If the sacrifices that accompanied the revival of Israel were for the sake of survival of the Jews, Israel may be a precarious place for that and the strength of the American center today cannot be dismissed as secondary. Indeed, without Israel and its living Jewish language, no modern, secular Jewish culture can survive. But from the experience of Jewish history, we cannot assign superiority, or higher security, to either one or the other.

3.3   The Assimilationist Model, which sees the Jews and their descendants in each country as part of the respective nations and societies. Here we may include the intellectual movement of the "Canaanites" in Israel, who wanted no link to the Jews, their forebears. Many assimilated Jews may still preserve some social affiliation with Jewish religious institutions, or some vestiges of Jewish identity-questioning. Today in the U.S., religion among Jews is the best fig leaf for assimilation. Outside of their social affiliation with a Jewish religious framework or attendance at some "Jewish" events, the daily and professional life of those people are as of any American.

Those Jews who embraced assimilation developed no far-flung ideologies or political parties for that purpose, because the Jewish identity-question is not part of the general discourse to which they had assimilated. Discussing it would mean reopening their vestige Jewishness. They don't need any explicit ideology to justify their move into another culture; the fact itself is sufficient.

3.4   At first glance, these three models seem mutually exclusive, yet selecting only one of them implies an essentialist fallacy or an ideologically motivated view of history, often derived from present-day personal concerns or politics. It is impossible to explain many phenomena in the history of the Jews without invoking all three models and shifting between them. Indeed, in actual history, people often vacillated between one model and another, or simultaneously related to several identities in messages to different addressees.

The irony is that after the Holocaust, which was based on a racial category, Jews deprived of any other cultural identity fall back to the biological (racial) identity: I am a Jew because my parents were Jews. An individual may admit that he/she is a Jew but doesn't know or is not interested in much more. Admittedly, this is an inconvenient self-definition and some individuals will seek farther to justify their categorization as a Jew.

3.5   In reality, the winning model today around the world is assimilationist, with marginal corrections. We must include in that the Hebrew culture of Israel: from the perspective of their countries of origin, all immigrants to Israel had to assimilate to a strange and powerful culture and paid for it as for any such dislocation. Rachel Katznelson, one of the pioneers of the revival of Hebrew, wrote, "We had to betray Yiddish, even though we paid for this as for any betrayal."[5]

3.6   To be philosophical about it, it was the dispersion of the Jews around the globe that had saved them from disappearing: when one community was destroyed, another budding center took over. The "innate" immigrant instinct of the Jewish masses may have been a safer bet than all the argued ideologies.

4   THE MODERN JEWISH REVOLUTION OR RENAISSANCE?

4.1   The term Revolution implies a sudden overthrow of a political or ideological system and a reevaluation of all values, world views, beliefs, and norms of behavior. In the modern age there have been several competing options for such radical changes in Jewish existence. The revolution went through the hearts and minds of each individual, his behavior and choices. Ben-Gurion spoke of a "Zionist Revolution," but that was only part of a wider, global "Jewish Revolution," a centrifugal movement catapulting Jews in all

---

5   *Language in Time of Revolution*, pp. 139–40.

directions: Zionism, Communism, Yiddish culture, Hebrew culture, assimilation, and so on. Vis-à-vis his father or grandfather, a totally assimilated Jew embodies a revolution that was not less radical than the Zionist utopia.

4.2   As I pointed out in my book *Language in Time of Revolution*, one common denominator of all those trends was a revolt against the pan-historical and pan-geographical conceptions of Talmudic Judaism and a return to history (including immediate interests, political parties, and Realpolitik). Another impulse was the shift from communal to individual consciousness (hence the centrality of literature).

Leon Wieseltier, Literary Editor of *The New Republic*, in a sharp and topical article "Against Ethnic Panic" (*The New Republic* 05.27.02) argued against the "typological thinking about history," which is "ahistorical thinking." In modern times *"a revolution in the Jewish spirit"* [emphasis mine—BH] has occurred, a return to "historical thinking" which is concrete, empirical, practical, secular. "The lesson they learned was called Zionism."

But, surely, it was not only a matter of spirit but of action and building new institutions. And it was also the lesson of the socialist and Yiddishist Bund, the Jewish anarchists, the thousands of Jewish Communists in Soviet Russia and around the globe, the millions of Assimilationists, and all other options taken by Jews—millions of Jews who did not go to Palestine but actively shaped their language and mode of existence. Wieseltier himself, a former Yeshiva student, is literary editor of an influential (non-Jewish) American political weekly and certainly not an "ahistorical" thinker, as this article confirms once again.

We must free ourselves from the habit of arranging Jewish history according to the Zionist narrative, based on a habitually slanted selection of information.

4.3   Renaissance, a term launched by Martin Buber in Germany, was used within the Jewish world itself. In Hebrew it was called: tehiya (literally: "coming to life," or "resurrection"), in Russian, the ideological language of many East-European Jewish intellectuals: Vozrozhdeniye (this was the name of a small Jewish intellectual party before World War I) and in Yiddish: renesans. In Yiddishist circles in the beginning of the twentieth century, there was an exhilarated feeling of a renaissance of Jewish culture, as expressed in the new Yiddish and Hebrew poetry, literature, theater, political thought, scholarship, secular education, and so on, with all those domains reinforcing each other. A stamp issued by the Yiddishist "Kultur-Lige" in Kiev 1919, featured the three writers pronounced as "Classics" of Yiddish literature: Mendele Moykher Sforim, Sholem-Aleichem and Y.L. Peretz only a short time after their death (in 1915–1917). The Yiddishist Chagall talks about "our renaissance."

To reduce this Renaissance to merely Hebrew is wrong for the understanding of the Hebrew revival itself, which came about through a far-reaching dialogue and competition with the other options.

4.4   Thus, the term "Renaissance" connotes the cultural revival inside Jewish culture in all languages, the sense of immense achievement (after 2000 years of stagnation). In the Hebrew sphere, we can trace it back to the "culture argument" within Zionism in 1897–1902, tapping the East European Zionists against Herzl's merely political and formal Zionism. A key text was Ahad-Ha-Am's influential "Revival of the Spirit" ("Tehiyat ha-ruah," 1902). I assume that Buber drew his concept of the Jewish Renaissance from this context or specifically from Ahad-Ha-Am's seminal essay.

4.5   The concept of Renaissance implies a) etymologically: a biological metaphor of a nation, that was once alive, then semi-dead for 2000 years (Arnold Toynbee called the Jews "a fossil of history"), and is coming to life again; b) conceptually: a parallel to the Italian Renaissance in art and literature (especially as interpreted by the then influential Jacob Burckhardt), which shifted the focus from God to the individual human being—as center of a painting and of the universe.

This double idea had been expressed already by the nineteenth-century Hebrew poet of Vilna, Adam Ha-Cohen, who related the life of the Hebrew language to the life of the nation and called for the revival of Hebrew as a spoken language and a language that covers all human disciplines and crafts (1859[6]). Here was the source of another Lithuanian Jew, Feldman, who renamed himself: Eliezer Ben-Yehuda, and his zealous appeal for the "Revival" of the Hebrew language in order to revive Hebrew literature. With the victory of Hebrew as the base language of a society, Adam Ha-Cohen's dream came true and was expanded to all domains of culture, adopted in the new Hebrew language.

4.6   What is the relation between those two terms? Revolution connotes an upheaval in the social and semiotic systems of the nation and of the individual, whereas Renaissance connotes the new achievements following that revolution. The terms are complementary, though partially overlapping.

6   See *Language in Time of Revolution*, p. 120.

It is, of course, possible—but, I think, it would be unwise—to enlarge the scope of the term "Renaissance" to include the achievements of Jews in the general domain. Marx, Freud, Durkheim, etc., are symptomatic of the modern Jewish Revolution but are not part of any Jewish Renaissance. Renaissance in its internal use connotes the productivization of the former "Luft-mentshn," flourishing of culture and scholarship, Jewish political revival, and the building of the state of Israel. It is a Renaissance within Jewish history, whereas the achievements of individual Jews in the general sphere are part of the history of general disciplines or non-Jewish national cultures, and only biographically part of the history of the Jews.

We could include these extrinsic trends, too, in the term "Renaissance," but that would imply a biological (racial) metaphor of the nation that came to life. Jews are often proud of the achievements of other Jews; even Jews within the Jewish cultural domain will boast of such "non-Jewish Jews" as Einstein, Freud, or Jonas Salk. But the link between the two domains could only be racial.

4.7   The contributions made by Jews to the general culture and science of the twentieth century can be explained by an intricate confluence of three major factors: a) traits acquired by Jews throughout history, socialized and stereotyped; b) a cluster of modes of "Jewish" discourse and behavior, deriving from the so-called "Talmudic" learning, simplified and folklorized in Yiddish, and then transferred to the behavior of Jews in other languages; c) opportunities—the modern expansion of possible fields of activity and openness of modern societies to new ideas and new fields of knowledge and creativity.

4.8   It is important to note that such achievements by Jews entering the general culture were made within the systematic, rigorous, and sophisticated frameworks of European ("Christian") science, thought, economies, etc. They were implemented by the modern Jewish Revolution, which catapulted many Jews as individuals from the confining communal domain of the *shtetl* world to Western society, its values, behavior, thought, and semiotics of discourse.

5   THE CONTEXT OF THE JEWISH REVOLUTION IN THE RUSSIAN EMPIRE

5.1   The transformation of the Jews in Eastern Europe proceeded in two interlocked stages. From a historical perspective we can see that the Modern Jewish Revolution was based on a unique phenomenon in Jewish history: the crystallization of a Jewish nation in the Russian Empire, with a Jewish majority in a network of towns over a vast territory, a self-sufficient social and cultural structure and a unifying Jewish language, Yiddish, that was long separated from its German source. The language mediated between the Hebrew-Aramaic religious tradition and the surrounding culture, and was spoken in Eastern Europe for half a millennium. This sense of being a nation (Dr. Chaim Zhitlovski called it "Yiddishland") laid the ground for the unifying and modernizing moves of the new secular trends.

5.2   The roots of this Jewish nation lie in medieval Poland, the largest country in Europe, where most of world Jewry lived in the sixteenth–eighteenth centuries. Here the Jews enjoyed a full-fledged autonomy, including tax collecting and separate jurisdiction over the Jewish population.

When Poland was dismantled toward the end of the eighteenth century, Russia received the bulk of the Jews—they came with the territory—and kept them enclosed in the same area. Renamed the Pale of Settlement, it was a huge geographical ghetto, comprising what is today Ukraine, Belarus, Lithuania, Latvia, eastern and central Poland.

In many ways, twentieth century anti-Semitism and even the state of Israel are indirect results of the partition of Poland in the late eighteenth century without resolving the Jewish problem. That includes the massive influx of former Polish Jews, marked by their foreign and much derided German accent, into Berlin and Vienna, which became a breeding ground of modern anti-Semitism.

5.3   In the nineteenth century there was a veritable demographic explosion among the Jews. Between 1800 and 1880, the Jewish population in the world rose from 2.2 million to 7.5 million. The bulk of this growth was in the Russian Empire, where the Jewish population grew at least five-fold. This growth fostered poverty (as mimicked and ridiculed by Mendele Moykher Sforim, evoking the Jewish situation in Lithuania in the eighteen fifties), but also initiative, creativity, and upward mobility.

The reasons for this growth are not quite clear. One reason could be the better health resources available to Jews, access to doctors and awareness of the importance of medicine; another may be the higher consciousness of their precarious existence. When Marc Chagall, a poor boy from the Pale, was bitten by a mad dog at the age of four, he was immediately whisked off to a doctor in St. Petersburg, even though Jews were forbidden to live there. Jews were town dwellers; even a small *shtetl* was an urban community after all.

A more important reason may be the early marriage age (often at 12–15, sometimes even before puberty), reinforced by the snatching of Jewish boys to serve 25 years in the army of Tsar Nicholas I. In addition, there were the typical serial marriages of Jewish men: when the first wife died in childbirth, or of an illness or exhaustion after having many children, the widower, aided by the socially arranged matchmaking, would promptly remarry. It was normal for Jewish families to have 8, 9, 12 children, even 18 and 24 from two consecutive wives.

This was enhanced by a veritable demographic puzzle: the preponderance of women vs. men among the Jews. In all the towns of Vitebsk province there were 88 men to 100 women among Jews. Indeed, many men emigrated abroad or overseas. Were the numbers of emigrant males enough to explain the disproportion? It may appear as a mystical biological "compensation" for the Jewish losses in pogroms and persecutions. In any case, the fecundity of the Jewish population in the nineteenth century was striking.

5.4   On average, the Jews constituted about 12–15% of the population in the Pale of Settlement. But this is a misleading picture. Eighty-five to ninety percent of the Christian population lived in villages, where there were only 1.5% Jews. In the towns, however, Jews constituted two-thirds of the population. In all the towns of Vitebsk province together, 66.3% of the inhabitants were Jews. In the big cities, their number was between a third and a half or more. In Vitebsk, capital of the Province, 52.4% were Jews vs. 37% Russians and Byelorussians together (the rest were Germans, Poles, or Latvians). This preponderance of Jews in the towns was mainly a phenomenon of the nineteenth century. Thus, Yakov Leshschinsky showed for the city of Vitebsk that between 1772 (the partition of Poland and its annexation to Russia) and 1815 (after the Napoleonic wars) the Jewish population grew six-fold while the gentile population less than doubled.

Whereas in Western Europe Jews were always a small, scattered minority, lived in ghettos or on the margin of cities (the *Judengasse* in Worms, Rothenburg, Vienna, or Frankfurt), in Russia they typically lived in Jewish towns. It was the first time in Jewish history in the Diaspora that Jews dominated a whole area, based on interlinked cities and small towns The Jewish presence, thus, was dominant on a large territory, a polka-dotted map, where all cities and towns were linked by one cultural and economic network.

The geographic structure of this Jewish nation in Russia was similar to the structure of the Jewish Yishuv in Palestine in the nineteen thirties, which was seen as a Jewish state. Yet the Jews in Palestine were a minority and their prospective state covered a network of dots on the map (Kibbutzim and Jewish or mixed cities), just as in Eastern Europe.

5.5   A major factor in this sense of a Jewish nation in the Russian Pale of Settlement was the negligible role of the peasants in the growing economy and culture. Until 1861, the peasants (about 85% of the population) were serfs, who could be bought and sold with their villages. By the end of the nineteenth century, just a generation or two after their liberation, they were economically and psychologically still suffering from that subjugation.

We may compare it to the situation of American blacks, who were liberated about the same time and complain about the effects of slavery to this day, a century and a half later. In Russian literature the "people" were characterized by apathy or fatalism; were still dependent on the landowner and breadgiver, and could not easily move to another place without permission of the village council (*Obshtshina*). Thus, the villages and peasants hardly counted in the economic and cultural life of Western Russia; and in the active part of the population the Jews were not a minority at all.

5.6   It is a mistake, or at least a skewed picture (driven by either Zionist ideology or a post-Holocaust victimhood identity), to depict Jewish history in the Diaspora as a chain of persecutions. Between one wave of pogroms and another, the Jewish nation was flourishing. Jews in the Pale of Settlement had no civil rights but could prosper in the economy. Marc Chagall, a poor provincial boy with a Yiddish accent in Russian and no Right of Residence in St. Petersburg, was awarded the Second Stipend in the Imperial School for the Encouragement of the Arts in the capital. Was this anti-Semitism or philo-Semitism?

In the Pale of Settlement in the nineteenth century, Jews developed and owned most of the industrial production, banking, foresting, artisan crafts and trade. In Vitebsk province, even the export of hog-bristle (for making brushes in England) was a Jewish trade. Only the power structure was not in their hands: they were rarely represented in local administration, army, police, churches, even among postmen.

An objective measure for the economic status of the Jews can be seen in the number of their memberships in trade Guilds, bestowed by a government not necessarily sympathetic to the Jews. By 1855, in all cities and towns of Vitebsk province there were 6 Christian and 58 Jewish merchants of the First and Second Guild. In Vilna there were 21 Christians and 199 Jews of

the Third Guild—an overwhelming majority. Among the officially classi-
fied "burghers" (*meshtshane*) in Vilna, there were 5,280 Christians and 11,845
Jews, again, over two-thirds of the total. If we discount the villages, this was
very much a Jewish country.

True, thousands of peasants moved to the cities before the Revolution, especially to the capitals, and laid the foundations of the proletarian class, that
later carried the burden of the Revolution; and many peasants became merchants. But the prominent place of Jews in Western Russia and their readiness
to learn and move had prepared them for a new social place after the October
Revolution.

5.7   Simultaneously, the Jewish population as a whole was on the move;
there was a mass migration from small towns to the cities and overseas, which
enveloped most of the young and left no family without migrants. In this
Diaspora mentality, Jews had no attachment to the "soil" or to a particular
country or language, and the image of the "Wandering Jew" was internalized,
as in some of Chagall's paintings.

After the Revolution and the demise or emigration of many Russian aris-
tocrats and intellectuals, combined with the enormous expansion of the government apparatus and mass education, new cadres were urgently needed.
Furthermore, in the small towns the Jews were neither peasants nor proletarians—the two ruling classes—even when poor, they were small traders and
considered "petit-bourgeois"; hence going to the universities and the big cities
saved them from the categorization as a class enemy. The Jews filled that va-
cancy; they were a protected and trusted group, loyal to the liberating Bolshevik regime. They filled the universities, the educational system, the industry,
the secret services, the party, the academy, and so on.

But the same statistical asymmetry led to a reversal of the situation. In
the thirties, with the intense urbanization and industrialization of the Soviet
state, a new cadre of peasant origin moved into positions of power in the new
regime. The large numbers of Jews in those places were in their path and an
inevitable clash ensued. The Stalinist purges of the thirties (especially against
"Trotskyites") engulfed a disproportionately large number of Jews and actually pushed the Jews out of their prominent position in party and government. The purges of the late forties (against "cosmopolitans") pushed them
out from many positions of culture. The harsh numerus clausus in the universities under Khrushchev was threatening to complete the process.

5.8   Jews were never attached to the soil nor confined to their village, as the Slavic peasants around them were. The tradition of Jewish itinerant tailors and peddlers, moving from village to village and returning for Sabbath to the town; the dense network of trade relationships connecting the backward villages with the towns, the towns with the cities, and finally to Western Europe—all in the same language—made them habitually mobile.

Individuals who left their small *shtetl* looked back at their single *shtetl* with disgust or nostalgia, or both. But it was not the single *shtetl* that was the Jewish territory in Russia—the *shtetl* was the fictional locus of literature only—but rather the network of *shtetls*, connected to one city, with Rovs, teachers, and merchants moving back and forth. It was the second step, this Jewish territorial nation on the move, that produced the modern Jewish Revolution. The writers and the readers of the new literature were born in *shtetls* or villages but lived now in cities or went abroad. The *shtetl* served only as the iconic Jewish territory, the typical locus where Jewish types, behavior, languages, or problems could still be kept from the general urban landscape.

5.9   Jews were a transterritorial social group—both on the large European scale and in each local area. The network of Jewish settlements in the late medieval Polish East was established first when Jewish leasers of the land, *arrendars*, hired sub-arrendars, who scattered throughout the territory. Two phenomena contributed to the consolidation of this nation: Hasidism and the railroad.

In the eighteenth century, the Jewish nation was unified by the Hasidic movements, which overruled the religious autonomy of each community. All Hasidim tried to visit the Rebbe in his court, usually a small town, such as Lubavich with 1,660 Jews (67.3% of the population) or his much smaller summer place at the railroad station of Zaolshe. People from different places met there, got the Rebbe's advice or blessings, traded, concluded marriage agreements, shared Jewish gossip, etc.

5.10   In the second half of the nineteenth century, the railroad made connections easy and revolutionized Jewish life. Jews had the proverbial "shpilkes" (pins and needles in their seat, i.e., an urge to travel). Sholem Aleichem understood it when he moved the symbolic locus of Jewish existence from the *shtetl* to the railroad wagon. In Jewish terms, a province was like one large spider web with the knot in the capital city, connected, on the one hand, with neighboring spider webs and, on the other, with the capitals of Russia. Hence we are not just talking about a town of 500 or 3,000 inhabitants or a city of 30,000, but a province of 215,000 Jews (in the case of Vitebsk) living in interconnected towns (somewhat like the urban structure of contemporary North Carolina).

And toward the end of the nineteenth century, Jewish literature, newspapers, ideologies, and political parties unified the whole Pale.

The move into the cities in the Pale itself grew rapidly. Unlike the monolithic *shtetl*, cities were polyphonic, they hosted a great variety of cultural and political trends, in noisy argument with each other. For the newcomers, they were a microcosm of modern Jewish culture.

5.11   The Modern Jewish Revolution was prompted not by the *shtetl* culture, but by those who grew out of it and revolted against it. Already in the beginning of the twentieth century, the *shtetl* represented the "lost Jewish world." But if a writer or a painter wanted to evoke an authentic Jewish fictional society or anchor in it his criticism of Jewish life and destiny, he resorted to the mythified *shtetl* and its prototypes.

In the census of 1897, some 97.8% of the Jews declared Yiddish as their language. Yiddish permeated Polish Jewry sometime in the sixteenth century and lasted into the twentieth. It was the language of everyday life as well as of teaching and, later, modern literature. It unified Jewish existence, codified a unique Jewish discourse, and preserved the Jews as a distinct nation. For the first time in Jewish history, a Jewish language lived on for more than one generation in the territory of a different language group. (Yes, there is the case of Ladino, but there is no comparison to the multifunctional, ever-developing Yiddish.)

5.12   The massive Jewish population, stretching as far as the eye could see, which was culturally above the illiterate peasant of the surrounding villages and had no interest in communicating with him except for trade purposes, provided the ground for this linguistic identity. Most Jews of the Pale were not allowed into Russia proper and lived everywhere among minorities (Poles, Byelorussians, Ukrainians, Lithuanians). Their contact with Russian, the language of power and culture, was mainly through the Russian bureaucracy, that would have little contact with Jews. This reinforced the survival of Yiddish.

Yet toward the end of the nineteenth century, a whole generation learned Russian and Russian literature and through it acquired access to the values and norms of European culture. Some of them returned to their home base (in the wake of the Russian Populists) to build Jewish culture on Russian models, and European models mediated and schematized in Russian culture.

5.13   A major factor in the success of individual Jews in Russia was the harsh persecution in education. If only 1% of university students could be Jews, they were the best of the best and eventually they made important contributions to Russian culture. If others did not get in, they studied in the West and often came back to Russia with new cultural standards and European degrees in medicine or engineering. Similar phenomena were observed on the level of the academic Gymnasium.

Only 25,000 privileged Jews (university educated or merchants of the First Guild) lived in St. Petersburg in the beginning of the twentieth century, but many of them occupied important positions in Russian culture, literary criticism, law, even politics. Their ambivalent interaction with the masses in the Pale of Settlement was a moving force in the modern Jewish Revolution.

5.14   It was in the Russian Empire where almost all the intrinsic trends were created. Other Jewish communities were either extensions of this Renaissance, carried over by immigrants, or joined it sooner or later. To some extent, the revival was joined by another branch of former Polish Jewry: Galicia, but the major initiatives were Russian.

Political Zionism was, indeed, founded in the West, but Hibbat Zion (the "Lovers of Zion" in Odessa of 1881) preceded it. Furthermore, Zionism would not have become a reality without its implementation by Russian Jews, including the early waves of immigration to the Land, the revival of Hebrew and the creation of a Hebrew literature and a Hebrew society, encompassing a whole network of social and cultural institutions.

5.15   It is worth noting the important place ideologies played in Jewish society. The sudden leap from a primitive, "medieval" *shtetl* existence to the heights of modern sophisticated culture was bought at a high price.

Totalizing ideologies, especially Marxism, gave a young autodidact a handle for understanding the bewildering, new and chaotic world; it provided a discourse to understand and explain everything, red glasses to see the world with, and an impulse to rebel. It also denationalized the sense of suffering and wrongdoing, shifting it from a Jewish to a general human condition, to a systemic rather than private problem.

5.16   In the end result, the Modern Jewish Revolution was nurtured not by the *shtetl* or by the *shtetl* world in itself, but by the exodus from it. Self-awareness and the question of Jewish existence were highlighted in migration. It was the globalized network of the *shtetl* world that created the sense of a Jewish nation and empowered Jewish writers and ideologies. Yet this nation needed a radical modernization, openly joining the secular, modern world either inside the culture or in other languages. Both the writers and their readers were already living in cities or abroad. If the writers used the *shtetl* as a fictional locus, it was akin to the invented American West as an American mythology and a fictional locus for Western movies.

5.17   Jewish literature is a literature of migration, the literature of a transplanted nation. From the perspective of history, it is clear that this revolutionary time was a transitional period. Because of that centrifugal movement away from the source, it could not survive in the long run, except in the state of Israel. Yet it left a great, highly complex and contextually bound literature in our libraries.

2 MULTILINGUALISM

Throughout most of their history, the Jews were a multilingual nation, both in fact and as part of their identity consciousness. Their history was marked by the movements of a small Jewish minority from one land and culture to another, and by the multilingual library of texts which they carried with them. To understand Jewish multilingualism in Eastern Europe we must consider both the nature of Jewish history and their self-defined myth of origins as well as the exceptional historical situation of the Jews in Eastern Europe between the eighteenth and the twentieth centuries.

In an autobiographical book, the Israeli novelist Amos Oz, who was born in Jerusalem, described his Polish-Russian Jewish parents as follows: "My father could read sixteen or seventeen languages and speak eleven (all of them with a Russian accent). My mother spoke four or five languages and read seven or eight. They would talk in Russian and Polish when they didn't want me to understand (most of the time they didn't want me to understand). For cultural reasons they read books mainly in German and English. Their dreams at night were surely in Yiddish. But as for me, they taught me only Hebrew. Maybe they were afraid that knowing languages would expose me too to the temptations of wonderful and fatal Europe" (*A Tale of Love and Darkness*, p. 6). The Hebrew revival was one road to shedding the Diaspora existence and its hallmark, multilingualism.

This exuberant multilingualism was widespread among the first generation of Jews from Eastern Europe who broke out of the small-town *shtetl* existence, went to the cities and immigrated to the West, to America or Palestine.
Multilingualism was a moving force of the Modern Jewish Revolution, the total transformation of the Jews in the modern age, their place in geography and
history, their languages, education, professions, behavior, and consciousness.[1]

The number of languages usually mentioned by such individuals ranged
between five and seven and, in special cases, thirteen or fifteen. The standard
case would include Yiddish and Hebrew, Polish and Russian, German, perhaps
French, and the new world language English. Individuals who attended yeshivas or had private tutors in Hebrew education could read Aramaic; students
of a humanistic gymnasium (like Oz's father) would know Ancient Greek and
Latin. That brings us up to ten languages. In particular cases we may add other
languages, e.g., Lithuanian, Italian (Vladimir Jabotinsky, Leah Goldberg), or
Czech (as Oz's mother, who was a student in Prague, had to know). Those who
emigrated to South America mastered Spanish or Portuguese; knowledge of
the two extreme Slavic languages (Polish and Russian) made reading Ukrainian poetry easy; and in Palestine, many Jews studied Arabic. We don't know
exactly in what "ten languages" Oz's father could declaim poetry, but even if it
was an exaggeration, those multilinguals had at least some sense of the grammar, vocabulary, and poetry of several languages, drawn from at least three
out of four language groups (Germanic, Slavic, Semitic, Romance).

This phenomenon was not unique to intellectuals: "everybody's" grandfather in New York or Tel Aviv knew at least Yiddish and some of its component
languages: Hebrew, Russian, Polish, German, as well as immigrant English, depending on their life's itinerary. Many Jews of that generation were born in the
Pale of Settlement before the Revolution of 1917, moved to a city in Eastern Europe (Moscow, St. Petersburg, Vilna, Warsaw, Odessa), emigrated to Germany,
then to France, then to America, tried Palestine in-between. Some went from
Ukraine to Canada or the U.S., back to the Soviet Far East to build a Jewish state
in Birobidjan, then to Moscow, and eventually to Israel. Other itineraries wound
up in South America, South Africa, Australia, New Zealand, Uzbekistan.

In Medieval Europe, the same phenomenon prevailed on a smaller scale.
Whether because of persecutions and expulsions or because of grasped opportunities and lack of "rootedness," they had self-described "shpilkes" (Yiddish

---

1   See B. Harshav, *Language in Time of Revolution.*

for "pins and needles," literally: "pins in their ass"), unease in staying in one place, and frequently traveled between territories and languages. Their very existence in the Christian world was defined by the religious opposition: Jew vs. Christian. Thus, they acquired a critical perspective of biculturalism and bilingualism, as well as a sense of cultural relativity, flexibility, and irony. Typically, Jews specialized in the exchange of goods (trade), signs (languages), and signs of goods (money). In the twentieth century, the age of social sciences, Jews were prominent among American Nobel-Prize laureates in Economics and in theoretical linguistics and anthropology: Bréal (founder of Semantics), Durkheim, Levy-Bruehl, Levi-Strauss, Freud, Boas, Sapir, Bloomfield, Jakobson, Chomsky, Lakoff, Derrida—all born on the boundaries of languages.

BASIC CONCEPTS

Multilingualism is the knowledge of more than one language by a person or a social group and the ability to switch from one language to another in speech, in writing, or in reading. Other terms describing this phenomenon include: Bilingualism, Polylingualism, Plurilingualism, Diglossia, Languages-in-contact. Recent scholarship in the U.S. favors the term "bilingualism," derived from the binary problems of immigrants and social institutions such as "bilingual education." The term "diglossia" (suggested by Charles Ferguson) indicates complementary languages, used by the same person for different functions in social communication. Uriel Weinreich called his classical book *Languages in Contact*, thus stressing the linguistic forms of impact one language has on another when used in proximate communities.

Multilingualism may be personal, social, or inter-subjective. Personal multilingualism refers to the knowledge and verbal behavior of an individual, not necessarily shared by the whole community. Social multilingualism refers to a nation, a tribe, or another social group that sustains two or more languages. When Shmuel Nigger, the prominent Yiddish literary critic in New York, wrote at the eve of the Holocaust a book in Yiddish, *Di tsvey-shprakhikeyt fun undzer literatur* ("The Bilingualism of our Literature"), he did not imply that every Jew reads both Hebrew and Yiddish, but that there is a larger, national entity ("*our* literature") which includes both, by that time quite separate literatures. In the beginning of the twentieth century, many Yiddishists would not include Hebrew in "our" literature (the literature of "the people") and the Hebrew culture in Palestine would not include Yiddish in "our" literature. Nigger's book was, among others, a statement of cultural politics, an attempt at saving Yiddish literature as part of Jewish culture. Indeed, by that time, most speakers of one Jewish language didn't know or didn't read the other.

On the other pole, Professor Dr. Yosef Klausner, who occupied the first chair of Hebrew Literature in Jerusalem, wrote a multi-volume *History of Modern Hebrew* [sic!] *Literature*, which included detailed biographies of all the Hebrew writers. Yet Klausner did not include the Yiddish texts most of them had written. Thus, he discussed the founder of both Yiddish and Hebrew modern literatures, Mendele-Abramovich's books of Hebrew fiction but not their original Yiddish versions. Professor Klausner was a nationalist-Zionist and strove towards one language on one land by one Hebrew (rather than Jewish) nation. But Mendele's response was: I like to breathe with both my nostrils (Yiddish and Hebrew). On the other hand, neither Nigger nor Klausner included Kafka or Freud in "our" literature, as it is often done today in courses on "the Jewish experience" in the U.S., based on a tacit assumption of Diaspora pluralism.

In modern times, Jewish society in Eastern Europe included the use of Yiddish, Hebrew, Aramaic, Russian, German, perhaps Polish—all in the same community and even in the same family, but not all known by all individuals. Many women, especially of the lower classes, knew Yiddish and some "Goyish" (the local Slavic dialect), though their husbands knew also some German as the lingua franca of trade, and the languages of Jewish learning, Hebrew and Aramaic. Yet the society as a whole knew those five or six languages as "family resemblances." Hence, we can observe a third, inter-subjective kind of multilingualism, spread among many individuals in a given society, but not obligatory for every one of them.

In discussions of multilingualism we face three entrenched stereotypes. First, people tend to base their description of language on the spoken word, hence bilingualism is described as speaking in two languages. Yet much of culture is preserved in writing and in print, as is the case of the Jewish religious library, and an acquired written language may be overwhelmingly richer than the spoken language. Medieval knowledge in Europe was recorded in Latin, though most scholars spoke in vernacular. Hebrew and Aramaic were the source of all Jewish knowledge and were taught in the spoken language, Yiddish—a multilingualism based on three languages in two different media (speech and print). Related to this topos is the Romantic idea of authenticity in language, "imbibed with the mother's milk," i.e. in the *mother tongue*. Yet this "natural" acquisition of a language in childhood is countered by the important learning processes in all stages of life. Most Israeli Jews, including most Hebrew writers in the twentieth century, use Hebrew as their *base language*, although it was not their mother tongue.

Thirdly, the nation-state ideology promoted the ideal: "One nation, one land, one language" (and one Leader). Forces of power and/or cultural authority worked to enforce this unity, identifying the ethnic and political boundaries with language borders. And if this national unity did not match the facts, it was imposed upon deviant persons or groups. Thus, many dialects were suppressed or erased in France in order to impose one national language. In Yiddish in the twentieth century, mainly through the school system and mandatory unified spelling, the Yiddishists imposed a unified "standard language" on its various dialects. Similarly, in Palestine in the beginning of the twentieth century, the "Sephardi" pronunciation was imposed on immigrants who were fluent in various Ashkenazi dialects of Hebrew. Yet the assumption of overlapping identity of nation, land, and language is an essentialist fallacy. In history, there was a great deal of asymmetry between those three categories. The language/ ethnic group/ nation/ state identity must be seen as a horizon, a force for the homogenizing of larger social groups, and a goal of nationalist and cultural movements.

THE STRUCTURE OF MULTILINGUALISM

In a society or a state there is never one language and never language alone. Not one language, because various minorities live among the dominant language group and because the official language itself presides over a motley of dialects. In the Austro-Hungarian Empire, there were many languages and cultures on their own territories in a common state, dominated by the German language. Not language alone, because every language is a repository of cultural values, images, and memories ("semiotics of culture"). The boundary between semantics of language and semiotics of culture is blurred: multilingualism shades into multiculturalism.

The boundaries between dialects and languages are fuzzy too: there is often a gradual shading from one dialect to the next, until a new language appears on the map. The differences between the German dialects of Berlin and Bavaria are more prominent than the differences between the Russian and Byelorussian languages. A person speaking both Bavarian and High German is practically bilingual. Yet for historical and political reasons, the first pair are considered dialects of one language and one nation, Germany, whereas the second pair became two languages and two states. In Jewish life, there was intense animosity between Litvaks, Galitsianer, and Polish Jews, based on their different dialects, yet those did not crystallize as languages because of the overarching power of a common religion, alphabet, nationalism, and anti-Semitism.

Societies are multilingual in different ways. To begin with, the participant languages can relate to each other horizontally or vertically.

In Horizontal Multilingualism the participant languages are parallel to each other in their use. They include several modes:

1) *Bilingualism* proper—two alternative languages are co-extensive: either they reside in the same territory or in the same mind. Typical examples of personal bilingualism are individuals with two parents speaking different languages. Social bilingualism occurs when the territory of a weaker language is occupied by a stronger language, either militarily or culturally (English in India, Greek in Hellenist Eastern Mediterranean); or, the opposite, a weaker language immigrates to the territory of a stronger language (Spanish or Yiddish in the USA). Usually such bilingualism is transitional and after a generation or two, the stronger language prevails. In the interim period, however, the weaker language (Spanish) has a sufficient group of reference (Hispanics) to be dominant in that secondary framework. In bilingualism, two languages are synonymous and interchangeable, and are used depending on the addressee and situation.

2) *Diglossia*—two languages are complementary. They are both necessary for a person's verbal behavior but fulfill different communicative functions, covering different semiotic domains. Thus, the immigrant language is used at home, often with one's spouse or older people, while the dominant language is used at work or with one's children.

3) *Lingua franca*—a basic vehicle of communication between separate language communities (Swahili in East African nations, English in former British colonies). It establishes several bilingual relations with each of the local languages, and diglossia relations when the semiotic functions are complementary (official business vs. home).

In Vertical Multilingualism, the languages enter hierarchical relations with each other in a three-tier structure:

4) Local dialects, professional idiolects, or languages of origin, indicating a person's home language or professional attachment.

5) The standardized national language, where all differences are neutralized. From this common base, the speakers can move to any dialect or professional idiolect or to any text in the past.

6) A *Supra-language* for international communication. This vehicle is usually the language of a current or former colonial power (Russian in Chechnya, Ukraine and Kazakhstan), political power (English in the third world or even in the European Union) or cultural power (English in the language of high-tech). Whereas lingua franca covers the intellectually lowest levels of culture and immediate personal communication, the supra-language covers the highest levels of science and culture and is complementary to the national languages. Thus, in contemporary India, a person uses (1) his/her dialect and often the dialects of the neighbors; (2) the national languages Hindi (in present) and Sanskrit (in the past); and (3) English as the language of education. Thus, English serves both the low and the high: as a basic lingua franca between all Indian "tribes" and as the language of politics, technology, mass communication, and science. In the past, similar functions were filled by Greek, Latin, Arabic, Russian, etc. Printed Hebrew fulfills a similar function among the scattered Jewish communities speaking different languages around the globe.

Each tier in this hierarchy can have several options: several interacting local languages, several competing national languages and several competing Supra-languages (English competing with Russian in the states of the former Soviet Union). Worldwide, academic reading and writing use the Supra-language (mostly English), while creative writing and national culture are in the national language.

Thus, the language of Israel is not Hebrew alone, but a trilingual structure: Hebrew as the language of national identity and separateness, the language of the literary tradition and of statehood, law and the bureaucracy; English as the Supra-language of science, international culture and the international media; and the language of immigrant groups (rather than dialects), speaking Russian, Georgian, Arabic, French, Hungarian, Yiddish—with their own publications and daily newspapers.

In this complex horizontal and vertical grid of languages, there are obvious influences of languages in contact upon each other—and a largely scholarly literature investigating it. In many societies, there is a perennial struggle against foreign words imported into their national language ("Le drugstore" in Paris) and, on the other hand, incessant importations of such expressions—to match the knowledge and cultural distinctions obtained in other languages. The rapid growth of modern Yiddish and modern Hebrew was enmeshed in this process.

RELATIONS BETWEEN LANGUAGES AND THEIR USERS

1. A state of multilingualism may be achieved *naturally*—a person grows up with two parents speaking different languages, or is a member of a minority, or lives in a multilingual community—or *acquired* later in life, through immigration or learning.

2. The media of communication in each participant language may vary: conversation, writing, reading, symbolic systems. Those do not necessarily overlap. Thus, in the Jewish religious tradition, the law is given in Hebrew texts, its discussion and explication—in Aramaic texts, and the process of interpretation, study, and education—in the spoken Yiddish (or spoken modern Hebrew, English, etc.). Latin and Hebrew in the Middle Ages were "dead" or merely textual languages, whereas the scholars spoke in the vernacular.

3. The functional relations between the complementary languages in a multilingual situation are divided by the implied addressee (learned discourse in Latin or Hebrew vs. family correspondence in the vernacular) and by the semiotic domains addressed (religious texts vs. daily life, or social behavior vs. science).

4. Except for cases of precise bilingualism, there is asymmetry between the participant languages. Usually one of the languages becomes a *base language*, which provides the syntactic frame of the multilingual discourse. From this base, the speakers may depart into other languages, invoke historical layers of the "same" language, quote texts scattered in geography and history, or unfold professional and scientific idiolects. The earliest base language may be a person's first language, the so-called mother-tongue (in Yiddish: *mame-loshn*), intimate and emotive. But with time, the relationship may invert and an acquired language takes its place as the base language of a person or a whole society.

5. We may distinguish between the base languages of an individual, a society, and a text. Not every individual shares the base language of the society and an individual may write a text not in his own base language.

There are constant attempts to match those with each other, according to the principles of *mirroring* and *asymmetry*.[2] An individual will try to mirror the base language of a society by eliminating asymmetries between them. Or, on the contrary, a creative text or a social group may deviate from the standard language and, in the process, create new asymmetries.

6. The scope of a person's knowledge of each language may vary greatly, along the following scale: a) "mastering" the language with its textual tradition and a large, pan-historical vocabulary; b) competence in the rules of syntax of the current language and confidence in its use; c) elementary communication; d) traces of that language in the form of words and expressions included in the syntax of another language (Hebrew and Yiddish words in American English; Russian words in Israeli Hebrew fiction).

INTERNATIONAL SEMIOTIC DISCOURSE

Intersecting with the grid of languages in a multilingual society, there is a semiotic grid of human knowledge, which offers international discourses or secondary "languages" (in a metaphorical sense). Such are the discourses of religion, Christianity, psychoanalysis, physics, politics, yoga, the form of the sonnet, etc. Those are "languages" of culture, or discourses: they originate in a specific language in a specific cultural situation and are then transported into other languages and cultures. The spread of the new discourse occurs either by the adoption of its terminology in new languages or by coining calques for the original terms. The growth of a natural language is determined by its absorption of such domains of discourse. Most of the knowledge in our national dictionaries is international, though adapted to the phonetics, morphology and lexicon of each particular language.

Thus, the international word "telephone" (part of the discourse of communication technology) coined from two Greek roots, was first adopted in German, then pushed out for more Germanic roots: "Fernsprecher" ("distance-speaker") without changing its semantics. In Hebrew, the word telefon is preserved but it is adapted to Hebrew spelling (using almost only consonants: TLFoN). Furthermore, from the noun, the necessary verb is coined: leTaLPeN ("to call by phone"), according to the rules of Hebrew phonetics

---

2   See in Harshav, *Language in Time of Revolution*, p. 93.

(P is equivalent to F) and matching Hebrew morphology (TiLPaNti or the colloquial TiLFaNti, "I called by phone," and TaLFeN li, "call me").

Both Yiddish and Hebrew grew immensely in the last century to a large extent through such acquisitions of large semiotic domains. At first, the original term was included in the language, then a substitute, based on a Hebrew or Yiddish root, was often invented. Thus, in Hebrew, "culture" was first called kultu'ra, then it became tarbu't. Even when the foreign word is preserved, there are modes of secondary adaptation. Yiddish coined trage'dye, kome'dye with penultimate stress, as in Russian, rather than the German stress on the last syllable of these words and the English on the first. This process occurred subconsciously in the Jewish languages in the modern age, which absorbed a large international vocabulary primarily via its Russian forms. It usually entered first the Yiddish discourse of political speeches, "publitsistika" and newspaper culture, and then was taken over by Hebrew.

In this multilingual situation, an international network of words, idioms, and other expressions emerged, that have equal signifieds (semantics) but different signifiers (sound structure, morphology, lexical roots). This layer of multilingual discourse, embedded in all languages, was enhanced by the international nature of the *genres of discourse*: the language of a sonnet, of a newspaper news item, an editorial, or a romantic letter are international within the framework of Euro-American culture. Culture is anything but the monolingual existence of isolated monolithic social groups; the unity of language is not in one morphology but across languages, in one semiotic discourse.

MULTILINGUALISM IN JEWISH HISTORY

The Jewish national myth is based not on one cradle or homeland but on a bipolar pattern. From one place they were either exiled or fled into another, opposite place, positive (Exodus from Egypt, celebrated every Passover) or negative (Exile from the Holy Land). With the fall of the First Temple they were exiled from Palestine to Babylon. This national tragedy was remedied by the return of the nation to the Holy Land. A similar pattern was repeated with the fall of the Second Temple and exile of the Jews from Eretz Israel to the Diaspora (Galut), scattered around the globe. Exile to the Diaspora echoed the exile of Adam and Eve from Paradise.

The foundational event of this territorial bipolarity is recorded in Genesis

Chapter 12: the Lord sends the father of the Jewish nation, Abram, from his native Mesopotamia ("Aram Naharayim, Aram of two rivers") "to the land I will show you," the land of Canaan, occupied by Canaanites. This chapter was perceived as a Zionist message, sending Abram to the Promised Land. Yet it is also the first expulsion of the Jews as a nation; for the Lord commands Abram: "Go forth from your land and your birthplace and your father's house." In the ears of Diaspora Jews, "Moledet" (birthplace) meant also "homeland" in the national sense: Abram was expelled from his homeland. And "Lekh-lekho" ("Go forth!") with its repeated harsh sounds, was expressive of the coarse command: "Get out!" Sholem Aleichem finishes his saga of Tevye the Milkman with the chapter "Lekh-lekho." The expression "the chapter of Lekh-lekho arrived," meant in Yiddish: the time of expulsions came (in this case: expulsion of all Jews from the Russian villages).

With the second Exile, the Jews scattered, in several stages, around the world. As all immigrants do, they adopted everywhere the local spoken language, and some of them acquired the dominant language of culture or the language of power. In Palestine, in the first centuries of the common era, the masses spoke Aramaic, the elite spoke Greek, and the learned carried on the knowledge and writing of Hebrew. Thus the term for a Hebrew liturgical poet was *paytan*, derived from Greek *poietan*. Adjusted by Hebrew morphology, the poetry was called *piyut*: a Greek cultural term, describing poetry written by an Aramaic-speaking Hebrew writer.

Micah Josef Berdichevsky, who studied the Aramaic Talmud at the elite Volozhin yeshiva in Lithuania with other liberal-minded students, became a prominent Hebrew secular fiction writer, lived in Berlin and wrote criticism and essays in Yiddish and German, defined this essential Jewish bilingualism in his essay "Hebrew and Aramaic," which uses the story of Jacob and Esau as a metaphor: "Two nations in your womb, [two peoples from your loins shall issue]" (Genesis 25:23). . . "still clash within us, and our tongue became two languages—Hebrew and Aramaic" (Berdichevsky 101). He claims it is immaterial whether the nation of Israel, that came from Aram, first spoken Aramaic, then learned in Canaan to speak Hebrew, and later returned their language to its Aramaic origins, or whether Hebrew preceded Aramaic and the Israelites learned the latter in their political and cultural contacts with their Aramaic-speaking neighbors. "The fact is that we deal with *two languages*, which, though neighbors, are radically different from each other, not in words and expressions but in their *soul*. . . *We are Hebrew-Aramaic in our language*" (102). This pair was supplanted by the Hebrew-Yiddish bilingualism in Eastern Europe, fulfilling a similar functional division (see S. Nigger).

Even in the days of their independence in ancient Canaan, the Jews were a small nation on the crossroads between Egypt, Syria, and Mesopotamia and were in contact with the neighboring languages (there are Aramaic texts in the Hebrew Bible). Yet the full complexity of Jewish multilingualism developed in the Diaspora. It combined their own languages (Yiddish, Hebrew, Aramaic) with the local dialects, on the one hand, and the language of the majority and of power, on the other hand. In addition, they shifted from the language of their old country, to the language of the new land where they went in their wanderings. Thus the Ashkenazi Elye Bokher (Elias Levita) moved from Germany to Rome and Venice, was a teacher to cardinals, wrote a grammar and versification treatise in Hebrew, and epic romances in *ottava rima* in Yiddish, and published a four-language dictionary: German-Latin-Italian-Hebrew, reflecting his origins and his two homelands (Germany and Italy).

In their cultural heritage, the Jews absorbed elements of the languages and modes of discourse which they acquired from other languages in the past. Thus, Arabic metrics, adopted by Hebrew poetry in ninth-century Spain, continued to be mandatory in Hebrew poetry in Christian Spain and, from the thirteenth to the eighteenth century, in Italy, where there were no Arabs and no Arabic knowledge. Nevertheless, unlike Arabic, the prevalent rhyme gender in medieval Hebrew poetry in Christian lands was feminine (penultimately stressed), as prevalent in the poetry of their Romance language neighbors.

The special trait of the Jewish Diaspora was the unprecedented preservation of a Jewish community throughout history, in spite of the repeated expulsions, migration, and assimilation. In every new language territory, the second generation adopted the new, non-Jewish language, but kept traces of the previous language. The so-called "Jewish languages" (Judeo-Arabic, Judeo-Greek, Judeo-German), which Jews spoke among themselves for generations, were not really different from the dominant language but were marked variants of it. The new formation was marked as a Jewish language in several respects: 1) Jewish languages were written in the Hebrew alphabet. 2) They preserved some expressions of the earlier language. E.g., Romance words (kreplakh, cholent) and names (Yentl from Gentilla) were preserved in German-based Yiddish. 3) Some Jewish cultural markers were included in the new languages (the tradition of the Bible, Hebrew poetry, Jewish cuisine, Yiddish words, semantics of proverbs, etc.). 4) Only part of the scope of the new language was

assimilated in the Jewish version. Large parts of German (the language of philosophy, high poetry, bureaucracy, etc.) never visited Yiddish.

The Jews did not disappear in history, largely because they kept their holy
language Hebrew for written communication, unharmed by the spoken, external and changeable vehicles. This split of communicational vehicles according
to media contributed to the preservation of the "Holy Tongue" (Hebrew and Aramaic) throughout the ages. It was founded on a complex and detailed network
of religious beliefs and behavior, based on the Book of Books and a library of
texts and commentaries, studied in mandatory education. The spoken vehicle,
however, absorbed cultural elements from the surrounding languages, folklore
and verbal behavior. This was not an accidental but an essential multilingualism
which enabled the functioning of the Jews in a bifurcated existential situation.

INTERNAL MULTILINGUALISM

The languages known to Eastern European Jewry were of three kinds: Internal
languages,[3] External languages, and the internalized multilingualism of Yiddish. The autonomous stratification of Jewish social institutions within the
larger state was implemented in Ashkenaz in three internal languages, all written in the same, Hebrew alphabet: Yiddish, Hebrew, and Aramaic. Professor
Dr. Yosef Klausner, a leader of the modern revival of Hebrew and the first professor of Hebrew literature at the Hebrew University in Jerusalem, maintained
that Hebrew is not one language but four: Biblical, Mishnaic, Tibbonite[4] and
Modern; any speaker of one language would not understand the other. Indeed,
we could add several more Hebrew languages: the innovative language of Palestine liturgy of the Byzantine period; the neo-Biblical language of Spanish
Hebrew poetry. We must also mention Ashkenazi Rabbinical Hebrew—a "synthetic" language, combining words from several historical layers of Hebrew
with some Aramaic quotations; it was alive in writing from Rashi to Mendele
Moykher Sforim. These Hebrew "languages" appeared in history in spurts and
isolated developments, without the continuity of a spoken language.

Jewish Aramaic, too, was at least three languages: 1) the variants of classical Aramaic of the Bible and Bible translations; 2) the colloquial Aramaic of

---

3   In my book *The Meaning of Yiddish*, I called it Polylingualism, stressing the fact that we are
    dealing not with complete languages but with a polyphony of glimpses in several language
    directions. For more detail, see there.
4   The medieval Spanish-Provençal scientific Hebrew, influenced by Arabic.

Talmudic discourse; 3) the artificial medieval Aramaic of the thirteen-century *Zohar*—the classical book of the Kabbalah, and shorter texts, such as the *Kaddish* or the *Had Gadya*, a European pattern song, translated from German into Aramaic, and sung at the Passover Seder.

Aramaic was the Yiddish of an earlier millennium, it mediated between the spoken and the written world. With its demise as a spoken language among the Jews, it was sanctioned as part of the Holy Tongue. Yiddish tried but never achieved this status in print, but compensated for it in the educational process. Learning was conducted in Yiddish dialogue discussing the Aramaic dialogue about the Hebrew monologues of the Bible.

But from the position of religious learning, hence the position of Yiddish, all those historical variants of Hebrew and Aramaic are one language, *loshn-koydesh* ("The Holy Tongue"), kept in one library and often on one page. What brings them together are the unique identity of nation and religion, their validity as arbiters of both daily life and theology, their unifying Hebrew alphabet, separate from all neighboring writing systems, and the scholarly settings in which texts in all those languages were discussed as one continuum. On one page of the Talmud you encounter separate texts in Biblical Hebrew, Mishnaic Hebrew, Ashkenazi Rabbinical Hebrew, classical Aramaic and Talmudic dialogical Aramaic, all organized as a highly controlled, graphically deployed and canonized mosaic. On a stratified page of a later-day family Torah, you encounter Biblical Hebrew, two Aramaic translations, Rashi and Rabbinical Hebrew of the major commentaries, and Yiddish translations of both the Bible and commentaries.

Nevertheless, new writings distinguished between the different languages which compose *loshn-koydesh*. Since the components of the Holy Tongue were not spoken, they kept their independence in writing, as separate genres of discourse. Aramaic was much quoted in Yiddish, but rarely written in independent sentences and texts. Books, correspondence, community chronicles, and legal proceedings were written in a Hebrew framework, with embedded Yiddish and Aramaic phrases. Hebrew poetry throughout the ages was predominantly Biblical in its lexicon. In some realistic Hebrew fiction in the period of Revival, Aramaic represented the spoken language of the characters, Yiddish (Mendele, the narrative poems of YaLaG Gordon). Realistic prose used a synthetic language, including many Aramaic expressions (Brener) beside European and Yiddish imports.

Selected chapters of the Torah and prayers—in printed (rather than written) Hebrew letters—were studied in Heder, the elementary school, mandatory for all boys from the age 3 or 4 until Bar-mitzva at 13. The more difficult Aramaic was studied by boys in their teens in yeshivas—the elite academies that produced certified Rabbis for hundreds of communities and became the breeding ground of modern, secular Hebrew literature.

EXTERNAL MULTILINGUALISM

In the middle ages the Jews were expelled from most European states and concentrated in the Kingdom of Poland and Lithuania, as well as in parts of Italy and some German towns, and in the Mediterranean shores of the Ottoman empire. Few in numbers, they were always outsiders and a small minority. They kept their internal languages in writing and acquired, to various degrees, the spoken dialects of their neighbors as well as the "King's language" of the state. Few medieval Jews read the Latin alphabet, hence the need to write German texts in Hebrew letters.

In the nineteenth century, in the Russian Pale of Settlement, most Jews did not live among the Russians but among speakers of local dialects or minority languages. Jews were exposed to Byelorussian and Ukrainian (the language of the peasants), Polish (the language of the landlords), Russian (the language of the state) and German (language of culture and yearly fairs, that could be seen as an extension of their internal Yiddish). This situation encouraged the preservation of their own spoken language, Yiddish. Living on the interstices of languages and nations, they could communicate with the Low (the colloquial language) and the High (the language of power and culture). Their knowledge of those languages was not complete and primarily oral, but they had a foothold in several languages, conspicuously belonging to several language families.

INTERNALIZED MULTILINGUALISM: YIDDISH

According to the great historian of the Yiddish language Max Weinreich, Yiddish was born in the Carolingian empire at the end of the first millennium. Indeed, from a Yiddishist ideological position in the twentieth century, there is one continuum of a spoken language going back to the tenth century. The earliest extant Yiddish texts are from the end of the thirteenth and the fourteenth centuries, notably a manuscript of a German romance in Hebrew letters, found in the Genizah in Cairo, Egypt. Some mature literary texts were written since the fifteenth century, notably the European romances Buovo d'Antona [Bove Bukh] and Paris and Vienna, written in Italy in the early sixteenth century in Yiddish/German in Hebrew letters and in ottava rima strophes by the multilingual scholar Elias Levita.

Looking, however, from the past forward, we can see in these Yiddish texts little difference from German, except for the use of certain Hebrew expressions and a few Romance language words. The Jews behaved as other immigrants and adopted the language of their host nation. The critical difference from other dialects was found in writing, in the use of a separate, Hebrew alphabet. The Hebrew alphabet opened the gates to the other partner of Jewish multilingualism, the library of books, prayers, and Rabbinical judgments in the Holy Tongue. This Jewish-German language (Jüdisch-Deutsch) lived on the margins of German and only in the eighteenth century was it called Yiddish (Jüdisch). When Yiddish wandered to Venice or Amsterdam, it lived there basically for one generation, until full assimilation ensued.

The radical change occurred when Yiddish settled in Slavic territories, in a language environment that is not similar to Yiddish. Here they preserved the language for many generations. The earliest Yiddish texts in Poland, where the majority of world Jewry lived, are from the sixteenth century. It stands to reason that the Jews who lived in Slavic lands beforehand spoke Slavic languages, Czech or proto-Ukrainian. In the sixteenth century, a new influx of Jews from Germany, supported by a religious and moralist revival, imposed the Yiddish language as the language of the Jewish autonomy in Poland. The earlier spoken Slavic languages served as a substratum to the Germanic Yiddish, much as spoken Romance languages underlay the Germanic vocabulary of the Jews in the beginnings of Yiddish. The syntax and vocabulary of Yiddish carry the Slavic impact to this day.

In the eighteenth and nineteenth centuries a unique phenomenon in Jewish history occurred: the Jews became a majority on a polka-dotted map over a vast territory of the Russian Pale of Settlement (encompassing what is today Byelorussia, Lithuania, Ukraine and more). Of course, in absolute numbers the majority population were peasants, but the peasants were hardly an economic force, they were serfs, attached to their villages until 1861. The Jews, mobile, well connected through a network of trade and full of initiative, constituted two-thirds of the population of all towns and at least a third or a half of the population of the larger cities. Though deprived of citizen rights, they built and owned most of the local small industries, banking, and local as well as international trade. In medieval German cities there was a *Judengasse*, the Jewish street, whereas here most of the town was Jewish, except for the Russian administration, police, and churches, serving the whole area. The Yiddish language served as the cement and communicational network of this nation. Its Russian and German components served as a natural bridge to the language of power, Russian (earlier: Polish), and the languages of culture, Russian and German.

Yiddish is German-based: most of its vocabulary is of German origin, though in many cases there is a Hebrew or Slavic subtext in the semantics of the ostensibly German words. One can write pure sentences using only the German, but not any other component. The secondary, but stylistically decisive partners are Slavic languages (Czech, Polish, Russian), the Holy Tongue (Hebrew and Aramaic), and a large international vocabulary.

As Max Weinreich argued, Yiddish is a language of fusion: it uses components of several languages and melts them in one linguistic system. Thus, *shlimezalnik* is composed of three elements: schlim + mazl + nik (German + Hebrew + Russian) and the general European "doctor" gets a Hebrew plural: *doktoyrim*. But this fusion is not as complete as an independent Yiddish ideology would have liked to have it. Americans hardly pay attention whether an English word comes from one source or another, whether *legal* and *loyal* are from Latin and French, *nation* is French, and *right* is Anglo-Saxon, or vice-versa. But in Yiddish there is high consciousness of the component languages and the literature uses their differences for stylistic purposes. Yiddish speakers lived among the Slavs in a Hebrew library and were close to Germany. The fusion of Yiddish is not as complete and the different components behave often according to the grammars of those languages. Thus, the Hebrew *mokem* has a Hebrew plural form: *mekoymes* (rather than the Yiddish plural: *mokems*). Furthermore, while the process of fusion in English was accomplished, Yiddish never had strict boundaries. Yiddish is to some extent a language of fusion but it is also an open language; its speakers can easily roam in the reservoirs of the Holy Tongue, German or Polish and Russian and bring in whatever concept is needed at the moment. People of learning will use more expressions from the Holy Tongue, acculturated Europeans will use more German, there is more German in the Yiddish of Lodz or Silesia and more Slavic expressions in the Ukraine. Yiddish has a core, common to all its users, a wider circle of component-conscious words, and an open frontier into its component languages.

Yiddish is in its nature a multilingual language and its speakers are by definition multilingual (as poor as their grammar in those languages may be). The open borders of Yiddish, which allowed a massive influx of words from all its component languages and the modernization of the language in the modern age, also served as a bridge in the other direction. Yiddish speakers could easily adapt to speaking German (Yiddish minus Hebrew and Slavic words) and Yiddish speakers revived modern Hebrew. Thus Yiddish was the bridge between the internal tradition and European culture, between internal and external multilingualism.

With the abandonment of both Yiddish and the exuberant multilingualism of a wandering people, the Jews became "normal": as everybody else, they use one base language and one or two acquired languages of learning (Hebrew and English, English and French, etc.), depending on a person's profession and context.

References

Berdichevsky, Micah Josef. 1987. "Hebrew and Aramaic" [in Hebrew], *Poesy and Language*. Selected and edited with an Introduction and Notes by Emanual Bin-Gorion. Jerusalem: Bialik Institute.

Grosjean, Francois. 1982. *Life with Two Languages: An Introduction to Bilingualism*. Cambridge, MA: Harvard University Press.

Harshav, Benjamin. 1999. *The Meaning of Yiddish*. Stanford, CA: Stanford University Press.

———. 1999. *Language in Time of Revolution*. Stanford, CA: Stanford University Press.

Holquist, Michael. 2003. "What is the Ontological Status of Bilingualism?" in Doris Sommer, ed., *Bilingual Games: Some Library Investigations*. New York: Palgrave Macmillan.

Nigger, Samuel [S. Charney]. 1941. *Di tsvey-shprakhikeyt fun undzer literatur* [The Bilingualism of Our Literature]. Detroit, MI: Louis Lamed Foundation for the Advancement of Hebrew and Yiddish Literature.

Nigger, Shmuel. 1990. *Bilingualism in the History of Jewish Literature*. Translated from the Yiddish by Joshua Fogel. Lanham, MD: University Press of America.

Oz, Amos. 2004. *Sipur al ahava ve-hoshekh* ["A Tale of Love and Darkness" in Hebrew]. Jerusalem: Keter.

Weinreich, Max. 1973. *Geshikhte fun der Yidisher shprakh*. 4 volumes. New York: YIVO.

Weinreich, Uriel. 1953. *Languages in Contact: Findings and Problems*. New York: Publications of the Linguistic Circle of New York—Number 1.

3 THE CRISIS OF JEWISH IDENTITY

S.Y. Agnon's *Only Yesterday*[1]

S.Y. (Shay) Agnon was born as Shmuel-Yoysef Tshatshkes in the town of Butshatsh in eastern Galicia, formerly a part of the great Kingdom of Poland, and between 1772 and 1918 incorporated in the Austro-Hungarian Empire (today in Ukraine). The Polish spelling of his and his town's name—Czaczkes of Buczacz (read: Cháchkes of Búchach)—sounds almost grotesque, and his flight from the name was a symptom of his flight from the shtetl world.[2] In local parlance, the Jewish name of the town was Bichúch, and Agnon imitated the name in his fictional Shibush, a decaying, valueless, dying world, as portrayed in his novel *A Guest for the Night*. Hebrew critics made a great deal of this symbolic name—*Shibush*—for its dictionary meaning is: breakdown, disruption, blunder—and this sounded like a death sentence on the Jewish Diaspora. Furthermore, breakdown is a cognate of Thomas Mann's *Buddenbrooks*, representing the breakdown of the bourgeois world. Yet in the living language—the Hebrew incorporated in Yiddish—Shibush (pronounced: Shíbesh) means: a worthless thing, a negligible value: if something costs a shibesh, it practically costs nothing (derived from a worn-out penny, the

---

1   Introduction to the Israeli Nobel Prize winner for literature, S.Y. Agnon's novel *Only Yesterday*, translated by Barbara Harshav, Princeton University Press, 2000.

2   The facts on Agnon's life are based primarily on Dan Laor's *S.Y. Agnon: A Biography* [in Hebrew] (Tel Aviv: Schocken Publishers, 1998); and on the still-classical biography of Agnon by Arnold Band, *Nostalgia and Nightmare* (Berkeley and Los Angeles: University of California Press, 1968).

smallest coin with the Emperor's face rubbed off). And this perception evokes Y.L. Peretz's Yiddish romantic poem "Monish": "In kinigraykh Poyln / Nit vayt fun der grenets / ligt zikh a shtetele / groys vi a genets" ("In the Kingdom of Poland / Close to the border / Lies a town / As big as a yawn.").

In fact, considering the demographic structure of that time, Búchach was not a small shtetl but quite a large town, a center of a whole district, well connected to a network of similar towns around Galicia. The town sent a delegate to the Galician Sejm and later to the Parliament in Vienna, as well as a delegate to the first Zionist Congress in Basel in 1897. In 1890, when Agnon was three years old, the town counted 6,730 Jews, about 70 percent of the total population, as was typical for towns in Eastern Europe. Since 1874, the town had an elected City Council (12 Jews, 9 Ukrainians, 9 Poles) and between 1879 and 1921 Berysh Stern, the son of the head of the Jewish Kehilah, was mayor of Buczacz—not quite a Jewish exile. The Jews engaged in trade (indeed they conducted the trade of agricultural products for the whole region) and in crafts: they were the tailors, furriers, carpenters of the area. There was also a vigorous political and cultural life: Hasidim and their opponents, the Misnagdim, enlightened Maskilim, semi-secular, and worldly; there was a Jewish Socialist party and a Socialist-Zionist party, and so on. The language of the Austrian state, army, bureaucracy, and university was German (which was relatively easy for Yiddish-speaking Jews to acquire, especially when they had ties to German market cities, such as Leipzig and Danzig), while Polish had an autonomous status in Galicia and enlightened Jews studied in Polish Gymnasia. On the other hand, the Jews spoke Yiddish and had close relations to their brethren on the Russian side of the nearby border, and infused it with the two languages of study, biblical Hebrew and talmudic Aramaic (both together were called "The Holy Tongue"). Thus, the minimal education of boys was in five languages (girls often studied French).

Agnon was born on 8/8/1887, yet he claimed he was born on 8/8/1888 (lucky number) which fell on Tish'a Be-Av, the ninth of the month Av in the year 5,648 since the creation according to the Hebrew calendar. This claim is simply wrong, because that date fell on August 17, 1888. The ninth of Av is a most significant date: it is a day of fasting to commemorate two events of apocalyptic proportions in Jewish history: the Destruction of the First Temple and the First Exile from the Holy Land and the Destruction of the Second Temple, causing the two thousand year long Exile. It is also, according to one tradition, the day the Messiah will be born. Agnon lived in a mythological universe, in the ahistorical world perception of Talmudic Judaism, where dates were less important as points in a chronological narrative but rather as significant moments in a universe of meaning.

In a similar way, Marc Chagall, who was born a few weeks before Agnon on the other side of the Russian border, claimed he was born on 7/7/87 (the actual date was June 24, 1887, according to the old Russian calendar, i.e. 6/7/87). But for Chagall, the magical number was an omen of his chosen destiny as an irrationally creative artist (see his "Self-Portrait with Seven Fingers"), while Agnon's fictional birthday was linked to the two great Destructions of the Jewish nation in the land of Israel (and perhaps, to the nation's Salvation, as mentioned in the first sentence of this novel). Did Agnon see himself in his innermost soul as the Messiah, the visionary prophet who would find the lost key of Jewish destiny, or perhaps as the witness to a final Destruction, *Khurban*, as represented in his two great novels?

Agnon received a traditional Hebrew education from the age of three until the age of ten, then was tutored by several private teachers and embarked on an intensive course of study and reading. His father was a furrier, was steeped in traditional Jewish learning. He prayed in the prayer house of the Chortkov Hasidic sect, whereas his maternal grandfather was a Misnaged (opposed to Hasidism). His mother was an avid reader of German literature, and at an early age, along with extensive readings in the traditional Jewish Library, Agnon learned Polish and German, read modern Hebrew secular literature as well as European fiction, as mediated through Yiddish and Hebrew translations, and read German literature as well as the fashionable Norwegian writers Ibsen, Bjørenson, and Hamsun in German translations.

He began publishing in Yiddish in 1903 and published stories and poems in Yiddish and Hebrew. When he reached the age of twenty-one, rather than being drafted to the army, Agnon left Buczacz. After visiting Lvov, Cracow, and Vienna, in June 1908 he immigrated to Palestine, settled in Jaffa, in the new Jewish neighborhood of Neve-Tsedek, and worked as an assistant editor of a literary journal. Here, his first story, "Agunot" ("Abandoned Women") was published, signed: Sh-Y Agnon ("the teller of 'Agunot'"). In 1912, he lived for several months in Jerusalem, where Yosef-Hayim Brenner, the highest literary and moral authority among the Labor-Zionist settlers, published at his own expense Agnon's most important early novella, *And the Crooked Shall Be Straight*.

In October 1912, like most members of the Second *Aliya* (the wave of Jewish immigrants to Palestine between 1903–1914), Agnon left Palestine and returned to the Diaspora. He settled in Berlin, where he met Sh.Z. Schocken, a well-known German businessman, Zionist, and publisher, who became his lifelong patron. In 1918, the translation of *And the Crooked Shall Be Straight* was published in German titled: *Und das Krume wird Gerade*. In 1920, Agnon married Esther Marks from Königsberg, with whom he had a daughter and a son. In 1921 they settled in Bad Homburg, but in June 1924 the house burned down, along with Agnon's library and manuscripts. In October 1924, Agnon returned to Palestine and settled with his family in Jerusalem. During the Arabic pogroms against Jews in 1929, Agnon was moved to the center of Jerusalem and his house in Talpiot was badly damaged. In 1930 he traveled to Leipzig in Germany, where his collected writings were being edited in Hebrew (published by Schocken in four volumes in 1932). In the summer of 1930 he also visited Poland and his hometown Buczacz, which served as the basis for his novel *A Guest for the Night* (published in 1939). He was twice awarded the prestigious Bialik Prize for literature and twice (in 1954 and 1958) the highest Israeli award, the Israel Prize. In 1966, Agnon was awarded the Nobel Prize for literature, together with the Jewish-German poetess Nelly Sachs. Agnon died on February 17, 1970, and was buried in a state funeral on the Mount of Olives in Jerusalem.

·

As Agnon felt that this strangely intensive bygone world happened "only yesterday," but was timelessly valid, so his own fictional world was alive, pervading all of modern Hebrew culture "only yesterday," and can—and should—stand beyond its ostensibly parochial landscape as one of the great literary myths of the twentieth century.

Shmuel-Yosef Agnon's Hebrew novel *Only Yesterday* (*Tmol Shilshom*) was written in Palestine under British Mandatory rule in the late 1930s, finished in 1943 during World War II, before the full scope of the Holocaust was revealed, and published after the war in 1945. The prominent Israeli literary critic Barukh Kurzweil, who had a Ph.D. in German literature and was a leading authority on his fellow Austro-Hungarian novelist, pronounced: "The place of *Only Yesterday* is among the greatest works of world literature." Those were not parochial sentiments of a "minor literature"; similar opinions were voiced by Leah Goldberg, Hebrew poetess and polyglot, translator of Petrarch and Tolstoy into modern Hebrew, and first Professor of Comparative Literature at the Hebrew University in Jerusalem; and by Robert B. Alter, Professor of

Hebrew and Comparative Literature at the University of California at Berkeley, a discerning critic and scholar of the European novel.

On the face of it, it is a simple story about a simple man, Isaac Kumer, who immigrated from Austrian Galicia to that cultural and political backwater, the southern Syrian province under Ottoman rule—the historical Palestine and the new Jewish settlement, the *Yishuv*. He arrived with the Second *Aliya*—a wave of a few hundred secular idealists, mostly Socialist Zionists from Russia, who came to the Land of Israel between 1903 and 1914 to till the soil, revive "Hebrew labor" and the Hebrew language, and became the founding generation of Israeli society. Isaac, however, who was neither a Russian nor a Socialist but believed in their ideals of resettling the land, drifted back to the fold of Orthodox Jewry, the Guardians of the Walls in Jerusalem.

Yet on this most unbelievable margin of all margins, the great themes of twentieth century literature reverberated. Among the main concerns of the book are "the death of God," the impossibility of living without Him and the impossibility of returning to Him, the reversibility of the Siamese twins Homeland and Exile, the weight of the traditional Library and the hollow sound of inherited discourse, the power of suppressed eroticism, and the ambivalent and drifting individual consciousness in an age of ideology. The book was written after Schopenhauer and Freud, after Spengler and Lenin—and grounded in the most austere, minimal society, in an impoverished fossil of an ancient myth.

Summarizing the book would be a futile exercise since its strength lies not in events but rather in hesitations about events. The historical context is as follows: in the sixteenth through eighteenth centuries, when Jews were barred from most Western European countries, the great majority of world Jewry was concentrated in the largest European state, the united Kingdom of Poland-Lithuania, which included what is today most of Poland, Lithuania, Belarus, and Ukraine. Between 1772 and 1794 Poland was dismantled by its neighbors, Russia, Austria, and Prussia (which later became Germany). The majority of Russian Jews found themselves in a huge geographical ghetto, the Jewish Pale of Settlement in the Russian Empire, and a large community lived in Galicia, the southern part of former Poland, now incorporated into the Austro-Hungarian Empire. Yet the Austrian Jews obtained full citizenship under the rule of a benign Emperor. There was an enormous explosion of the Jewish population in the nineteenth century: from 2.2 million worldwide in 1800 to 7.5 million in 1880 and 16 million before World War II. The authentic

Jewish territory in Eastern Europe was a network of small towns, where they constituted between one-half and two-thirds of the population. What united them was not an administrative hierarchy, but a dense cultural network, a religion with a Library of texts and a modern network of social and cultural institutions: separate Jewish schools, cemeteries, philanthropic organizations, hospitals and hospices, publishing houses, books and newspapers, a literature in several languages, as well as modern political parties and social organizations. All this was conducted in three private languages: Yiddish (for daily communication, education, politics, and modern life), Hebrew (of the Bible), and Aramaic (of the Talmud), as well as the languages of state and culture.

Agnon continues to call his homeland "Poland" (*Polin*), though under Austrian rule its culture was increasingly Germanized; whereas the Jews in Russia rapidly accepted Russian culture and ideologies and were considered "Russian Jews." The revolutionary fermentation among Russian intellectuals, on the one hand, and the inferior status of Russian Jewry (deprived of the right of citizenship and disrupted by waves of pogroms), on the other, gave rise to a self-conscious literature and a whole gamut of political solutions and parties among the Jews of Eastern Europe, as well as the immigration of millions to the West and the U.S. This fermentation brought about a total transformation of the Jews, their languages, professions, education, their very place in general culture, geography and history, which we may call the Modern Jewish Revolution.[3] The Zionist immigration to *Eretz-Israel* (The Land of Israel) was a mere trickle in a great stream—although its eventual results changed the nature of Jewish culture and identity as we had known it for two thousand years.

In the 1880s, a movement of Lovers of Zion (*Hovevey Tsion*) emerged in Russia, centered in Odessa, propagating the revival of the historical Land of Israel. In 1881, a small group of young intellectuals, who called themselves BILU (an acronym for "House of Jacob, come ye and let us go," Isaiah 2:5), immigrated to Palestine and thus started the First *Aliya*, the First Zionist Immigration (1882–1903). This was the first wave of Zionist settlers in Palestine, the so-called New Yishuv (the "new settlement" or "new population"). They built Jewish settlements (or "colonies"), supported by Rothschild and ICA (the Jewish Colonization Association), and became farmers on the land. Only

---

3   See my book, Benjamin Harshav, *Language in Time of Revolution* (Stanford, CA: Stanford University Press, 1999).

in 1897 did Theodor Herzl proclaim the World Zionist Organization in Basel with the goal of establishing a Jewish State in Palestine by political means. Herzl's ideal swept the imagination of Jews everywhere, especially among the millions in Eastern Europe, but most Zionists paid the membership Shekel and stayed where they were. The real implementation of Herzl's dream came through the subsequent waves of idealist immigrants, especially those arriving from Eastern Europe.

There was also an Old Yishuv of a few thousand Orthodox, mostly old Jews, who came "to die in the Holy Land," yet raised families and maintained a Jewish presence, mainly in Jerusalem, Tiberias, and Safed. Many of them lived on the minimal "Distribution" (*Haluka*) given them by "Societies" (*Kolel*), according to their cities of origin, where the financial support came from. Traditional learning and reading religious books was a major preoccupation of the men.

The new Zionist immigrants regarded this subsistence off the Distribution, poor as it was, as the most abject, parasitic aspect of Jewish Diaspora life. Yet, as Agnon tries to show, winds of change penetrated these walls too: Some built new neighborhoods outside the Old City walls—a symbolic as well as practical move—and established the first agricultural colony in Petach Tikvah ("The Opening of Hope"), some were artisans and supported their families with productive labor.

After the first wave of settlers ebbed, the Second *Aliya* arrived (1903–1914). Their ideological fervor was carried by young Socialist Zionists, mostly from Russia (fiercely debating between Marxist and anti-Marxist positions on Zionism). The immediate impulse was the pogrom in Kishinev in 1903, and the self-defense against the pogrom in Homel the same year (at the age of fifteen, young Rosa Cohen, mother of Itzhak Rabin, was one of the fighters and immigrants). The new pioneers intended to work the land, but work was scarce or nonexistent and the landlords of the First *Aliya* preferred cheap Arabic labor to the inexperienced socialist and secular bachelors. Collectives of Hebrew itinerant laborers emerged, reviving the Hebrew language in public communication and, after World War I, erecting the first agricultural communes (*kibbutzim*) on national land. All in all, there may have been three thousand pioneers in the Second *Aliya*, most of whom abandoned the Land after a year or two; according to Agnon, only two hundred Jewish workers remained. In 1908 there were sixty members of the Marxist party *Poaley Tsion* and ninety of the anti-Marxist Socialists, *Ha-Poel Ha-Tsa'ir*. Their slogan was: "Hebrew land, Hebrew labor, Hebrew language." And though Hebrew sentences were spoken throughout the ages, between 1906 and 1913 the Second *Aliya* created the first Hebrew-speaking society, a Hebrew city, and Hebrew schools.

At the same time there was an influx of secular Zionist immigrants to Jaffa and Jerusalem, and trade flourished. In 1909 Neve Tsedek, a Jewish neighborhood north of Jaffa emerged, which later turned out to be the beginning of the first Jewish city Tel Aviv. The first Hebrew high school, Gymnasiya Herzliya in Tel Aviv, and the Bezalel School of Art and Design in Jerusalem were the pride of the New Yishuv. During World War I, Jews were persecuted by the Turkish authorities, some were conscripted into the Turkish army (fighting with Germany against the Allies), and some were expelled from Palestine. But after the war, when Palestine became a British Mandate territory where a "Jewish Home" was to be established, and a new wave, the Third *Aliya*, came in 1921 from the Russian Revolution, the pioneers of the Second *Aliya* (Berl Katznelson, David Ben-Gurion, Meir Dizengoff) became the leaders of the new Hebrew Yishuv.

This is the context Isaac Kumer enters. The rough outline of his story is as follows: Isaac Kumer was born to a poor family in a Jewish town in eastern Galicia. Losing his mother at an early age, he turned his father's little store into a Zionist club and brought it to bankruptcy. A naïve bachelor, unlike most of his career-oriented generation, he consumed the Zionist phraseology lock, stock, and barrel, adapted it to his religious discourse, and actually went to realize the Zionist slogans. He went to the Land of Israel to plow its soil and revive it as in biblical times. But agricultural work was not to be found, since the earlier immigrants of the First *Aliya*, landowning farmers in new Jewish settlements, preferred cheap Arab labor to the rabble-rousing young socialists. Labor Zionism, too, turned out to be a pipe dream. Almost dying of starvation, Isaac found work by chance as a housepainter in Jaffa and then in Jerusalem, and instead of tilling the soil or building the country, he painted over old houses—a symbolic gesture as well as a practical, life-saving trade.

In Jaffa he neglected the religious commandments and drifted into secular behavior, common among his generation. He became intimate with Sonya, the daughter of a well-to-do family in Diaspora and a Gymnasium student. Like most members of the Second *Aliya*, Sonya was Russian, and for some reason she flirted with this Galician simpleton and later rejected him capriciously. But when he ascended to Jerusalem, he wound up back in the Orthodox and anti-Zionist religious world of the Old Yishuv. Inexplicably, he fell under its spell and eventually married Shifra, the daughter of an extreme Orthodox fanatic, who was paralyzed and could not object to the match.

One critic called the book "the Epic of a period," and another described it as "the most weighty and important attempt in our literature to depict the life of the Second *Aliya* in the Land of Israel." Indeed, one construct that Agnon offers the reader is a faithful and meticulous historical record, including descriptions of buildings and neighborhoods in Jerusalem, and mundane, humanizing anecdotes about legendary historical figures. Yet the documentary program resides only on the surface; behind its façade, enfolded in the novel's allusive and elusive, ironic and shrewd style, is a complex field of multidirectional and ambiguous meanings, raising a tangle of constructs, to be made by the reader and contradicted again, questioning the major aspects of the human condition.

The text is built on a series of ambivalences: Exile as a homeland versus the national Homeland as an exile; Jaffa versus Jerusalem; the liberated Sonya versus the Orthodox Shifra; subconscious drifting versus the dominant ideology of the collective Will, and so on. Actions and events "happen" to him, though usually he intended the opposite; and the motivations for those actions are always overdetermined, leaving the reader puzzled about which motivation to accept and which system of values is decisive.

But after several clues, planted yet unnoticed by the reader, there comes the powerful twist and the novel soars to Surrealist-Kafkaesque dimensions. Isaac playfully drips paint on a stray dog, writing "Crazy Dog" on his back in Hebrew. The dog Balak takes over the story: wherever he appears, he wreaks havoc, creates panic, and gets pelted with stones. Shifra's father is terrified into a stroke, and Balak has to flee into exile, to non-Jewish neighborhoods, where the Hebrew inscription on his back is illegible, and thus the dog becomes the embodiment of Exile. On the other hand, running around the city, he serves as the reader's guide to the precise geography and history of the neighborhoods and housings of Jews from various countries in early twentieth-century Jerusalem. The exuberant descriptions of Balak's predicament are among the most powerful chapters in the novel; the dog has been interpreted as an allegory of Jewish Exile, as Isaac's erotic projection, as the embodiment of the irrational, demonic force that subverts all Enlightenment rationality, as a guide to Jerusalem, as a satire of its outlandish Orthodox society, as a Kafkaesque parable and a Surrealist vision. He is probably all of those combined. Persecuted without understanding why, Balak really does go mad, and eventually bites his patron Isaac, who dies of the venom.

It was impossible for Isaac to stay in the fossilized religious world of Eastern Europe, which had come to a dead end and was abandoned by his peers, who chose assimilation in a foreign culture. Filled to the brim with a universe of codified discourse, it became impossible for him to live a normal, secular life. In the end, Isaac's improbable and irrational return to the outer reaches of Orthodox society was an anti-utopian move, a dead end, destined to fail, too.

In his tongue-in-cheek, "naïve" voice, Agnon takes on the great themes of Modernity in European literature from the most marginal margin possible. The Jews seemed absurd and alien in Christian Europe; they were further marginalized when they procreated and multiplied, according to the biblical commandment, and filled up hundreds of small towns that had been passed over by modern capitalism. The Zionists who called for an exit from Exile were actually marginal in Jewish society; and the "realizing" Zionist, who in fact carries out their ideals, was a mock-hero even in their own eyes. From the petit-bourgeois decency of Austro-Hungary, which had granted the Jews equal rights, and their beloved Kaiser Franz Josef, Isaac went to that backward country, the decadent, despotic, and corrupt Ottoman Empire, and to its most marginal province, Palestine, where the Jews were doubly marginalized: by the Turkish governors and by the Arab majority.

The pioneers of the Second *Aliya* landed in this situation, with their Socialist and Tolstoyan ideals of working the land. They were marginal to the religious Jewish society in Eastern Europe, which they fled, and were ostracized or feared by both the Orthodox Old Yishuv in Jerusalem and by the first wave of settlers in Palestine, the farmers of the First *Aliya*.

Furthermore, the Second *Aliya* itself consisted of a few hundred Socialist-Zionist ideologically motivated bachelors, coming from the revolutionary ferment and anti-Semitic pogroms in Russia; while Isaac was a fuzzy-minded general Zionist, a Galician Jew, alien to their ideological fervor and erotic liberties. He drifted to the Orthodox society in Jerusalem, a "medieval" fossil, stuck away in a backward province of a decaying empire, a society with little productive labor (the ideal of his youth), living in poverty on the alms of the Distribution (given by the "societies" of their hometowns), and guarding the graves of ancient Jewish glory and the texts attached to those bare stones. The Old Yishuv was excluded from the new revival of the Land of Israel and excluded itself from the spoken, secular Hebrew language and modern Hebrew literature. And Isaac was an alien intruder among them, too. It is hard to imagine a more exclusionary exile from all exiles.

Yet in all this historical specificity, some of the major themes of the twentieth century reverberate throughout the novel. They are not formulated in any ideological or philosophical manner, but are constantly evoked by this "naïve" witness and textual juggler. In a century that celebrated the Will and the will to power (as reflected in Herzl's resounding slogan: "If you will it, it is no dream"), Isaac is constantly led astray by encounters and circumstances, always turning up in the opposite place from where he set out to be, and it is impossible to ascertain whether it is predestination, God's hand in the world, or blind and accidental fate that conducts this absurd existence. As Professor Boaz Arpali of Tel Aviv University put it, "The truths suppressed by the hero, the decisions he flees, the internal forces he shuns, knowingly or unknowingly or refusing to know, gather momentum in his soul throughout his life, and break out in the end, destroying both his soul and his life."[4]

The first sentence of the novel begins in the name of a collective "us," quoting the official Zionist line as an accepted fact, namely, that it was the fellows of the Second *Aliya* who brought our Salvation, our redemption from Exile.

> Like all our brethren of the Second Aliya, the bearers of our Salvation, Isaac Kumer left his country and his homeland and his city and ascended to the Land of Israel to build it from its destruction and to be rebuilt by it.

Indeed, in Hebrew, *Geula*, Salvation, is the opposite of *Gola*, Exile, locked in an interdependent binary opposition. It is the basic religious terminology, describing the timeless Jewish condition as Exile from their Homeland, to be redeemed when Messiah comes; yet here the language was secularized and transferred to the historical and political views of Zionism, which believed it could be a human task, performed in our generation. Etymologically, the word "homeland" (*moledet*) means "the land of your birth" and is used in Modern Hebrew literature as "fatherland" in the European sense. Thus, Chernikhovsky's famous poem *HaAdam eyno ela*, which takes part in a dialogue between the national Homeland and every Hebrew writer's private homeland, like Chernikhovsky's own very concrete birthplace in the southern

---

4   Boaz Arpali, *Masternovel: Five Essays on* Temol Shilshom *by S.Y. Agnon* [in Hebrew], Literature, Meaning, Culture 23 (Tel Aviv: The Porter Institute for Poetics and Semiotics, Tel Aviv University, Hakibbutz Hameuchad Publishers, 1998).

Ukraine, begins: "A man is no more than a little plot of land / A man is no more than a pattern of the landscape of his homeland." And that is the homeland Isaac Kumer abandoned for the sake of the abstract "Homeland" of the Jewish nation. He did it, as the popular song of the pioneers proclaimed: *Anu banu artsa livnot ulhibanot ba-* "We came to the Land to build it and to be rebuilt by it."[5] The notion was that, as the Land was neglected and desolate, so were the Jews in Exile; the pioneers going to the Land to work its soil would rebuild their own "Diaspora mentality" by rebuilding the land; they would create a New Man and a New Jew, not hovering in the air and living on air, as modern Jewish literature described him, but physically productive, with a straight back and mind, with roots in the soil.

The centerpiece of this sentence is a verbatim quotation from God's commandment to Abram (before he became Yahve's Abraham), sending him out to the Promised Land. This is how Isaac Kumer, the naïve and wholesome Zionist, understood the biblical phrase: as an injunction to go to the Land on God's mission. Yet what a terrible price to pay! As the King James Bible translated it: "Get thee out of thy country, and from thy kindred, and from thy father's house, unto a land that I will shew thee" (Genesis 12:1). The double root *Lekh-lekho* ("Get going! Get out of here!"), with its drastic, harsh ring in the East European context, sounded as an expulsion, and in Jewish Diaspora semiotics (as opposed to religious dogma), the Torah portion, "Lekh-lekho," became a synonym for expulsion. The last chapter of Sholem Aleichem's *Tevye the Milkman* is called *Lekh-Lekho* ("Get Thee Out") and describes the expulsion of the Jews from all Russian villages, even though they were born there. Quoting literally from the Bible and providing his own contemporary translation, as was the customary way of teaching Torah, Tevye tells Sholem Aleichem (in the original, the words in italics are in Hebrew, their mock-translations are in bold in Yiddish): "What weekly portion are you reading now? Leviticus? With us, it is a different chapter: the chapter of *Lekh-lekho. Get thee out*—they told me—*you must get out* of here, Tevye, *from thy country*—from your own land, *and from your homeland*—from your village, *where you were born* and lived all the years of your life, *unto a land that I will shew thee*—wherever your eyes may carry you! . . ."

Agnon's contemporary Marc Chagall used the same biblical text in his

---

5   In Hebrew, *banu* ("we came") includes the past as well as the first-person plural; hence *anu* ("we" or "us") is redundant and betrays the Russian or Yiddish thinking of its authors.

painting, "The Red Jew" (1915). One scholar in Jerusalem used the Zionist interpretation and read it as Chagall's autobiographical message: Chagall returned from Paris to his homeland Russia in 1914. But Chagall read the Bible through Sholem Aleichem and Yiddish folk semiotics, where "The chapter of *lekh-lekho*" means simply expulsion from your home. Indeed, in 1915, hundreds of thousands of Jews were expelled "within 24 hours" from their home-towns, and many thousands came to Chagall's Vitebsk. There is no trace of Russian Zionism or Chagall's homecoming here: an Eternal Jew, his face as white as death, is about to get up and leave his town behind.

This was the duality of interpretation faced by Agnon: the overtly Zionist and optimistic ideology was subverted by a Diaspora reading. And interestingly enough, Agnon changed only one item: instead of "get thee out . . . from thy father's home" (a sense of guilt that haunts him throughout the book), he says: "from his town," the decaying town that was Agnon's emblematic representative of Exile. As the language of the Bible betrays, Abraham was expelled to the Promised Land, and in many ways, so was Isaac Kumer.

And here is a link to the hero's name. Agnon's admired poet Bialik began his poem on the Kishinev pogrom of 1903 with : *kum lekh-lekho el ir ha-hareygo*, which in Hebrew means "get up go thee to the city of slaughter." Why get up? And why is a conjunction missing between the two verbs (I Chronicles 22:16 says: "arise therefore, and be doing")? As the Hebrew critic Dov Sadan argued, *kum* here is in Yiddish (Bialik's daily language): "come, let us go," using the same biblical phrase, *lekh-lekho*, but this time he is told to come and see the city of slaughter. Agnon's protagonist is called Kumer, the one who came—to fulfill the commandment *lekh-lekho*, go thee to the Promised Land. Instead of Bialik's *kum lekh-lekho*, he heard *Kumer lekh-lekho*. But where did he go—to the Promised Land or to Bialik's devastation? In an important respect, the book is a sacrifice of Isaac, performed by himself.

When the book was published in 1945, before the establishment of the State of Israel, in a patriotic Zionist atmosphere, the opening sentence would have been taken seriously, at face value. It requires a long journey through the novel to discover that the opposite is true. The heroes of the collective myth, the laborers of the Second *Aliya*, are exposed as disillusioned and embittered remnants of an ideal, though Agnon does pay them reverent lip service. On the contrary, Agnon shows wherever he can that the Orthodox Old Yishuv also expanded beyond the physical and symbolic walls of the Old City. He set out to write the great epic of the Second *Aliya*, but wrote a novel about the escape from it. As Dostoevsky intended to write in *The Brothers Karamazov* "The Life of a Great Sinner," but didn't get to it and wrote a long antinovel instead, that is a mere preamble to what should (and probably couldn't) have been written, so Agnon ended his book with a formulaic closure:

> Completed are the deeds of Isaac.
> The deeds of our other comrades,
>   the men and the women,
> Will come in the book, *A Parcel of Land.*

Which, of course, he never wrote.

Amos Oz, in his rich and sensitive writer's book about an admired writer,[6] makes it clear that Agnon's mode lies in overdetermination: every move, activity, or event is explained by so many motivations that none makes sense. He uncovers the ironies and contradictory subtexts behind the ostensibly naïve façade of Agnon's style and argument. And he correctly places it all in the perspective of Agnon's Exile/Fatherland dilemma. Thus, the introductory essay begins with a quotation from Agnon about himself, and Oz's striking interpretation:

> *Because of that historical catastrophe when Titus the Roman Emperor destroyed Jerusalem and Israel was exiled from its land, I was born in one of the cities of Exile. But all the time I imagined myself as having been born in Jerusalem.*[7]

Those words, as all readers of Agnon know, are true. But, strangely enough, their opposite is also true. Had Agnon chosen to say: "Because of that historical catastrophe when East European Jewry fell apart, I became a Hebrew writer in Jerusalem. But I always saw myself as one who was born in one of the cities of Galicia and destined to be a rabbi there"—those words would also be true and right on target.

The tragedy of Agnon's vision lies in his perspicacity: long before the Holocaust, he saw the degeneration, ruin, and end of Jewish Eastern Europe; for him, there was no way back to the Diaspora. Yet, the Zionist vision he embraced was far from a secure conquest, and its champions were far from idealists. Agnon's satirical view of the Makhersons (literally: operator) and

---

6   Amos Oz, *The Silence of Heaven: Agnon's Fear of God*, translated by Barbara Harshav (Princeton: Princeton University Press, 2000).

7   Y. Agnon, *From Me to Me* [in Hebrew] (Tel Aviv: Schocken Publishers, 1976), p. 85.

Makherovitches was relentless. There was no utopia in Agnon. But precisely for that anti-utopia in a utopian society, he could put the future in brackets and explore all problems of modernity in the fictional worlds of the past.

The quotations in the opening of the novel—from the Bible and from a pioneer song—are culled from Isaac's consciousness. The narrator presents him and his mind in the third person, thus either being faithful to Kumer's perceptions or creating an ironic distance, or both. Thus the narration is conducted on two levels in a Combined Discourse of the narrator and the hero's focus. The narrator leads the text and the hero is the observer. The narrator appears with his Royal We, sometimes representing the Second *Aliya* or the Zionist revival and collective ideology, sometimes representing Isaac's conscious or subconscious sensibilities, sometimes left alone with Isaac or serving as his voice, and always hovering just above him, yet shifting from reproducing his internal monologues to taking a distance and mocking him. Indeed, there is no specific person behind the "We," but an empty slot of a grammatical first person plural, to be filled in as variously as the text allows. And the same "We" takes over the dog Balak's consciousness in the second part of the book, interprets his innermost thoughts and observes him from the outside as well. There is no omniscient narrator here, for at every junction, the omniscience is suspended for the sake of a focused point of observation: Isaac's, hovering above Isaac, or the dog Balak's.

The fictional world of the novel is presented with very little concrete and descriptive material, but is rather reflected through Isaac's responses to it. A constant stream of consciousness drifts through his mind, yet it is not consciousness that we are offered directly, but strings of quotations and formulaic, pious discourse. If ever there was a text to pervasively using what M. Bakhtin called "alien discourse" (what has later been renamed "intertextuality"), it is surely Agnon's. Isaac has ready-made phrases, stories, anecdotes, and formulae for whatever his eyes encounter. And those are excerpted not just from the Bible and prayerbook, but from the immense Hebrew library. But there is no distinction between religious and other sources: he uses the phrases and images of the most popular Zionist ideology (the image of the man with his plowshare) as well as official Austrian propaganda, stories of the marvels of Vienna as well as the exploits of the early pioneers in Palestine. It is not a stream of consciousness here, but a *stream of textuality*: consciousness takes a back seat to the mosaic of textual excerpts and patterns.

As witness to an apocalyptic event in Jewish history, Isaac Kumer is similar to the narrator in Kafka's "Great Wall of China." Kafka's narrator is paradoxically both a simple laborer, ordered to do monotonous physical work on a senseless national project, and a scholar of Chinese history, both within the process and above it in time. Isaac is both a simple housepainter, even a simpleton, who believes and understands anybody and everybody, and as learned a reader of the Hebrew library as Agnon himself. Yet all the uses of traditional turns of phrases are not meant as specific allusions to specific texts, but rather serve as a stylistic layer which represents a textual culture, where the texts are preserved but their interpretations are shaken. Agnon's Israeli reader, who does not know that library, certainly perceives it so. Moreover, many Hebrew phrases and words that look like quotations actually have a subtext from Agnon's (and his character's) first language, Yiddish. Thus, in Israeli Hebrew, *bitahon* means "security," while in Yiddish it means quite the opposite: "you must have *bitokhn*" (the Yiddish pronunciation) means "to hope for the best" in a situation that is rationally hopeless, because the term derives from the phrase *betakh beHashem*—"trust in God" (rather than man).

In many ways, *Only Yesterday* is an abstract modern novel. From the beginning, reality is often presented not in individual situations and encounters, but in plural and in long catalogues. For it is not the external fact that constitutes the fictional world, but the summary of such facts in Isaac's mind, filled with categories and catalogues. When he leaves home, we are told: "Isaac parted from his father and his brothers and sisters and all his other relatives and set out on the road." But for all his guilt feelings about abandoning his family to exile, we are not told here the names of his brothers and sisters nor how many of them there were.

Traveling on a train is most convenient for that mode of abstraction.

The train rolled on between villages and hamlets, cities and towns. Some were known for their great rabbis and others were known for their famous cemeteries. Some earned a name with the produce of their fields and the fruit of their trees, the fish in their rivers and the minerals in their mountains; and others earned fame with their poultry and livestock and other things in heaven and on earth. And yet other places have neither learning nor earning, but do have a Quarrel. Some sanctify the Name of the Holy-One-Blessed-Be-He with the Kedushah, *We shall sanctify You*, and others sanctify Him with *We shall bless You*, and they wrestle with each other and create a Quarrel. And another Quarrel, between Assimilationists and Zionists. The former want to be like all the other nations, and the latter want to be Jews, so they wrestle with each

other and create a Quarrel. And yet another Quarrel, between those who want
Salvation by miracle and those who want a natural Salvation, so they wrestle
with each other and create a Quarrel.

A neutral classifier summarizes his observations, takes no stand on the alternative options, and empties them of any concrete content. Yet between the
lines, we learn about the futility of the Jewish Quarrels that devour Diaspora
society and willy-nilly are introduced to the major theological issue of the
book and of modern Jewish history: Is Salvation to be brought by a miracle or
in the normal course of nature—all this in passing on a train through named
or nameless towns and cities.

He arrives in the legendary capital of his Empire, Vienna, and has several
hours of free time on his hands. But first he delivers a catalogue of all the remarkable places in the capital without having seen any of them:

> Isaac was all on his own and considered where he would go. Would he go
> to Leopoldstadt with its splendid synagogues whose beauty is unsurpassed
> throughout the world, or to the Prater, the joy of the whole city, or to the
> big house called Bunch of Grapes, or to their church that has a clock where
> every single one of its numbers is more than two feet high, or to the library
> where the Book of Psalms is written in gold letters on red parchment, or to the
> Emperor's palace, or to the Museum. Many were the things here that we heard
> about and now we can see them. And now we stand at the entrance of Vienna
> and we don't know where we shall go or where we shall turn. Isaac stood a
> while, his mind flitting from place to place but his feet aren't moving, for with
> so many things, his head is heavy and his feet are heavier than his head.

Even more remarkable is his hymn to the greatness of the Austrian Empire:

> The train wound its way up, and wound its way down. High mountains flew
> by and snow lay on them, and even though Passover was already past, the
> snow didn't budge. And so, Isaac sits and rides through the realm of Aus-
> tria, that same Austria that rules over eighteen states, and twelve nations are
> subject to it. One and the same law for the Jews and for the people of the
> land, their well-being is our well-being, for the Emperor is a Gracious King,
> he protects all who take shelter with him, Jew and non-Jew alike. Her earth
> is lush and fertile and the produce of her land is greater than the need of her
> inhabitants. She is blessed with everything and knows no shortage. One land
> makes wheat and barley and rye and beans and lentils and oats and corn; and

another land makes potatoes and fruit of the orchard. One land makes plums for confiture and Slivovitz, and another land makes hops for beer. One land makes wine and another land makes tobacco and flax, and all lands are full of livestock, animals, and birds. Some give milk and butter and cheese, and some give meat and wool and skins and feathers. One land produces horses, and another land chickens and ducks and swans, doves, and pheasants, and bees make honey and wax, and her lakes and rivers are filled with fish and her mountains with silver and copper and tin and iron and lead for paint and salt mines, and coal and oil. And her forests make wood, and there are high mountains there, covered with eternal snow.

"Her forests make wood, and there are high mountains there, covered with eternal snow." There are no specific names for trees, no specific places in the mountains. He does not use the realistic technique of describing one of those provinces or talking to one person who may have boarded the train. We don't even know which province produces what product. And more important, Isaac does not confront this paean with his Zionist ideology; if this Empire is so rich and Jews have equal rights in it, why is he going to that desolate Palestine?

The paucity of realistic details reflects both the relatively undifferentiated world of lower-class folklore and the Jewish Diaspora imagination, living in a fictional world of books, in a timeless Holy Land or Babylon, and not distinguishing between one tree and another or one mental situation and another. Nineteenth-century Hebrew dictionaries translated the names of specific birds or trees as "a kind of bird" or "a kind of tree." The great European fiction with its immense wealth of differentiated descriptive details of the physical world, nature, and civilization, as well as of states of mind, did not reach traditional Jewish society in Eastern Europe. The ways of resolving this situation (aside from writing a derivative European novel) were ways of abstraction and textuality.

The great Jewish writers of the twentieth century responded to this period of transition from a medieval, traditional society, religious in its framework and codified in its forms of behavior—to the world of modern, secular Europe, with its individualism, centrality of consciousness, and historicity. It was not a move exclusive to Jewish society, but here it was telescoped into a very short period of one or two generations, and dramatized by both the internal textual tradition of this people and the external perils to their existence. Agnon, Sholem Aleichem, or Kafka evoked that fault line and gave it mythological forms. Sholem Aleichem knew he was not Tolstoy, that he could not describe aristocratic drawing rooms in exquisite detail because the authentic Jewish world was the world of the small town, the so-called *shtetl*, poor in physical objects, whose inhabitants lived in an imaginary universe, a mishmash of folklore and snippets of learning. He diverted the level of concreteness from actual events and their historical causes to the stream of speech of his garrulous protagonists. Even when a wave of pogroms washes over Russia, Tevye the Milkman says, "when they began talking about pogroms." Thus Sholem Aleichem erected a fictional world in Yiddish, using the most authentic material of the Yiddish language: its associative, rambling talk, filled with proverbs, idioms, stories, and asides, and studded with shards of distorted quotations from the Hebrew Library. Writing in Hebrew, Agnon mined the historical layers of the written Hebrew language and created an illusion of textuality, using both phrases and anecdotes from the Library as well as syntactical patterns that imitated the traditional books. Kafka, on the other hand, lost both the talkative Yiddish and the Hebrew Library of texts. In his fictional work, Kafka moved out of the Jewish domain, yet his *realia* was just as poor in concrete details. He too resorted to abstraction, used catalogues of items in plural and presented the significant discussions of the "system" (in *The Trial*) in abstract, ideological terms.

In all of them, the front narrative was trivial; the real, profound issues were presented not in telling examples, but in the deep background, in ideological discourse. What remains concrete on front stage is *diverted concreteness*. Tevye talks, K. moves from one corrupt abode to another, Isaac changes places and jobs, but such concrete situations serve merely as occasions for verbal speculations and evocations, raising the great questions of human existence, the "rules of the game" in God's world, and the hierarchy of values or loss of them.

Thus, writing in Hebrew was not just a linguistic matter, but a resort to the totality of ways of seeing the world through the mountain of traces from a Borges-type Library. That Hebrew Library entailed a panhistorical and transgeographical view of Jewish existence: it does not much matter where or when the characters were, the essential conception of the Homeland-Exile dichotomy remained eternal, until Salvation comes. There is very little here about any problems of the Ottoman administration or the Arab majority in Palestine, the Russian revolutions or technological advances, the building of

Tel Aviv or the revival of Hebrew as a spoken language. Poverty in the most marginal marginality of Jerusalem under Ottoman rule means exclusion from the technological age. Isaac's escape from the workers of the Second *Aliya* also means escape from the age of ideology. Yet the traditional religious view did not allow for Salvation by human hands, for the Zionists' "pushing the end." Thus, the impasse is given, no matter what end it may take.

Furthermore, at first reading, the novel sounds like a naïve and meandering story about a naïve and drifting housepainter, until it explodes with the Mad Dog (the French translation of the novel is even titled, *The Dog Balak*). From here on (at least), all rationality is thrown to the dogs.

The discussion of the specific Hebrew substance of the novel, its ascetic minimalism, focusing on a nonintellectual, non-ideological antihero, must not obstruct our view of its deep European roots. Agnon was the last Mohican of Diaspora Hebrew literature, still able to invoke and visualize the religious world of the simple folk in East European Jewry, looking back from the territorial context of the Zionist revival in Palestine. Furthermore, Agnon did it while having read a library of European novels, though masking his modern concerns in the rhetoric of the traditional Library and its "naïve" readers.

Boaz Arpali, who analyzed the genres intersecting in Agnon's novel, called it a "Master-Novel" or "Super-Novel," written by a "Super-Master": "*Only Yesterday* is a Super-Novel, for it includes several models and central aspects of the European novel since its inception. It is a conglomerate in which those models and aspects obtain new meanings and functions both in themselves and one vis-à-vis the other, thus creating new and exciting relations among them." The plot of the novel, too, is at least a double plot: "On the one hand, from its very inception, it is mainly a picaresque, panoramic, episodic and comical plot with a strong social orientation. On the other hand, it is a plot of character and destiny (or, perhaps preferably: character that is destiny), a dramatic-tragical plot, whose links derive from one another in a tight causal chain with a psychological-existential orientation. The first story emerges in a consecutive reading from the beginning onward, while the shock brings us to the second story, in a retrospective reading from the end to the beginning."

4 AMERICAN POETRY IN YIDDISH AND ITS BACKGROUND[1]

AN EXPEDITION TO THE RIVERS OF MANHATTAN[2]

How long will Yiddish Literature be unknown among Gentiles?
How long will they think of us—in literature—as Hottentots?
　　—A. Leyeles, *In Zikh*, July 1923

So many years in America, such a fine literature created here, and we remain strangers to our neighbors as if we had lived in Siam or had written in some Eskimo dialect.
　　—A. Leyeles, *In Zikh*, March 1937

We learn the language of the mute and the deaf. We embark on anthropological expeditions to the jungles and mountains of Central America or New Guinea, we study the remnant tongues of Native American tribes. But what do we know of the poetry and fiction that flourished here, "on the rivers of Manhattan"[3] and other cities, dynamic and polyvalent, intensely American, but mute in its language, a one-way street with no return?

1　Introduction to Benjamin and Barbara Harshav, *American Yiddish Poetry* (Stanford, CA: Stanford University Press, 2008).

2　For examples of Yiddish poetry in translation, see: Benjamin and Barbara Harshav, *American Yiddish Poetry*, and Benjamin Harshav, *Sing, Stranger/A Century of American Yiddish Poetry: A Historical Anthology* (Stanford, CA: Stanford University Press, 2006).

3　*On the Rivers of Manhattan* is the name of a book of poetry in English by Charles Reznikoff, coined upon the Biblical "On the Rivers of Babylon" in the cultural center of the Diaspora.

There was once a rich, buoyant American literature in Yiddish, perhaps the most coherent and full-fledged literary institution in the United States outside of English. Except for its exclusive language, it was not a parochial phenomenon. It spanned a wide gamut of themes, forms, and ideologies—from utopian socialism to American *engagement*, from cosmopolitan universalism to Jewish nationalism—and encompassed a variegated range of styles and genres—from naturalist fiction to avant-garde experiments, from popular melodrama and stirring novels in newspaper installments to virtuoso sonnet garlands and hermetic free verse.

While English poetry was dominated by the exquisite elitism of T.S. Eliot and Ezra Pound and steeped in cultural allusions to the European past of Dante, Shakespeare, and the Provençal bards, Yiddish poets—shoemakers, housepainters, or "poor newspaper writers" as they were—often confronted American realities directly: the wonders of construction and city architecture, the subway, the harbors, labor unions, the underworld, the plight of the blacks, the trial of Sacco and Vanzetti, alienation of the individual in the jungle of the metropolis, social injustice, and immigrant longing.

At the same time, Yiddish poets were fascinated by contemporary international ideas. Modernism, Freud, the Russian Revolution, Buddhism, the Tao, Nietzsche, Baudelaire, Villon, Isaiah and Homer, Whitman and Rabbi Nakhman from Bratslav mark the range of intertextuality of American Yiddish poetry. Young Yiddish poets in New York talked "about eternity, death and grammar" (as Glatshteyn put it in his poem "On My Two-Hundredth Birthday," written at the age of twenty-five)—talking was at the heart of their culture.

They created a chorus of voices, inscribing with emotional and intellectual intensity their responses to the human condition—nature and the modern city, alienation and love, the "Golden Land" and the "Old Home" overseas—in existential or melodic lyrical poems or long, descriptive verse narratives. Because Yiddish poetry in this period was largely Modernist poetry—that is, consciously art in language—it employed the most specific characteristics of the Yiddish language and drew on its cultural density, creating unique combinations of diction, sound, and allusion. Indeed, it is hardly possible to experience the full impact of this poetry without having internalized the language and its emotive and socio-semantic dimensions.

American Yiddish poetry has two faces. On the one hand, it is a prominent expression of modern Jewish culture. It gave voice to yet another permutation of Jewish history: the migration of a whole people to a new world, the changes in their social fabric and value systems, the traumas and internal richness of Jewish existence, the ties and tensions between collective pressures and individual freedom. It also laid bare the treasures and the contradictions of the Yiddish language and the Jewish tradition. Yiddish poetry transformed the language of a popular, age-saturated, oral culture into the aristocratic and cosmopolitan forms of post-Symbolist poetry or the coarse and cutting metaphorical outbursts of Expressionist verse. And in its decline—perhaps like no other literature—it gave voice to the tragic vision of the Holocaust in Europe, enmeshed in the tragedy of the poet's own disappearing language.

On the other hand, Yiddish poetry was no mere vehicle for the expression of "Jewish" experience. This was a time of mass movement of people of Jewish origin into general Western culture, the business world, art, and academia. Yiddish poets were part of it. They responded to the modern world as human beings and as Americans, embracing the forms of Western culture while working in their own language. As the Introspectivist manifesto of 1919 put it, "poetry is, to a very high degree, the art of language . . . and Yiddish poetry is the art of the Yiddish language and is merely a part of the general European-American culture."[4] Thus, much of Yiddish poetry written in the United States was consciously and effectively a cosmopolitan, even American literature, expressing the emotions and thoughts of the individual in the modern metropolis. It was attuned to all facets of modern life and history, though written in the Yiddish idiom and using "Jewish" experiences (among others) as a language to express the human condition.

From an American perspective, Yiddish poetry must be seen as an unjustly neglected branch of American literature, a kaleidoscope of American experience and art entombed in yellowing, crumbling books, in the muteness of its own dead language.

From a "Jewish" perspective, Yiddish poetry was not the world of "our fathers," but of their sons, our cousins. In that great centrifugal move out of the old, medieval, jittery Eastern-European existence, Yiddish literature was one of the new cultural alternatives. Like those who invented Zionism, created modern Hebrew literature, or built the then unrealistic fantasyland of Israel; those who fell in the battles for Socialism; or those who assimilated into

---

4   For an English translation of the Introspectivist manifesto and other theoretical writings by the Introspectivists, see *American Yiddish Poetry.*

Western culture, contributing to its literature, art, and science and adopting new languages, ideas, and manners, Yiddish writers were carried on a revolutionary wave. They were creating a modern literature that would be "merely a branch, a particular stream in the whole contemporary poetry of the world" (as the Introspectivist manifesto put it), just as the founders of modern Israel wanted to build "a nation like all nations." For readers who could read themselves into their world, these writers produced a brilliant performance and eventually made a tragic exit from an empty hall.

They were our cousins, a branch of the same evolutionary tree that came to a dead end, a bough that bloomed and withered away or was uprooted by a tornado in a quirky twist of history.

ARCHAEOLOGY OF A CULTURE

In the past, Yiddish encountered formidable walls of prejudice. All the weight of Jewish inferiority complexes and the animosity of an alien world toward the "Jewish" image of the Jew were projected upon this language, which was seen as the embodiment of the "medieval," "provincial," primitive, devious, unassimilable Jewish subsistence. Masses of young Jews streamed into the richer, more powerful and rewarding general culture whenever possible—in pre-Hitler Germany, in postrevolutionary Russia, in the relatively liberal United States. Hence, no high-level effort was made to present the art of Yiddish in other languages. Halpern, Leyvik, Leyeles, Glatshteyn, or Teller (himself an English writer), who had the stamina to create a modern poetry in Yiddish in New York and about New York, rarely saw any collections of their poetry translated into English, although (or, as some would argue, because) there was no lack of Jews in the American literary establishment.

Today, it may be almost too late. The best achievements of American Yiddish literature were in poetry. Translating poetry is a challenging and frustrating task. It can rarely succeed in creating an equivalent that is close to the original in poetic stature. But beyond this crucial question, in recent translations one often observes a simple lack of knowledge of the full range and precise meanings and connotations of the original. A typical example is Leyvik's poem, "Here Lives the Jewish People." The poem starts with the line: "The towering life of the towering city," but one distinguished translator translated it: "The imprisoned life of the prison city," changing the whole meaning of the poem (in Yiddish, *turem*, "tower," of German origin, is similar to *turme*, "prison," which comes from Russian). She changed a hymn into a lamentation. In many cases, translators have used "feet" for the Yiddish *fis*, thus M.L. Halpern has a woman spread her feet rather than her legs. Yiddish is much more of a forgotten tongue than we are willing to admit.

One problem is that Yiddish poetry not only explored the full range of the Yiddish language and simultaneously enriched it in many ways but also benefited from the historically unique cultural junction at which the generations of its writers and readers found themselves. Hence, along with the historical layers and multilingual components of the Yiddish language itself, Yiddish poetry reverberated with the themes and images of the Hebrew-Aramaic religious, mythological, and cultural tradition, the reminiscences and figures of Jewish history. It also drew on the stories, allusions, and intonations of Slavic folklore and literature, as well as on some German literature and on the imaginary museum of modern (including Oriental) culture, mediated through those languages.

It may be said that modern Yiddish literature was written in the genres, forms, and conventions of Russian (and through it, European) literature, in a basically Germanic language that was impressed by layers of Hebrew texts and mythology and by "Jewish" images, typology, and intonations of speech. This complex and unique poetic language was open to the themes, motifs, ideas, and aesthetic trends of modern Europe. In this disheveled conglomerate Yiddish came to America, responded to its stimulae, and absorbed some influences of its literature, life, and ideological atmosphere. A reader or critic would have to travel the same road, at least intellectually, to perceive the full impact of the competing voices in a Yiddish text.

For example, A. Leyeles received a Jewish-Hebrew education growing up in the big-city atmosphere of the Jewish-and-German Polish city of Lodz under Russian rule, then lived for five years in London and spent most of his creative life in New York. Besides Yiddish and Hebrew, he knew Russian, German, Polish, English, and some French, and was well-read in those literatures. Leyeles was a master of Provençal poetic forms (probably under the influence of Russian Symbolism as well as of German and Yiddish Impressionism): he wrote sonnets, villanelles, rondeaux, ottava rimas, triolets, and terzinas in Yiddish and invented his own exact strophic patterns. At the same time, he created a variety of American-influenced but original and either "prosaic" or rhythmically intense free-verse forms. He translated an influential book of aesthetics by Broder Kristiansen from German into Yiddish, as well as poems

by E.A. Poe, Keats, Whitman, Paul Verlaine, Amy Lowell, Goethe, Lermon-
tov, Pushkin, and Stephen Spender. Leyeles's poems echo themes from Buddhism, psychoanalysis, American architecture, the Russian Revolution, the
Bible, Baudelaire, and the Holocaust.

This does not mean that every Yiddish poet was a multilingual walking
library, but that Yiddish poetry as a whole stood at this unusual intersection,
attuning its antennae to "Culture" and open to winds from all sides. The contemporary American reader or translator can hardly match the immediacy
and fusion of moods and modes that met at that junction.

Neither can it be done by the repeated nostalgic waves of fondness for Yiddish, which often rejoice in the sentimental, melodramatic aspects of lower-
class Yiddish popular culture and film—in the *shmates*,* the very mention of
which evokes derision or good-humored laughter. Along with the warmth of
a naïve humanity and a groping for some kind of "roots," nostalgia entails a
distancing gesture vis-à-vis the primitive, though endearing, "world of our
fathers" which, thank God, we have left behind forever. Clearly, nostalgia for
the vestiges of Yiddish popular culture, as well as the emotive connotations
of Yiddish words and expressions used in contemporary English or Hebrew,
fulfill a significant sociolinguistic function. But the relation between modern
Yiddish poetry and this stratum is not very different from that between English poetry, on the one hand, and American folklore, mass media, or Holly-
wood films, on the other.

In recent years, a revival of interest in Yiddish literature, and in American Yiddish literature in particular, has generated a new wave of translations
and dissertations. A number of books and anthologies have brought some of
the themes, names, and scope of Yiddish verse to the attention of the English
reader. Yet, unlike translations from French, Spanish, or German, we have little
hope of supporting our English renderings of Yiddish poetry with the full force
of the living context of the original looming in the background. If Rilke, Mandelshtam, or Baudelaire do not really come through in English translations,
the reader can supplement some of the lacks of the English text with a partial
knowledge of the source language and a feeling for the sound and sense of the
original, with a knowledge of its intellectual background, and with a cultural
belief in the halo of its importance. All this is lacking in the case of Yiddish.

---

*   *Shmates* is a loaded word, literally referring to rags, old cloth, or "junk," and colored by the
expressive sound of the derogatory cluster *shm-*.

The selection and density of poetic language communicates only when it can rely on a broad background, assuming the reader's familiarity with a wide body of texts in a society—written and oral, fiction, folklore, essays, ideology and philosophy. Very little of that background can be assumed in the reader's knowledge of the Yiddish world. Moreover, the artistic norms and values of Yiddish poetry itself are remote from the reader's expectations, and may often seem primitive, rhetorical, sentimental, or plain old-fashioned.

THE HISTORICAL CONTEXT

The oldest dated text in Yiddish is a rhymed couplet written inside the ornamental initial letters of a Hebrew word in the Worms *Mahzor* (prayerbook) of 1272. The oldest large Yiddish text, the so-called Cambridge manuscript, was found in Cairo, Egypt (in the famous Genizah). Dated 1382, it contains poems on Jewish historical topics (Abraham, Joseph, the death of Aaron), religious texts, and an otherwise unknown, earliest version of a German epic, *Dukus Horant*.

Many medieval Yiddish texts have probably been lost. Yet the variety of manuscripts and books extant from that period nevertheless shows the span of its writings: adapted German epics; epic poems on biblical topics written in medieval German meters; lyrical and historical poems in German and Hebrew verse forms; stories; plays; moral guidebooks, legal protocols, and private letters. From the first half of the sixteenth century on, Yiddish books were printed in Germany, Italy, Holland, Switzerland, and Poland and were distributed in the entire Yiddish realm: at one pole, Elia Levita's (Eliyahu Bakhur, Nuremberg 1469–Venice 1549) epic poem *Bove Bukh*, a Yiddish version in ottava rima of the European romance *Buovo d'Antona* (*Beve of Hampton*), written in Padua in 1507; and at the other, *Tsene verene*, a retelling of the Bible for women, which became so popular that it saw about three hundred editions.[5]

By the sixteenth century, the center of European Jewry had shifted to Poland, which was then one of the largest countries in Europe, comprising Poland (with Galicia, Pomerania, and Silesia), the Grand Duchy of Lithuania (including today's Byelorussia), and Ukraine, and stretching from the Baltic to the

---

5   On the history of old Yiddish literature, see Khone Shmeruk, *Yiddish Literature: Aspects of its History* [in Hebrew], Porter Institute, Tel Aviv, 1978. On Elia Levita's versification, see Benjamin Hrushovski, "The Creation of Accentual Iambs in European Poetry and their First Employment in a Yiddish Romance in Italy (1508–09)," in *For Max Weinreich on His Seventieth Birthday*, Lucy Dawidowicz et al., eds., Mouton, 1964, pp. 108–146.

Black Sea. In medieval Poland, Jews played an important role in developing cities and settling the eastern areas of Poland, mediating between the Polish landed aristocracy, on the one hand, and the peasants of various nationalities in this vast "breadbasket of Europe," on the other. In sixteenth-eighteenth-century Poland, there was a Jewish autonomous state within a state, headed by "The Assembly of Four Lands." A strong network of education and learning developed. Here, the Hassidic movement emerged in the eighteenth century and modern political movements, from Socialism to Zionism, rose at the end of the nineteenth. This became the base of the Yiddish-speaking masses.

Toward the end of the eighteenth century, the great Kingdom of Poland and Lithuania was devoured by its neighbors, Prussia (later: Germany), Austria, and Russia. Most Jews under Russian rule did not live in Russia proper but were confined to the formerly Polish-ruled territories, the "Pale of Settlement," a vast geographical ghetto that included the Ukraine, Byelorussia, and Lithuania, as well as the heart of Poland proper. The Jews of Galicia found themselves separated from their cousins and living in the Austro-Hungarian Empire.

In neither empire did the masses of Jews live among speakers of the state language but rather in the midst of various minorities: Poles, Ukrainians, Byelorussians, Lithuanians, Latvians, Germans, Rumanians, Hungarians. This fact enhanced the preservation of Yiddish in the densely populated Jewish towns. In 1897, 97.96 percent of all Jews inhabiting the Russian Empire claimed Yiddish as their mother tongue.

Throughout the nineteenth century, the Jewish population in Eastern Europe grew immensely, in numbers and in poverty. Millions emigrated overseas. In 1800 there were 2.2 million Jews in the world, of them, 1 million in Eastern Europe. By the eve of World War II these numbers had grown to 15 million Ashkenazi (and 1.5 million Sephardic and Oriental) Jews in the world.

Yiddish had a considerable body of folklore and a large written literature, which flourished in the sixteenth century and again since the nineteenth century, especially in the years 1862–1970. Its revival was part of the modern Jewish renaissance, which became a tidal wave after the pogroms in Russia in 1881–82, and which transformed the existence of the Jews and their descendants. This renaissance included mass migration overseas and to the West, as well as migration from small towns to big cities; assimilation and integration of many Jews into Western culture, economy, literature, and science; the emergence of political parties, from Socialists to Zionists; and the emergence of a modern literature in Hebrew and in Yiddish.

Toward the end of the nineteenth century, three "classical" writers—the "Grandfather" of Yiddish literature Mendele Moykher Sforim, Sholem Aleichem, and I.L. Peretz—lent prestige to a flourishing literary institution. In a short period, dozens of original authors created a literature with European standards, moving swiftly from the rationalist Enlightenment through carnivalesque parody to Realism, Naturalism, and psychological Impressionism, and then breaking out into the general literary trends of Expressionism and Modernism.

This became possible because of the secularization of the Jewish masses, the trend of abandoning traditional Hebrew religious education, and the strong wish to join the general world of modern culture and politics in their own Yiddish language. The growing political parties, especially the Folkists and the Socialists, supported Yiddish culture and education, seeing it at first as a tool for propaganda and a way to break out of the traditional religious framework and, later on, as a goal in itself. Hundreds of periodicals and newspapers appeared in Yiddish (the earliest was the newspaper *Kurantn*, published in Amsterdam in 1686). Libraries sprang up in hundreds of towns. A modern secular school system developed all over Eastern Europe (and to some extent in both Americas). Massive translation efforts brought to the Yiddish reader the works of Tolstoy, Kropotkin, Zola, Ibsen, Jules Verne, Rabindranath Tagore, Lion Feuchtwanger, Shakespeare, Yessenin, Ezra Pound, and many others.

It was, however, a tragic destiny. As Harvard Professor Leo Wiener put it in 1899, "there is probably no other language . . . on which so much opprobrium has been heaped."[6] Traditionally, Yiddish was dubbed the "Servant Maid" to the "Lady" Hebrew. With the onset of the Enlightenment among German Jews, Yiddish became the ugly symbol of everything that kept the Jews from entering civilized Western society. Indeed, from the point of view of a "pure" literary German language based in Berlin, Yiddish looked like a contortion, a corrupted medley with no aesthetic values. Moses Mendelssohn wrote that "this jargon contributed no little to the immorality of the common Jews," and demanded "pure German or pure Hebrew, but no hodge-podge." It was not merely a matter of language: Yiddish became the externalized object

---

6   *History of Yiddish Literature in the Nineteenth Century*, New York, 1899. See Joshua A. Fishman's survey, "The Sociology of Yiddish," in his anthology, *Never Say Die!: A Thousand Years of Yiddish in Jewish Life and Letters*, Mouton, 1981.

of Jewish self-hatred. Pressured by a Gentile society, Jews internalized many anti-Semitic stereotypes, blaming "Jewish" professions, character traits, mentality, and behavior for their lot among Christian nations. Moving out of the Jewish towns in areas of minority nationalities into centers of the state languages like Warsaw, Vienna, Berlin, Moscow, London, Paris, Tel Aviv, or New York, masses of Jews eagerly embraced the dominant language and culture. The movement of the young, bright, and successful away from Yiddish again left the language mostly to lower-class readers of limited culture, and thus reinforced the vicious circle.

To be sure, there was a vigorous Yiddishist movement counteracting both assimilation and self-abasement. Baptized in the famous "Czernowitz Conference" of Yiddish writers in 1908, it freed Yiddish from the demeaning label, "Jargon," and pronounced it "a Jewish national language." Yiddishism, too, the ideology promoting Yiddish as the language of Jewish culture, was part of the trend that was profoundly critical of the old ways of Jewish Diaspora existence (though it usually heaped the blame on religion rather than on language). A network of schools, publishing houses, libraries, and scientific institutions emerged, especially in post-World War I Poland and the Soviet Union. Textbooks were written, terminologies developed, elitist theater and poetry cherished, and so on.

In retrospect, however, it is clear that, in the long-range perspective of Jewish history, Yiddish culture was merely a bridge between traditional religious Jewish society and assimilation into Western cultures. Yiddish literature as an institution existed perhaps for seven centuries. But for each writer, it was a matter of only one (or, in rare cases, of two) generations. Most modern Yiddish writers had grown up with some Hebrew religious education, whereas their children were already steeped in the culture of another language.

The base of Yiddish culture in Eastern Europe, with its historical foundation, institutional network, and millions of native speakers, was destroyed by Hitler and Stalin. A third of the Jewish people perished in the Holocaust, but the destruction of Yiddish was total. Stalin killed Yiddish writers; Hitler killed Yiddish writers and their readers alike.

We must admit, however, that the trend toward assimilation was overpowering everywhere: in Soviet Russia after the Revolution, in Poland, France, England, Argentina, and the United States. The attempt to create a modern, cosmopolitan, autonomous culture in a separate Jewish language with no state of its own was doomed to failure.

THE YIDDISH LANGUAGE

According to its great historian, Max Weinreich[7], Yiddish emerged in the Rhine area around C.E. 1000, as the living speech of Jewish immigrants from Italy and France who adopted the German language of their new neighbors and gradually spread throughout Europe. Yiddish was an integral part of the culture of Ashkenazi Jews. It is not quite clear to what extent and at what time Yiddish really separated from German. In any case, the question is purely academic. From its inception, the language was used by a separate, tightly organized, international community with its own isolated world of knowledge, learning, history, and beliefs, and it was written in its own separate alphabet. Its typical features can be detected from the earliest documents. Yiddish was always a language of "fusion," in which elements from various German dialects, the Holy Tongue (the Hebrew and Aramaic of the texts of Jewish tradition), Romance languages (brought by Jews from Italy and France), and, later, from several Slavic languages were blended into one synthetic whole and one grammatical system.[8]

At the same time, throughout its history, Yiddish was an "open" language. In addition to those elements from its source languages that it had absorbed thoroughly, Yiddish speakers could at various times and for various purposes, draw from the resources of those languages and tilt their vocabulary in one direction or another. Indeed, Yiddish was the language of a multilingual society, moving among neighbors who spoke its component languages (especially German and Slavic) and preoccupied with books and with continuously multiplying texts and manuscripts written in the Holy Tongue.

The Jews were the only society in medieval Europe that had a mandatory education, at least for men. They devoted a great deal of time to learning and reading. The texts of that education—the holy books, the books of law and their commentaries, as well as the texts of prayers, Kabbalah, Hassidism, poetry, moral tracts, community annals, and so on—were in Hebrew and Aramaic. However, the processing of that tradition throughout the ages and in

---

7   Max Weinreich (1894–1969) was the founder and head of YIVO, the Jewish Scientific Institute in Vilna (1925) and New York. See his *History of the Yiddish Language* (in Yiddish), Vols. I-IV, New York; YIVO 1973 and the English abbreviated version *History of the Yiddish Language*, University of Chicago Press, 1980. I owe many linguistic observations to this book.

8   For a more detailed assessment of the Yiddish language, its historical contexts and semiotics of conversation, see my book, Benjamin Harshav, *The Meaning of Yiddish* (Stanford, CA: Stanford University Press, 1990).

all countries of the Diaspora involved not just passive reading and praying but active studying, arguing, interpreting, and writing. Books, commentaries, poems, legal Responsa, and epistolary texts were written throughout the ages in the Holy Tongue. But the Holy Tongue was mute, it was a "dead," unspoken language; and because Talmudic learning involved understanding, dialectical analysis, and argument, it needed an oral vehicle for the interactions of teaching and dialogue. The language in which this literature was taught and argued in Europe was Yiddish. Yiddish was also the language of daily life, conversation, trade, family affairs, storytelling, oral preaching, and a whole spectrum of genres of oral literature.

Thus Yiddish was merely part—albeit an indispensable part—of an interconnected cultural polysystem, and fulfilled only some of the functions of a "normal" language. It was the language of a society that brought to Europe a Hebrew tradition from the past, as well as a tradition of understanding and commenting on the Hebrew texts in another language (especially Aramaic, which itself became part of the textual tradition). In spite of its overt Germanic garb, Yiddish absorbed a great deal of the phraseology, vocabulary, conceptual world, conversational modes, and intonations of the Hebrew and Aramaic texts. It was also constantly exposed to the languages of its immediate neighbors (e.g., Polish or Ukrainian) as well as to the languages of the dominant power or culture (e.g., Russian or German), and was influenced by them. Indeed, in its grammatical structure as in its semiotic world, Yiddish provided a bridge between the traditional Jewish culture and the languages and cultures of Europe, their beliefs, folklore, proverbs, and images. This is why the living Yiddish language in America in the last hundred years could so easily absorb the stream of English words and expressions that flooded the language of conversation and newspapers (though this was bitterly contested by Yiddish purist educators and writers).

As with all other Jewish languages throughout history, Yiddish was separated from its source languages while using its own, separate alphabet. Hebrew letters had to be adapted for writing this basically Germanic language, much as European vernacular languages developed their independent spelling systems from the Latin alphabet. There was one exception: words of Hebrew origin, though pronounced differently in Yiddish, preserved their historical Hebrew spelling (although in Introspectivist writings and in Soviet Yiddish, these too were assimilated to the dominant Yiddish phonetic spelling).

The bulk of Yiddish vocabulary and many of its grammatical features are of German origin (deriving from various, mostly southern German dialects in their medieval stage). There are several thousands of Hebrew and Aramaic words and expressions, some of which entered other languages: *meshúge, tohu-vabóhu, Shábes, gánev* (thief), *balebós* (boss), *riboyne-shel-oýlem* (God), and so on.[9] Many words are recognizably of Slavic origin: *borshch, kashe, nudnik, shmate, podlóge* (floor). Some words still exhibit their Latin derivation: *bent-shn* (to pray, from "benedicere"), *leyenen* (to read, from "legere"), *kreplakh* (dumplings, cf. the French "crêpe"), *cholent* (dish kept warm for the Sabbath, cf. Old French "chalt," warm), and such names as *Bunem* ("bonhomme"), *Shneyer* ("senior"), *Beyle* ("bella" or "belle"), *Yentl* ("gentille"), and so forth.

A more interesting feature is the integration of elements from various sources, which occurred on all levels of the language, from phonology to beliefs. Thus the European *dokter* ("doctor") has a Hebrew plural: *doktóyrim* (*o* is pronounced *oy* in Ashkenazi Hebrew); the German-source *táyvl* ("devil") has a Hebrew plural *tayvólim* (like the Hebrew-derived *moshl-meshólim*, "parable"). The word *shlimázl* ("shlemiel") combines the German "Shlimm" ("bad") with the Hebrew "mazal" ("luck"); and a real shlemiel is a *shlimezál-nik*, adding the Slavic suffix *-nik* to the other two source languages. *Ikh núdzhe zikh* ("I am bored") has a Slavic root embedded in a Germanic verb form; *aróyf-ge-tshépe-te* ("attached to, hooked on to") has a Slavic root (*tshepe*, "to touch") encased in three Germanic morphemes.

Of special interest is the plural suffix *-s*, a contamination of the Old French plural *-s* (preserved in Yiddish and English but not in German) with the Hebrew plural *ot* (pronounced *-es* in Yiddish). This is used with words of all sources: for example, *khále-khales* ("Chalah") and *megíle-megíles* ("scroll" or "long list, long-winded talk"), of Hebrew origin; *khate-khates* ("hut") and *shmate-shmates* ("rag"), from Slavic; or *bite-bites* ("request") and *túrem-tú-rems* ("tower"), from German.

Naturally, synonyms of various origins developed separate meanings. Thus *seyfer*, from Hebrew ("book"), means "religious book written in Hebrew or Aramaic," whereas *bukh* means "secular book, in Yiddish or other languages"; and *dos heylike ort* (literally: "the holy place") means "cemetery," but its Hebrew synonym *mokem koydesh* means "synagogue."

---

9   It is important to remember that the Hebrew component in Yiddish is pronounced differently from the contemporary Israeli Hebrew. In American usage there are many compromises between the two.

Many expressions and idioms overtly using words of German origin actually have a Hebrew subtext. For example, the collocation *tsezéyt un tseshpréyt* ("sown to the wind," "scattered and dispersed") may be used for a person's family, his disorderly clothes, or his books published in various places, but the major allusion is to a central image of Jewish historical consciousness—namely, the dispersion of the Jews. The subtext is in the book of Esther (3:8): "There is a certain people scattered abroad and dispersed among the peoples in all the provinces of thy kingdom." The pair of Hebrew adjectives in the biblical source, when read in Ashkenazi pronunciation, is linked by alliteration of its stressed syllables (and pervasive sound parallelism): *meFUzer umeFUred* ("scattered and dispersed"). This has been transposed into words of the German stock with an end-rhyme, a form favored in Yiddish folklore: *tsezEYT un tseshprEYT*. In a statistical count, the phrase has only German components, but its subtext is Hebrew and its semantic substance is specifically Jewish.

Furthermore, this Yiddish idiom is often augmented to *tsezéyt un tseshpréyt oyf ale shíve yámim* ("scattered and dispersed on all the seven seas"), adding a "Jewish" tone by spicing the idiom with an emphatically Hebrew phrase, *shive yamim* ("seven seas"). In normal Yiddish, however, these Hebrew words are not used: the plural of *yam* ("sea") in Yiddish is *yamen*, and the proper phrase would be *oyf ale zibn yamen*. By using a phrase in real Hebrew rather than in the Hebrew that merged into Yiddish, the impression of an authoritative quotation is achieved. In reality, however, this Hebrew phrase does not exist in the Bible and is, paradoxically, coined from the European "seven seas." The semantics and vocabulary of the German and Hebrew components have thus been reversed.

A new layer joined the Yiddish fusion in the nineteenth and twentieth centuries. This consisted of so-called Internationalisms—namely, words of French, Latin, or Greek etymology that were accepted in most modern languages and that entered Yiddish via Russian, Polish, German, or English to represent new areas of modern civilization, science, art, and politics. The Introspectivist manifesto of 1919, a most consciously Yiddishist literary document, does not shy away from declaring that:

> Yiddish is now rich enough, independent enough to afford to enrich its vocabulary from the treasures of her sister languages. That is why we are not afraid to borrow words from the sister languages, words to cover newly developed concepts, broadened feelings and thoughts. Such words are also *our* words. We have the same rights to them as does any other language, any other poetry.

Thus A. Leyeles, interested in Ouspensky's "fourth dimension" and Oriental mysticism, wrote a poem on "Symmetry" as rest in mid-movement, the ecstasy of universal unity beyond the divisions of time and space, man and woman, God and demon. The second stanza reads:

Simétriye—	Symmetry—
Gimátriye fun mistérye.	Anagram of mystery.
Mistérye fun rytm	Mystery of rhythm
Oyf yener zayt zoym	On the other side of the seam
Fun tsayt un roym.	Of time and space.

The concepts and words for "symmetry," "mystery," and "rhythm" are modern Internationalisms; *gimátriye*, however, though matching these terms in sound as well as in its Greek origin, is a Kabbalistic term, referring to numerology. Yet, beside *gimátriye*, Yiddish also has *geométriye* (geometry). "Mystery" seems related to the Hebrew term for Kabbalah, *torat ha-nistár*, "knowledge of the concealed," and its Hebrew cognate, *mistorin*. "Time and space" reflect the interest in Einsteinian physics among Jewish intellectuals, but *tsayt* (time) is an old Yiddish word, whereas *roym* in the sense of cosmic "space" is Yiddishized from the German *Raum*.

In his sonnet "Evening," describing Madison Square at nightfall, Leyeles underlines the modernity of the impression with a profusion of Internationalisms. We transcribe the first and last stanzas, emphasizing the "modern" words (in upper case):

Shoybn blitsn, shoybn tsindn zikh in SKVER.
S'finklen likhter oyf FANTASTISH, POLIGONISH.
DRAYEKS, ROMBN, halb SETSESYE, halb HARMONISH,
Tantsn freylekh oyf in fentster—GROD un KVER.

....

A DEBOSH in SKVER. ELEKTRISH-LEGENDARISH
Roysht er op a sho, ORGYASTISH un VIRVARISH—
Zelbst-farshikerte KHIMERE, UMREAL.

Windows flash, flare up above the square.
Lights sparkle—polygonal, anonymous.
Triangles, diamonds—part Secession, part harmonious—
Dance joyfully on windowpanes, straight and queer.

....

Debauchery in the square. Electrically fantastic
Carousing for an hour, boisterous, orgiastic—
A chimera drunk on itself. Unreal ball.

More than half of the words in the fourteen lines of the Yiddish sonnet are used in English as well: square, fantastic, polygonal, Secession, harmonious, sardonic, gold, laconic, sprinkled, virile, carnival, debauchery, electrical, legendary, orgiastic, chimera, unreal. Most of them could be adopted from English or from other languages. They are, however, domesticated with Yiddish sounds and suffixes and are part of modern Yiddish. *Wirrwarr* is a German noun for "chaos, confusion, noise," and is used in Yiddish too; but here it is made strange by transforming it into the adverb *virvarish* by means of the German-stock suffix *ish* (not used in German for this root), and by being aligned with other attributes of modern exhilaration (elektrish, legendarish, poligonish). *DRAYEKS, ROMBN, GROD, KVER, geVINKLt* are new Yiddish terms of geometry (triangles, diamond shapes, straight line, diagonal, angle), here used to evoke the paintings of Klimt, of the Viennese "Secession." And all this is naturally conjoined, by the unifying flow of the metrical rhythm and Yiddish grammar, with the simplest and most domestic Yiddish words: *shoybn, fentster, likhter, himl, tantsn, freylekh, vinkn, flekn, sher, roysht, sho, farshikert* ("windowpanes, windows, lights, sky, dance, joyful, wink, stains, scissors, noise, hour, drunk").

As a language of fusion, Yiddish is similar to English in many ways. But Yiddish speakers are highly "component-conscious"—that is, aware of the differences between the source languages, their extensions beyond the accepted domain of Yiddish proper, and their rich stylistic interplay within a Yiddish text. The expression *Di mayse fun der geshikhte iz aza min historye* ("the history of this tale is such a story") is a parodic exposure of this characteristic, using three synonyms for "story," derived from Hebrew, German, and French (via Slavic), respectively. Modern Yiddish poetry based a great deal of its stylistic force on the selection of words from its component languages, on their various emotive overtones, and on the interplay between them.

The special role of Yiddish as a vehicle for conversation and oral communication in the unusual Jewish society, with its stress on trade, international ties, and rapid contacts between strangers, contributed to its characteristic features. Also crucial were the use of Yiddish for teaching and Talmudic analysis and argument, and the lack of a tradition of systematic treatises, essays, or philosophical writings in this language. Hence Yiddish speech typically has a high proportion of conversational expressions and dialogue markers intended to draw the listener's attention and to convey the speaker's emotive attitudes to the words and topics of his discourse. Yiddish discourse is talkative, associative, unsystematic; uses a wealth of proverbs, generalizations, quotations, anecdotes, and exemplary stories; and proceeds by asking many questions and answering questions with questions, rising constantly from language to meta-language and back, raising alternatives to a situation or argument, and undermining the assumptions of an assumed opponent.

PROSE AND POETRY

At first, modern Yiddish poetry did not know what to do with these properties of the language. On the contrary, it embraced metrical verse, well-measured and sound-orchestrated, as a vehicle for refined poetic feelings, an aesthetic antidote to the colloquial coarseness of "the cholent language," as the poet Frug dubbed it in the 1880s.[10] This dialogical language tried to imitate the monological forms of the European lyric. At the beginning of the twentieth century, Yiddish developed a poetic language for metrical poetry; largely in the Impressionist vein, it reached accepted standards, but its achievements were not Yiddish-specific or spectacular.

Indeed, the renaissance of Jewish literature in Russia in the late 1880s and 1890s created great fiction in Yiddish, based on the properties of the conversational language and the composition of the rambling, associative prose of its characters. This is epitomized in the best work of its classical writers, Mendele Moykher Sforim and Sholem Aleichem, two literary pseudonyms meaning, characteristically, "Mendele the Bookseller" and "How-Do-You-Do?" But the best poetry—in the eighteen nineties and nineteen hundreds—was written in Hebrew (especially by Bialik and Chernikhovski). It was based on the Romantic identification of the poet as the prophet of a society and on the poetic use of biblical Hebrew in tension with the fictional situations of the poems, which were created in European thematic and generic modes.

Only after World War I did Yiddish poetry truly respond to the special characteristics of its own language. The various Expressionist and Modern-

---

10   *Cholent*—a delicious dish containing meat, potatoes, beans, and other ingredients and kept warm for 24 hours for the Sabbath (when Jews do not cook). In the antireligious sentiment, as evoked here, it symbolized something stale, mushy, old-fashioned, and superstitious.

ist trends encouraged such an opening up of poetic language to all possibilities and intonations of the spoken idiom, including dialects, slang, political
and scientific rhetoric, and so on. Now fiction could be "lyrical" and lyrics
could sound "prosaic," and Yiddish poets did not refrain from marring the
subtle poetic instrument with coarse, ironic, dialogical, and "Jewish" markers. Glatshteyn always understood this problem and felt uneasy with poetry
that was too refined for "the wise prosaic smile of the clever tongue."[11] A
master of the dramatic monologue, he reached out, time and again, to mine
these resources, even at the expense of losing his grip on the rhythms of verse.
Glatshteyn embedded his most personal feelings in the simple ramblings
of his protagonist, a gregarious mystic, the Hassidic rebbe Rabbi Nakhman
from Bratslav, who would spice his Yiddish with noticeably Slavic and Hebrew
expressions.

Associative talking—a national sport in Yiddish—is a long, exuberant,
and rambling affair. It is a joy as well. When Glatshteyn's Rabbi Nakhman
from Bratslav turns up in heaven, losing all his words, he complains: "What
will you do from now to eternity? / No tales, no melodies. / Poor soul, you are
naked. / You are a mute in heaven." Eventually, he awakens from a dream, is
back on earth, and draws the moral of the dream: "May I be damned if I'd like
/ To sit on a heavenly rock. / Here, in the sinful world—/ To talk and talk and
talk" ("Hear and be Stunned").

YIDDISH TALK-VERSE

The unusual mode of Yiddish *talk-verse* may be as fresh, effective, and surprising as the language of metaphorical imagery was in Western Modern poetry
(though perhaps less familiar to its readers) and fulfills a similar function in
discourse. The reader has to imagine the character who does the talking, to
reconstruct him from his speech. The talk and the inverse characterization
of the talker create a double-directed semantic dependence, with an added
ironic perspective of the narrator or persona of the poet standing above the
text. Readers who judge Yiddish poetry by the ways it attempts to achieve
what English poetry does will miss the unique aspects of an ironic, allusive,
evaluative, conversational, and talkative medium, even when reduced to the
abbreviated codes of poetic selection.

---

11   See "Chronicle of a Movement," No. 27, *American Yiddish Poetry*, p. 802.

Moyshe-Leyb Halpern raised this art to an almost parodic degree in his long, aggressive, politically charged monologue to himself (addressed to his year-and-a-half-old listener), "This I Said to My Only Son at Play—and to Nobody Else." He uses in verse the technique of associative concatenation—a mainstay of classical Yiddish fiction—to present a kaleidoscope of his bitter personal vision, an existentialist-anarchist political slashing at life in general and American capitalism in particular, interspersed with coarse curses and surprising situational analogies.

In a long, wildly associative tirade, the speaker, Moyshe-Leyb, warns his son against war, shifting from invective against the powers of this world and false messiahs to the child's play and back again. Instead of epithets or metaphors, *analogue situations* are flashed at the reader, comparing the high and the low, the drastic and the sentimental. Especially effective are the similes bringing something enormous down to a domestic detail. Thus everything prepares for war:

Forests supply whips and gallows-wood
And flagpoles for a warship that lies at foreign shores
Like an inkstain on a loveletter.

What a peaceful simile for gunboat diplomacy! And suddenly the figure of Christ appears, hovering, bound to poles, with nails in his hands and "not even a bottle-stopper on his pierced body." His blood is not mentioned, but is reflected in the red sky:

And not merely the cloud above
In the gleam of a city fire—
The bedbug on our bodies, too, is red in the light—
Like the sun at dawn, like measle-sunset on baby-skin!

The miseries of daily life of the poverty-stricken Moyshe-Leyb seem to be as devastating—and as familiar—as the grand images of history and class warfare.

The concatenation is endless, leading from one thing to its opposite by analogy or associative whim, and then to a continuation of the new situation until a new link is sprung on us. Of course, all the links compose one ideological universe, one antiwar pathos and existential anguish, but the poem has scarcely any structural backbone or hard-edge subdivisions. Hence, all examples we may quote must cut something out of their context. Eventually, the son is warned against the president's call for war. I excerpt just a few links from the complex chain following it:

> And if the President—who is everyone's father, only God knows how—
> Should call, let him go first, to see
> That sky-plum and hungry-face are blue
> In the enemy's country, too!

In typically Yiddish fashion (as in Sholem Aleichem's *Tevye the Milkman*), instead of a description of reality, we have a dialogue embedded in a dialogue about that "reality": the son is instructed what to say to the president in a hypothetical situation. There is also a typically Yiddish aside, commenting on the word "president" and rising to meta-language that expresses the speaker's attitude and exposes the meaning of "father." (Note also the indirect metaphor in the uneasy analogy of "hungry-face" with the telescoped metaphor of "sky-plum.") Halpern continues:

> And he can hire himself out to a shoemaker.
> Ruling is not a craft. It is old-fashioned, like a squeak in new shoes.

This again is an associative shift from the low but practical profession of shoemaking, suggested as a better alternative to the presidency, to the phony fashion of squeaking shoes. From here we shift to other old-fashioned garb; the obsolete crowns, which merely keep the sun from bringing light into our heads; the "top hat," that symbol of the bourgeois in Georg Grosz's paintings; and then to the following chain:

> Yet a top hat will not let through one drop of air—
> Thus says medicine,
> Which protects even a fly so the spider won't get sick,
> Because we need spiderweb for science, as Caesar's patriot
> Needed pork on Jehovah's altar.

Simplified, the associative chain goes like this: president → crown → top hat → theories of fresh air → the use of medicine to protect the spiders → capitalist science → Roman desecration of the conquered Temple in Jerusalem → anti-Semitism as a weapon for diverting popular protest:

> And blood spilt in vain can be diverted to the Hebrews.
> All he has to do is wash his hands like Pilate

And at your table eat (if it's the Sabbath) *gefilte fish*,
Which is sweet like guests as long as they are fresh.

The symbolic "washing his hands" of blood spilt in vain has become trans-formed into the innocent Jewish ritual of washing the hands before eating, which leads to the Jewish dish that the Goyim are supposed to love, "gefilte fish." From here—with no thematic justification, out of sheer whim or mal-ice—Halpern inverts the proverb, "a guest is welcome like fresh fish: after three days he stinks."

Thus we have gone from the president's call for war to his eating fish. But this may be dangerous: he may choke on a bone; and this again, in a usual in-version, leads to a positive event: Moyshe-Leyb's son's friend, the little Negro, will rejoice at the president's death. But the little Negro—like Moyshe-Leyb's son, for whom war is a mere play with bottles on the stairs—does not under-stand a thing; suddenly, from happily rambling on, Halpern again transforms the little Negro's dance with an unexpected stab at the reader:

But he [the president] must watch out not to choke on a bone,
This may bring so much joy—that your friend, the little Negro,
Will go dancing. That's how he rejoiced
When they burned his father alive—
Two years ago, as he walked by a bakery, the smell of bread
Struck his nose—and he said "Good Morning" to a white broad.

This is a simple, direct description, strung in an associative chain, and not anticipated by anything beforehand, language that leaves us breathless at the end of the poem.

THE MODERN LITERARY RENAISSANCE

In spite of the seven hundred years of Yiddish writing, the history of Yiddish literature was not a living presence that engendered its modern stage. Rather, from the position of a new culture, created in the spoken language and mod-eled upon European literature of the modern age, scholars and critics set out to recover and reconstruct the past of their language and literature. Only Yiddish folklore was felt as a living tradition, eagerly collected and imitated. Hence, when new generations of writers entered Yiddish literature, they felt the frustration and elation of having to create and enrich both their literature and their language, as if they were just beginning. It was not merely a Modernist stance when the Introspectivists stated: "We have no tradition. We have found very little that could serve as tradition for us. The tradition begins perhaps with us, strange as it may sound" (*In Zikh*, March 1923).[12]

At the beginning of the twentieth century, Yiddish assumed center stage in Jewish culture and society. The modern Jewish intellectual confronted several languages and cultures—Hebrew, Russian, German and, later, English—all of which were thrown into great turmoil and ferment with the emergence of Modernism, i.e. precisely at this juncture. He toured an imaginary museum of periods and styles in several languages which was opened to the eager outsider who came to observe the history of those literatures from a panoramic vista. As I have pointed out elsewhere,

> for reasons of cultural history, Yiddish literature had not shared the development of its neighbors for hundreds of years; consequently, when the East European Jewish intelligentsia, in one grand leap, landed in the general twentieth century, Yiddish poetry undertook not only to catch up with Europe's deepened appreciation of the classics and the modernistic trends of recent generations, but also to take an active part in the discussion of the most timely cultural problems and in the artistic movements of the environment. [13]

We must remember the unusual condition of the Yiddish poet. Almost no poet learned Yiddish literature in school, as poets in other languages did. Most Yiddish schools were founded in Europe after World War I—after the major writers and poets appeared, using their authority for validation. Naturally, they imbibed a vivid Yiddish language spoken in their homes and environment, but only in rare cases did they acquire knowledge of Yiddish literature from their parents. Most Yiddish poets had an elementary Hebrew religious education; some continued in general schools in other languages; and all made up their own, private university by reading books in a number of languages, including the rapidly developing Yiddish library. Many Yiddish poets even began by writing poetry in other languages (Leyvik, in Hebrew; M.L. Halpern, in German; Leyeles, in Russian; Malka Heifetz-Tussman, in English) before switching to the intimate language that was warmly referred to as "*mame-loshn.*"

12 See "Chronicle of a Movement," No. 14, *American Yiddish Poetry*, p. 794.
13 "On Free Rhythms in Modern Yiddish Poetry," in Weinreich, Uriel, ed., *The Field of Yiddish*, New York, 1954, pp. 219–266.

The multilingual intersection, coupled with the international scope of Yiddish literature and the migrations of its writers, was extremely fruitful for Yiddish poetry; at the same time, it also contributed to the great shifts and zigzags in its history. A poet could switch from writing Russian poetry to Yiddish (S. Frug, in the 1880s) or from Hebrew to Yiddish and vice versa (Bialik, most Hebrew poets of the beginning of the twentieth century, Uri Zvi Grinberg, Aron Zeitlin). In each of those literatures, there were different poetic norms at any given time. Yiddish poetry in any given generation was different in America, in Europe, and in the Soviet Union (somewhat like the differences between American and British poetry). Since the poets tended to continue their personal style, migrating or shifting from one of those countries, languages, or orientations to another often led at least to a partial transfer of norms, and hence to changes in the receiving literature.

For example, S. Frug (1860–1916), who "made it" as a Russian poet in Petersburg in the 1880s, writing sad lyrical poetry and sentimental verse on Jewish themes, adopted Russian meters as a matter of course and brought them along, unwittingly, when he began writing Yiddish verse, thus causing a revolutionary change in the history of Yiddish and Hebrew versification. Similarly, Moyshe-Leyb Halpern brought German poetic rhetoric from Hoffmansthal's Vienna to the Russian-oriented verse of the Yiddish "Young Generation" in New York of 1910.

It is important to realize that when a Yiddish poet wrote poetry, that poetry was not part of a normal nation-state with a stratified society. The Yiddish poet did not have Yiddish schools, universities, philosophers, sociologists, research institutes, police stations, bus drivers and such all around him. Literature was "everything." It was a substitute for religion and for statehood, it was a state in itself, "Yiddishland"; to abandon it was to abandon the whole culture. Hence the enormous importance of literature in the eyes of its adherents (reinforced by the Romantic view of the poet as prophet of a society, acquired from German philosophy via Russian literature), and the despair of its isolation. To be sure, literature fulfilled that role in conjunction with the Yiddish press and some social organizations linked to the same cluster. But the close relations of Yiddish writers with the popular press, on which their existence depended, were love-hate relations; succumbing altogether would have meant giving up the "elitist" dream of a separate culture.

·

In its lifetime, Yiddish literature hovered between the illusion of literature as art and the awareness of its precarious existence. Indeed, its best works may serve as a classical parable for the central dilemmas of modern literature. Yiddish writing reflected all the modern tensions of a self-ironic society in the process of losing a traditional value system: the throes of urban alienation gripping the scattered descendants of a close-knit feudal community; the tensions between the demands of Modernist art on the one hand and the repeated search for new forms of mimesis and expression on the other; and the critical problem of language renewal in a text-burdened culture. All this was magnified by the traumas of Jewish history, from which the poets tried to escape through the forms and myth of modern poetry, and into which they were pulled back by the intimate ropes of their Jewish language.

THE OPTIMIST IMPULSE

After World War I, a true mass movement of Yiddish readers and writers carried the day. Centers of Yiddish literature emerged on the new map in Poland, the Soviet Union, the United States, with minor centers in Rumania, Argentina, Israel, France, England, Canada, South Africa, and elsewhere. Yiddish newspapers, schools, libraries, unions, and theaters spread everywhere. With the participation of artists such as Marc Chagall and El Lissitzky, Modernist Yiddish journals were published in Warsaw, Berlin, Paris, Moscow, New York, and other cities.

Indeed, the early nineteen twenties were the best years of Yiddish poetry. Yiddish never really had a tradition of a high-style language or a Latin-oriented poetry. The Yiddish language was colloquial, "juicy" and expressive. With Expressionism in Germany and Futurism and Revolutionary poetry in Russia, the new trends were amenable to absorption of the spoken language in verse—including ironies, puns, harsh sounds, wild associations, and conversational gestures—as well as to opening the doors of poetry to dialect, slang, Hebrew allusions, and the international vocabulary of urban civilization. Yiddish poetry came of age and became part of the international movement. It learned the lessons of Yiddish fiction, worked on the unique features of its language, and faced the imaginary world of Jewish historical existence head-on.

Yiddish literature enjoyed an atmosphere of confidence in the value of its work and in the talents engaged in it. Hebrew was an age-old culture, the oldest continuous culture (except for the Chinese), wise, with high moral values, permeated with a sense of its historicity and—as some saw it—burying its energies in ancient learning of irrelevant issues under the aegis of a rigid religious code of behavior written in a language incomprehensible to the masses. Yiddish would speak directly to the people in their own rich and living language; express their experiences in the present as full-fledged, free human beings; communicate to them the events, works, and ideas of the modern world; and evoke their vitality and folk wisdom, the only guarantors of a rejuvenation from within.

In a Yiddish literary journal, *Shtrom* (Stream or Torrent), published in Moscow in 1922, a Soviet commissar of art, writing on the question of whether Jews, who had never created graphic art, could achieve it now, concluded:

> I myself know very well what this little nation can achieve.
> Unfortunately, I am too shy to utter the words. It's really something,
> what this little nation has done!
> When it wanted—it showed Christ and Christianity.
> When it wanted—it gave Marx and Socialism.
> Can you imagine that it will not show the world some art?
> It will!
> Kill me if not.

The conversational tone of this essay is typical, sentimental, ironic Yiddish speech. The bravado is revolutionary style. The author was Marc Chagall. Such optimism about the possibilities of the new creative impulse among Jews was widespread and gave Yiddish literature, along with other manifestations of this sweeping trend, its boom years of the early nineteen twenties (some gloomy thematics that often appeared in it notwithstanding).

The exuberant atmosphere, hard realities, and world-embracing ambitions among young Yiddish poets in New York are nostalgically recounted in Leyeles's long poem, *A Dream Under Skyscrapers* (1947), the stock-taking of a generation, written in virtuoso-rhymed Byronian octaves that cannot possibly be translated without losing the effect of their metrical patterns and the play with Yiddish sound-and-language fusion. We quote here four separate stanzas in English prose paraphrases:

> In the soaring checkered buildings
> Of the magnificent, tumultuous metropolis New-York,
> Young people sit cramped-in, careworn, careless,
> And the skyscrapers are alert witnesses
> To a new edifice being erected—here, in the marketplace.
> With the heritage of fathers and grandfathers,

A tower-of-words is built; the builders are young,
They lay the bricks in joy and in sorrow.
. . . .
The dreams of that generation were enough
To erect Pithom, Ramses and a Pillar of gold.
All around, wealth has unfurled and unrolled.
But the restless youth have secretly
Forged a new burden, a new freedom.
And created, and wanted pie in the sky,
And measured themselves with the brightest lights,
And founded a guild of proud, new poets.
. . . .
By the rivers of New York I sat down
And confined my dream to the new, free, wide-open air.
I dreamt a rich dream, I built a vision
Through days and nights, under heavy skyscrapers,
Under stone—not palms, poplars or cypresses.
Often, unaware of the change from evening-gold
To morning-red, I watched over the lights
Of a stubbish Jew, a Yiddish poet.
. . . .
And in our own domain? A new style and genre
Blew in our street too, on our road.
Not in vain did we swim to the new, distant shore,
Not in vain have we read the American poem
And inhaled, absorbed the Whitman tone
Through restless nights after hard workdays.
The land America was home, not a guest-house,
We loved the land with no pedigree, no castes.

YIDDISH POETRY IN AMERICA

A little book of Yiddish poems appeared in the United States in 1877, and the first journals were published in the 1870s, but the real life of Yiddish literature in America began in the 1880s. It was part of the massive immigration of Yiddish-speaking Jews from Eastern Europe and of the institutional network that the immigrants built in New York and other American cities, so admirably described in Irving Howe's *The World of Our Fathers*.

Yiddish writers in America often felt that they were refugees from a great literature; that the Jews in America were too pulverized, too busy making a living or assimilating, for a vital, educated literary audience to be established; and that the real, deeply rooted base of Yiddish was in the Jewish masses of Eastern Europe. Actually, a new, quite different literature developed in Yiddish in the United States, independent of its counterpart in Europe. In Dubnovian terms, the historical center of Jewish life and culture wandered from Poland and Russia to the United States, where it remolded the old forms—among them, Yiddish literature—and at the same time developed new forms, more organic to the environment and institutionalized in the English language or integrated in the general American framework. Simultaneously, a second center grew in Eretz Israel, with Hebrew as its communicational vehicle, to form what is now a bipolar, Hebrew-English, new historical axis of Jewish existence.

Yiddish literature in America was based to a large extent in the daily and periodical press, which included literally hundreds of publications unhampered by the censorship that plagued Yiddish publications in Russia. The first daily newspaper appeared in July 1881.[14] In certain periods, the combined circulation of Yiddish dailies was very high (about 700,000 in 1916). Many of the young and the intelligent kept leaving the Yiddish-speaking enclave and thus drained its intellectual resources. But for almost a century, the culture was able to sustain itself.

The Yiddish press felt that promoting culture and knowledge was one of its chief responsibilities. It became a major vehicle of Yiddish literature and criticism, published the works of the best authors, and eventually gave many writers who were willing to practice journalism a livelihood and a forum in which to express their opinions on culture, politics, society, Jewish history, and world events. At first, "selling oneself" to a newspaper was considered degrading for a real artist, and some "held out" longer than others. "If there is a profession in the world which rubs off words like coins changing hands, it is the anonymous journalism which provides bread and butter for Glatshteyn's table" (*In Zikh*, July 1934) wrote his friend and fellow poet A. Leyeles, who himself earned his daily bread as a journalist and editor in the daily *Der Tog*. But journalism also fulfilled a real need of the Yiddish writer, who was constantly reminded of

---

14   In Russia, a Yiddish newspaper was founded in Petersburg in October 1881, but it was a weekly. The earlier weekly, *Kol mevaser*, which practically launched modern Yiddish literature, appeared between 1862 and 1873.

the problematic aspects of existence and of the intentional choices that had to be made in any effort against the current in this turbulent and politicized century. "Every genuine poet," Glatshteyn wrote on another occasion, "should have a lot of opportunity to write journalism so that he can write it out of his system, steam it out of himself, so that when he comes to writing a spoken poem, he is already shouted out" (*Sum and Substance*, p. 131).

Thus, the "anarchist" paper, *Di Fraye Arbeter Shtime* (The Free Workers' Voice), edited from 1899 by S. Yanofsky, published some of the best Yiddish writers, promoted new talent, and published essays on theoretical issues. The *Daily Forward*, founded in 1897, though ostensibly socialist and actually rather sensational and popular, did a lot to support major writers or bring them over from Europe. All papers published poems as well as literary criticism. In addition, there were countless monthlies, cultural journals, little reviews, and periodical collections devoted to literature, to social and political matters, or specifically to poetry. There were many Yiddish publishers, and hundreds of books appeared. In this abnormally unbalanced culture, where the language could not serve any broader political purposes and where the system of daily life and the bureaucratic and educational networks were increasingly conducted in English, literature was the heart of the culture. Poets, however, kept complaining, remembering the idealized mission of the poet as a prophet of a society in post-Romantic Russian and Hebrew literature, and forgetting that it was not easy to publish Modernist poetry in English, either.

Yiddish culture in America was active for over a century. It sustained the continuous life of several newspapers, publishing houses, schools, and institutions, but there was little continuity of human resources and a mere vestigial internal development of new generations. The continuity of this culture was, rather, supported by wave after wave of new immigrants. Most Yiddish writers in America, no matter when they crossed the ocean, came from religious homes in Eastern Europe. They left their parents behind, in the "Old Home"; at the same time, they left the old world of Jewish existence in Eastern Europe and its overpowering traditional religious framework. Theirs was a radical revolt—part of a youth trend in the old country—against those two ancient and conventional social frames. It was accompanied by the emotionally upsetting move of leaving one's parents' home, often at an early age. The sculptor Chaim Gross and the poet Moyshe-Leyb Halpern left their parents at the age of twelve and went first to the big cities in the Austro-Hungarian Empire (Vienna and Budapest) to make it on their own even before they moved to

America. Many of their readers had shared this experience. When they came to America and rebuilt their lives and personalities with the strong motivation of becoming "American," some of them joined the already existing institutions of secular Yiddish culture.

Most Yiddish American poets came to the United States as young men in their late teens or early twenties. They had not yet formed their poetic personalities, not yet integrated into the Yiddish literature of their old homes, and hence were able to feel the exhilaration of creating a new literature in a new country—and their own lives with it. They were both old enough to have imbibed the atmosphere of a full-bodied Yiddish language and culture, and too old to embrace English as a creative language. Jacob Glatshteyn arrived in New York at the age of eighteen. A. Leyeles came at the age of twenty, but had left his parents' home in Lodz for London when he was sixteen. Halpern arrived when he was twenty-two and had already published some poems in German in Vienna; he had left his parents' home in Galicia at the age of twelve. Leyvik came from Siberian exile at age twenty-five, but had been arrested and taken from home as a young revolutionary at eighteen.

An analysis of the ages of immigration of all the poets included in the two comprehensive anthologies of American Yiddish poetry published in Yiddish shows that these examples are representative. Of the thirty-one poets included in M. Basin's immense anthology, *Amerikaner Yidishe Poezye* ("American Yiddish Poetry," 1940), about two-thirds were 18–23 years old when they reached America. The average age was 20.5. (However, some stopped over for several years in London or elsewhere, i.e., left their homes at an earlier age.) M. Shtarkman's anthology, *Hemshekh* ("Continuation," 1946), included fifty poets, with a larger proportion of the younger generation. Here, the average age of immigration was sixteen years. Two-thirds of the poets came at ages 14–19.[15]

The younger immigrants grew up in the early 1920s, in an atmosphere of great hopes for Yiddish literature around the world, when joining it was still interesting and possible. A telling example is J.L. Teller, who came to America at the age of eight, was an *iluy* ("genius") in Hebrew and Talmudic studies, and had an excellent English education (culminating in a Ph.D. in psychology from Columbia University). As a young man, he was obviously influenced by contemporary American poetry, notably by "Objectivist" verse; he also wrote books of

---

15   Three others were born in America, four came as children, and only six came to the U.S. at ages older than twenty.

history and journalism in English, but in poetry opted neither for English nor Hebrew but for his mother's tongue, Yiddish—still an option in 1930. His friend Gabriel Preil, who began as a Yiddish Introspectivist poet, did shift to Hebrew and became one of the most interesting Hebrew poets in New York.

In contrast, few immigrants of an older age joined the ranks of the Yiddish poets. This was a new poetry of a new country, although written in Yiddish; to be able to understand the situation and contribute to it, you had to build a new life here. Furthermore, those young writers who established themselves in the still-vital Yiddish literature of Europe became part of the literary establishment there. Only a few recognized poets reached American shores as refugees: Kadya Molodovsky in 1935, Aron Zeitlin in 1940, Chaim Grade and others after the Holocaust.

A comparative analysis of the biographies of American graphic artists of Jewish origin, who came from the same Eastern-European background, shows that most of them arrived at a somewhat earlier age: Ben Shahn was eight years old; Max Weber, ten; Louis Lozowick, fourteen; Raphael Soyer, thirteen; Mark Rothko, ten. They were young enough to enter American culture proper, receive an American education, and create art, but were not rooted enough in the language to be able to write significant poetry. The few immigrants who did write in English, like Andzia Yezierska, Abraham Cahan, or Judd L. Teller, did so in prose rather than poetry. Their writing still reflected a Yiddish-speaking society. It took another generation for creative Jews like Saul Bellow or Philip Roth—the American-born children of immigrants—to have an impact on English literature.

Thus Yiddish poetry in America was created mostly by young immigrants. It was, nevertheless, a truly American literature, as an internal analysis of the poetry demonstrates. Leyeles's *Rondeaux* or *Fabius Lind*, Glatshteyn's *Free Verse* or *Credos*, J.L. Teller's *Miniatures*, Berysh Vaynshteyn's *Broken Pieces*, or M.-L. Halpern's two posthumous volumes of *Poems* published in 1934 are as American as anything written in English in that period. It was in America that the poets sensed freedom of thought and ideas, that their conscious perceptions of literature were formed and their poetic language crystallized. America was both the real and the imaginary space from which the material of their poetry was drawn; where they made their acute observations with the fresh eyes of involved participants; and where the overwhelming power of the melting-pot metropolis found them unprotected and sent them off to political protest or to "escapist," individualistic lyrical fictions. Even their recollections of the "Old

Home"—negative and derisive at first, and nostalgic later—were made from an irreversible position on American ground. Calling M.-L. Halpern, the author of *In New York*, a poet from Galicia makes no more sense than calling T.S. Eliot a "poet from Missouri" or Ben-Gurion a "Polish politician." But while their peers the graphic artists became part of the accepted history of American art, and their contemporaries writing in English (like Charles Reznikoff) are part of American poetry, the Yiddish poets—who could certainly match them in form and theme—were quarantined within their alien language.

The trends of Yiddish poetry created in America were rarely extensions of Yiddish literature in the old country but rather evolved from the concrete dynamics of the independent American Yiddish literary center. Though its poets often felt like the young branch of a lush tree, refugees washed out on a strange shore, American Yiddish poetry actually developed concurrently with the Yiddish literary renaissance in Europe, and even preceded the latter in its major achievements. The "orphan" feeling merely meant coming to terms with the isolation of the modern poet—and this by people who were used to the warm embrace of an admiring society—or so it seemed at a distance.

True, many American Yiddish poets still read European languages and often drew on various sources from the Jewish and non-Jewish culture of Europe to which they had grown attached in their youth. These influences, as well as the autonomous development of an American Yiddish poetry and poetics, made their writing different from the English poetry next door. But no generation of American Yiddish poets was part of any worldwide Yiddish poetic trend. The atmosphere of life in the United States, which included not only harsh working conditions but also a more peaceful scene and sense of freedom, contributed to this difference, as did the impact of American poetry and social ideas. The terrifying events of the twentieth century shook Yiddish American poets to the quick, but those events did not occur in the streets of their own cities and spoke, rather, to their more general historical sense of humanity and Jewish destiny.

THE GENERATIONS

We can observe four major groups of Yiddish poets that emerged in the United States:

1. The "Proletarian" or "Sweatshop" poets of the end of the nineteenth century were mostly Socialist- and Anarchist-inspired, but at the same time

expressed panhistorical despair about Jewish destiny in the Diaspora and even dreamed of Zion. They were known for their personal involvement in the life of the sweatshop proletariat, their concern with social and political issues, and their direct, revolutionary rhetoric, and were popular with Jewish workers. They also considered themselves inspired "Poets," however, and wrote poetry on "lofty" subjects like love, nature, or the art of poetry, vacillating between their interests in "Jewish" and "cosmopolitan" themes.

An account of the Yiddish poets in America, published in a Russian Jewish newspaper in 1905, demonstrates their plight:

> [Many of them had to suffer] the most bitter poverty which has shackled the poetic imagination in chains and destroyed the beautiful, rich aspirations one after another. We mean, of course, the writers who did not agree to accept compromises with their concept of art, who did not want to sell out their inspiration for a mess of pottage, did not want to serve with their pen purposes which have nothing to do with literature. In the end, they were forced into factories, into sweatshops, into the streets and marketplaces to peddle newspapers, apples and suspenders. Look what happened to our best poets: one died in the flower of his youth of tuberculosis [David Edelstadt], a second one is confined to a madhouse [Joseph Bovshover], a third, sick with consumption, has a tailor's shop in Colorado [Yehoash], two or three write news items and articles in the daily papers, and others have neither time nor courage to create poems in the prosaic, oppressive atmosphere of American hustle-bustle. (H. Alexandrov, quoted by Sh. Nigger in the *General Encyclopedia* in Yiddish, vol. *Yidden G.*, New York, 1942, p. 123.)

2. "The Young Generation" (also known by their Yiddish name, *Di Yunge*) emerged with their first journal in 1907. They were interested to a large extent in art for art's sake, in exquisite Impressionist poetry of mood and atmosphere, in mellifluous, masterfully formed verse, written in smooth, "poetic" diction. They would not harness their verse to any political purposes, not become "the rhyme department of the labor movement," as Zisho Landoy expressed it; rather, they centered on the experiences of the individual. They translated much from world poetry and, in general, introduced a cosmopolitan spirit into American Yiddish literature. In some respects, their poetry was akin to English Edwardian verse or to the general European neo-Romantic trend, but it was also influenced by the playful irony of Heine's lyrics. The Young Generation was a purely American product. Though influenced by a

general European mood, its poets had little in common with contemporary Yiddish writers in Europe, where prose carried the day. Their counterparts were a few Hebrew poets in Europe and Eretz Israel who were exposed to similar Russian and German influences, though the two groups hardly knew of each other at the time. The Young Generation had established in Yiddish poetry the mastery of verse forms, a cultured tradition of poetry translations, and children's poetry of high literary quality.

We should not be amazed by the fact that the best poets of the Young Generation in New York were simple workers: Mani Leyb was a shoemaker; Landoy, a housepainter; Leyvik, a wallpaper hanger; Halpern, a poverty-stricken jack-of-all-trades. These were not traditional proletarians who turned to writing. They were eagerly reading and discussing the poetry of Pushkin, Blok, Rilke, Hofmannsthal, Baudelaire, Verlaine, and Rimbaud, while publishing translations from European, Chinese, Japanese, or Indian poets. Shoemaking was merely a necessity of life (Moyshe-Leyb recommended it to the American president); after all, a poet had to make a living, and professorial jobs were not yet available. Besides, socialist ideology enhanced the poet's pride in being a real shoemaker, which, along with tailoring, had been the most despised profession in Jewish folklore. In accordance with the folk consciousness of the East Side Jews in general, the Young Generation viewed being proletarian and poor as a transitory stage, a temporary necessity brought about by the hard course of history, while aristocracy of the mind and ambitions to achieve the highest intellectual and artistic standards were inherent in being Jewish or—as they would think—in being human. This is not unlike the theory of the split mind advocated in Hassidism: while half of one's mind is steeped in the dark of everyday work and worries, the other half should be kept separate, rising high and unifying with God.

3. The "Introspectivists," a trend launched in 1919, began a theoretical and practical revolt against the dominance and "poeticalness" of the Young Generation (see the next section). For the Introspectivists, a poem presented a kaleidoscope of broken pieces from the historical world, as perceived in the psyche of a sophisticated urban individual and as expressed in a unique rhythmical "fugue." Theirs was a post-Symbolist poetics, stressing free verse, open thematics and language, and an end to the poetic ivory tower. But they, too, were radically different from their Yiddish contemporaries in Warsaw, Berlin, Kiev, Moscow, or Tel Aviv, who screamed in a loud voice the slogans of Expressionism, Revolution, and Zionism. The Introspectivists developed a rather Anglo-American poetics of irony, dramatized and objectified poetic

situations, and intellectual understatement; they formed a much more mature, antisentimental, and honestly harsh view of the real world.

4. The leftist poets of the twenties and thirties clustered around the "Proletpen" and more or less openly Communist journals, such as the daily *Frayhayt* and the monthly *Hamer.* Communist ideals had a great fascination for many justice-seeking Jewish writers in the face of the harsh aspects of American capitalism. Communism was also a dignified way of shedding the burden of Jewish particularity, or so they thought. Furthermore, it fed on the nostalgia for the Russia of the books, its literature, "open soul," melancholy songs, and revolutionary spirit. The memory of the liberation of the Jews from unbearable tsarist oppression (which many remembered with horror from their own childhood) was still fresh; so was the impression of the truly equal rights accorded them by the early Soviet regime and of the visible role many Jews were able to play in the new Russian culture, science, and government. Furthermore, Jewish Communists in America had a real audience and readership devoted to the cause and to Yiddish international culture, and a collective spirit that lured many a lonely poet.

The writers of the left did create some interesting poetry of naturalist description of urban realities and social protest, ranging from the obligatory topic of Sacco-Vanzetti to a book-length poem on *Little Rock.* But the pressures of Soviet-inspired policies, with their demands for flattening the language of poetry and making it a propaganda tool or rhetorical jingle of Socialist Realism that could be "understood by the masses," coupled with their anti-Zionist attitudes (especially their pro-Arab stance during the Arab uprising and anti-Jewish outbursts of 1929 in Palestine), estranged most of the important poets from their fold.

Many creative poets did not belong to any of these groups. Furthermore, certain basic trends and historical events had an impact on writers of various directions, and there was a great deal of infighting and mutual influence among them. In many ways, the description of literature in such groupings reflects the clusters of typical alternatives more than absolute differences among poets. For instance, Moyshe-Leyb Halpern and H. Leyvik began their poetic development with the Young Generation. But the young Introspectivist, Jacob Glatshteyn, while dismissing the Young Generation altogether, sensed even in 1920 the different poetic value of these two poets.[16] Indeed, Halpern exhibited

16   See "A Quick Run Through Yiddish Poetry," "Chronicle," No. 2), *American Yiddish Poetry,*
    p. 787.

strong Expressionist features in the 1920s, and Leyvik and Leyeles shared a certain tendency to an aura of mysticism in their verse (as well as a lifelong friendship). From the mid-1920s on, the achievements of all these trends as well as the influences of English contemporary poetry became common property. Poets of various backgrounds used them according to their personal development, as was the case with Modernism in other literatures.

After World War II, an influx of refugees from Europe brought a number of important poets to America and for a time increased the number of Yiddish readers. The Holocaust in Europe, disenchantment with Stalinism, recognition of the great light coming from the State of Israel, and dissolution of any firm body of Yiddish readership huddled all the writers together in one community.

Almost no new Yiddish writers were added after the 1950s, however. With the dying out of the poets of the generations that had emerged in the 1920s and 1930s, Yiddish literature in America dwindled to a tiny band. The famous daily Yiddish newspaper, *Forward*, which epitomized Jewish immigrant life in America and the struggles of the Jewish world for eighty-five years, and which had often lowered Yiddish culture to the level of the street but had also published some of its best writers, including Nobel-prize winner Isaac Bashevis Singer, stopped daily publication in 1983.

INTROSPECTIVISM: A MODERNIST POETICS[17]

The Introspectivist movement can serve as an outstanding example of the critical ambience in American Yiddish literature. The so-called Introspectivist manifesto of 1919 and the excerpts selected in the "Chronicle of a Movement," document the main theoretical ideas of its poets. Similar problems—concerning the relations between art and life, language and form, the individual and social reality, the "Jewish" and the "universal"—preoccupied other trends and generations in American Yiddish poetry. Yet, the Introspectivists formulated a consciously Modernist poetics, supported by their own creative work and related to Modernist poetics in the international context.

After eighty years of literary theory and criticism in Europe and America, the theorizing of the Yiddish poets around 1920 may seem somewhat naïve, but theirs was a more mature and complex view of poetic art than the one formulated in the early manifestos of Anglo-American Imagism. Theorizing by poets in manifestos, programmatic articles, or criticism uses a different

17   See the section "Documents of Introspectivism," *American Yiddish Poetry*, p. 773–804.

language and serves a different function than academic theory or criticism. It should not be judged by such standards, but rather as a direct expression of artistic ideology and polemics in a specific cultural context.

The Introspectivists absorbed the ideas on art that were developed in recent Modernist movements. In their arguments one can find traces of Italian and Russian Futurism, German and Yiddish Expressionism, English Imagism and Vorticism, as well as ideas expressed by Nietzsche, Croce, Freud, and T.S. Eliot. Sometimes it is hard to tell to what extent such echoes derive directly from primary texts and to what extent they are part of a cultural aura available to intellectual readers after World War I. The important point is the attempt to integrate such trends into a single coherent, "classical" Modernism, rather than voicing the slogans of one extreme position.

In 1918, A. Leyeles published his first book of poems, *Labyrinth*, each page of which was appropriately adorned with a frame made of swastikas, the ancient Indian symbol. Though still steeped in neo-Romantic moods and forms, his was a radical individualism and a sophisticated intellectual stance. As such, it was hardly acceptable either to his contemporaries, the poets of the Young Generation, or to the politicized environment of Yiddish cultural life in New York following the First World War. Some time in 1918, two young students, Jacob Glatshteyn and N.B. Minkov, came to Leyeles with their poems and "actively raised the idea of a new [poetic] trend." All three were intellectuals, well-read both in general and in Jewish culture; they met and talked continuously, developing the ideology and poetics of a new, Modernist trend in Yiddish poetry.[18] At the time, they published their poems in H. Gudelman's journal *poézye* ("Poetry," like the name of its English-language counterpart and Marinetti's *Poesia*), together with members of the Young Generation and several European Yiddish poets.

In 1919, the three poets formulated the principles of their trend and published them as an introduction to an anthology, *In Zikh* ("In Oneself"), including their own poems as well as those of several like-minded young poets. This introduction, entitled "Introspectivism," became the so-called manifesto of their movement. It is written as a declaration of principles, although in a discursive and didactic tone addressed to the general Yiddish reader. The anthology appeared in January 1920, and the first issue of the journal, *In Zikh* ("Inside Yourself") appeared shortly thereafter. In time, the title of the jour-

---

18   See A. Leyeles, "Twenty Years of 'Inzikh,'" *In Zikh*, April 1940.

nal was contracted into one word, *Inzikh*, and became the Yiddish name of their trend, "Inzikhism," and of its poets, "Inzikhists."

In Zikh was a typical little review, devoted primarily to poetry and also publishing poetic theory, criticism, and polemics, as well as political and cultural essays written by the poets. It appeared, with several interruptions, from January 1920 until December 1940. In all, 100 poets and writers participated in *In Zikh*, among them some of the young European Yiddish Modernists, such as Dvora Fogel (the friend of Bruno Schulz and author of "Geometrical Poems") and the Vilna poet Abraham Sutskever.[19] Though suffering from the lack of an intelligent readership and from vicious attacks by newspaper critics and party hacks, *In Zikh* became the standard-bearer of Yiddish Modernism in America.

At the end of the 1930s, the plight of the Jews in Europe diverted the focus from the theory of poetic language to the problem of art in an age of destruction. The poets, however, never abandoned their concern with art and language, as is clear from Glatshteyn's essays of 1945–1947, collected in *Sum and Substance*[20] and several subsequent collections. The shift of emphasis was also accompanied by a shift from Leyeles's dominance in the early years as a theoretician of poetry and free verse to Jacob Glatshteyn's prominence as the major Yiddish literary critic and poet after the Holocaust.

In Zikh, the first journal of its kind, was soon followed by Yiddish Modernist journals published in Warsaw, Lodz, Berlin, Moscow, and Paris, and devoted primarily to poetry, poetic theory, and graphic art. Such journals as *Shtrom* (The Torrent), *Khalyastre* (The Gang), and *Albatros* published a new, Modernist poetry in Yiddish, a poetry influenced primarily by Expressionism and Futurism, and the impact of the Russian Revolution with its messianic mood, futuristic utopia, and atrocities. The American Inzikhists did not share the horrors that the European Yiddish poets experienced in World War I and the pogroms of 1919 in Ukraine, nor did they share the Expressionist poetics of "Scream" about "Horror" and the "Twilight of Humanity" and the politicized views of literature (communist or Zionist). They were, however, aware of these European waves.

The name "Introspectivism" seems to be a direct challenge to the slogan of Expressionism that swept Europe. The opposition of Expressionism versus

---

19   J. Birnboym, "The Journal *In zikh*," [in Yiddish] in *Pinkes far der forshung fun der yiddisher literatur un prese*, New York, 1972, pp. 28–49.

20   This is Glatshteyn's own translation of the book's title. The Yiddish name, *In tokh genumen*, was the title of Glatshteyn's column in the Labor Zionist cultural weekly, *Yidisher kemfer* ("The Jewish Fighter"); a closer translation of this title would be "The Heart of the Matter."

Impressionism was used to describe the radical shift from an art registering external mood and atmosphere—the subtleties of air, light, and psychological nuances—to the coarse and pathetic expression of the rhythm and spirit of modern, urban civilization, with its technology, wars, masses, radical politics, and the destruction of bourgeois morality. Impressionism seemed to be the last art of mimesis, not essential for real expression. In his manifesto, "On Expressionism in Literature" (1917),[21] the German writer Kasimir Edschmid wrote: "The world exists. It makes no sense to repeat it. To explore it in its every last tremor, in its innermost core, and to create it anew—this is the greatest mission of art."

The Introspectivist manifesto echoes the initial assumption of this statement, opposing mimesis as the principle of art, but seeking its object elsewhere: "The world exists and we are part of it. But for us, the world exists as it is mirrored in us, as it touches *us*. . . . It becomes an actuality only in and *through* us." They promoted Introspectivist poetry as an intellectual insight into one's self, as a personal reflection of an internalized social world, rather than as a mere vehicle for the expression of a *Zeitgeist*, a political mood, the "essence" of the world or of "Man" in general. The poet's major concern was to express the organic relation between outside phenomena and the self, and to do it in an introspective and individual manner: "*In an introspective manner* means that the poet must really listen to his inner voice, observe his internal panorama—kaleidoscopic, contradictory, unclear or confused as it may be."

This is not an escapist, ivory-tower poetry, however. A major antinomy of Introspectivist theory is between the emphasis on individual experience and the range of the world it reflects. A key passage in the "manifesto" reads:

> For us, everything is "personal." Wars and Revolutions, Jewish pogroms and the workers' movement, Protestantism and Buddha, the Yiddish school and the Cross, the mayoral elections and a ban on our language: all these may concern us or not, just as a blond woman and our own unrest may or may not concern us. If it does concern us, we write poetry; if it does not, we keep quiet. In either case, we write about ourselves because all these exist only insofar as they are in us, insofar as they are perceived *introspectively*.

The list of thematic domains in this statement represents an Expressionist

---

21   Kasimir Edschmid, "Über den Expressionismus in der Literatur und die neue Dichtung," Berlin: Erich Reitz, 1919, p. 56.

grasp of political and cultural realities, though observed when they become part of the personal world of a modern man. It mixes religious attitudes and daily politics, world events and personal emotions, universal history and Jewish news in one kaleidoscopic whirl. One must not be misled by the individualism of the label, "Introspectivism." Theirs was a poetry acutely attuned to the historical and political world, although personally internalized by each poet. The major influence of Anglo-American poetry on the New York Yiddish poets lay in the tone of understatement and irony typical of Glatshteyn, the Leyeles of *Fabius Lind*, or the early Halpern, as opposed to the noisy screams of the Yiddish "big-city" poets in Europe. The Introspectivists were essentially political poets, though in a party-line sense they were the most apolitical poets in Jewish New York.

This conception also abolished the simplistic opposition between "Jewish" and "universal" topics and put an end to the escape of the Young Generation poets from national themes for the sake of pure poetry. It also prepared the Introspectivists—Glatshteyn, Teller, Minkov, Leyeles—to react naturally, as poets, to the Holocaust, and to grasp it in an individual poetic language, as part of their personal experience.

Thus the Introspectivists met the challenge of Expressionism to find a response to the political and social realities which entered personal life as never before. (They certainly determined the personal lives of Jews on the move, whose very channels of existence depended on the political climate.)

The Introspectivists fought an ongoing battle against accusations that they were knowledgeable but cerebral poets. (Leyeles "knows" how to make poems, therefore he is not a poet.) The distinction between "poetry of feeling" and "poetry of thought" was meaningless for them ("there is no boundary between feeling and thought in contemporary man"), as it was for T.S. Eliot. Those who adhered to either were "dualists" (compare Eliot's "dissociation of sensibilities") who created monotonous rhythms. Just as for other Expressionist or post-Symbolist trends, for them, "everything is an object for poetry": "There is no ugly or beautiful, no good or bad, no high or low." This opening of all thematic boundaries did not imply, however, any general permission for laissez-faire: they proposed a specific theory allowing the inclusion of all elements in a poem, under the slogans of "chaotic" and "kaleidoscopic."

The idea that poetry should present "the chaotic" rather than neat, well-made poems was in the air. For the Expressionists, this meant being truthful to the real world. Uri Zvi Grinberg, a soldier and deserter in World War I, wrote in the manifesto of his Yiddish journal, *Albatros* (Warsaw, 1922):

> *This is how things are.* Whether we want it or not. We stand as we are: with slash-lipped wounds, rolled up veins, unscrewed bones, after artillery bombardments and cries of "Hurrah," after gas-attacks; after bowls filled with gall and opium and the daily water: disgust. And the foam of decay covers our lips.
>
> *Hence the atrocious in the poem.*
> *Hence the chaotic in the image.*
> *Hence the scream in the blood.*
>
> . . . *It is imperative to write such poems.* Atrocious. Chaotic. Bleeding.

The translation of this ideology into the actual language of poetry meant promoting a chaotic composition, avoiding any continuity of time and space ("death to time and space," called an Italian Futurist manifesto), showing defiance to overt coherence and closure, and constructing a random collage of discordant elements in one text. Moyshe-Leyb Halpern is an extreme example of such a poet: after his first book, he abandoned the Impressionist poetics of the Young Generation and the well-rounded strophic poem, and became increasingly demonstrative and whimsical in the disordered, chaotic compositions of his poems, especially in his rambling dramatic monologues.

The Introspectivists found the chaos in their own psyche: "If the internal world is a chaos, let the chaos be manifested [in the poetry]." Chaos is not merely—and not primarily—the chaos of the modern world breaking out of all rationality, but the chaos of our personal stream of consciousness: "The human psyche is an awesome labyrinth." A person's "I" is subject and object at the same time, present and past, part and whole, his present life and the metamorphosis of previous lives; all exist in him simultaneously: "He is simultaneously at the Ganghes and at the Hudson, in the year 1922 and in the year when Tiglathpileser conquered and terrorized the world. Therefore, the Introspectivist is chaotic and kaleidoscopic" (Leyeles; see Appendix A, "Chronicle," No. 11, in *American Yiddish Poetry*). Hence their opposition to the Imagist ideal of concentration. Concentration and well-roundedness create a poem and a mood that is cut-off, isolated, and this is simply "a lie," the artificiality of art in relation to real "life," because the impact of any phenomenon on the human psyche stimulates a whole galaxy of moods, feelings, and perceptions.

The basic idea is similar to the concepts of "simultaneity" and "intersecting planes" in Italian Futurist plastic art, as the following passage from the manifesto shows:

> When the poet, or any person, looks at a sunset, he may see the strangest things which, ostensibly, have perhaps no relation to the sunset. The image reflected in his psyche is rather a series of far-reaching associations moving away from what his eye sees, a chain of suggestions evoked by the sunset. *This,* the series of associations and the chain of suggestions, constitutes *truth,* is life, much as an illusion is often more real than the cluster of external appearances we call life.

In Leyeles's "Autumn," "Symmetry," and other poems, we find motifs of this perception, which often has elements of Freudian psychoanalysis as well as of Oriental-type mysticism and Ouspensky's "fourth dimension."

The poetic equivalent to this psychological conception is the theory of kaleidoscopic art. Rather than mere "chaos," as promoted by the Expressionists and, instinctively, by M.-L. Halpern, the kaleidoscopic vision is an organized presentation indicating elements from various discordant situations. Instead of the one image of the Imagists, here the poem has many faces; instead of similes, they preferred colorful splinters of direct images. As N.B. Minkov pointed out in a later article devoted to the poetry of Leyeles (1939), this resulted in an inherent contradiction: while introspection itself is analytical, the kaleidoscopic method is synthetic. The excellent poet Minkov was biased himself, always tending to the former, immersed in a mystifying Introspectivism, although the analogy to Synthetic Cubism (as opposed to the earlier Analytical Cubism) was apt: the idea was to present, like Picasso, a conscious construct of broken pieces simultaneously representing several discordant aspects or points of view. Whereas the Expressionist chaos had its unifying force in its loud, Whitmanesque voice or political pathos, Leyeles was looking for a unifying force in an all-pervasive rhythm, constituting the "soul" or the "essence" of the poem. As the kaleidoscope is opposed to the single image, so the "fugue" of a free rhythm is opposed to the monotonous "air" presented by one meter.

The concept of the kaleidoscopic method thus brought together several modern principles: the psychology of the stream of consciousness, the multidimensional nature of modern life, simultaneity of experience, representation through a splinter element rather than a full description, and the conscious

organization of a poem as a "fugue" or a "symphony" of heterogeneous elements playing together in a single integrated whole. This concept describes
the art of T.S. Eliot in "The Waste Land" or "Ash Wednesday" and Pound's
"Cantos" better than the Imagist theories stressing the "thing," the individual
"image," or "concentration."

In their actual praxis, not all Introspectivist poets implemented the kaleidoscopic principle with full vigor. Glatshteyn used it in "1919" and then preferred to base the composition of a poem on a particular, possibly unrealistic,
situation. Leyeles, after using it in such texts as "January 28" and some of
his city poems, found a solution in the poetic cycle, such as "The Diary of
Fabius Lind" or "To You—To Me." Though each individual poem of a cycle
centered on one mood or situation and employed one rhythmical structure,
the cycle as a whole contained consciously heterogeneous topics—erotic, political, urban, and so on—presented in an intentional rainbow of rhythmical
forms. Thus the cycle "To You—To Me" has a framework written in a special
eight-line strophe, in precise meter and rhyme; it is, however, interrupted in
mid-strophe and mid-line—where a number of greatly varying metrical and
free-verse poems are inserted (among them, "Bolted Room" and "Fabius Lind
to Fabius Lind")—to be resumed thirty pages later in the middle of the interrupted line and completed in a formal closure. On a higher level, the whole
book, *Fabius Lind*, is such a diary of a contemporary, in which the personal
and the social, the trivial and the metaphysical alternate—matched by an ostensibly random alternation of a broad spectrum of formal and free verse—to
present a kaleidoscope "of metamorphoses, pain, transformation, elation and
achievement over a range of a lived piece of life." As Glatshteyn described it:
"In this book, ten years in the life of a highly cultured, unsettled, searching,
refined Jew were fixed forever"; hence, ipso facto, "for me, Leyeles's ten years
are also—and primarily—ten Jewish years."[22]

The second principle accompanying introspection was individuality of expression; according to the Introspectivist manifesto: "Because we perceive the
world egocentrically and because we think that this is the most natural and
therefore *the truest and most human* mode of perception, we think that the
poem of every poet must first of all be *his own* poem." This principle is applied
equally to content and form: "We insist that the poet should give us the authentic image that he sees in himself and give it in such a form as only he and

22 See "Chronicle," No. 25.

no one else can see it." Each poet must develop his own poetic language and his own poetics, which may eventually subvert any principle of the group.

Here, again, there is a paradox: by individuality the Introspectivists did not mean relativism in value judgments. They insisted that the poet should not only be a "person" in his own right but an "interesting," "contemporary," "intelligent, conscious person . . . capable of expressing the seen, felt and understood in his own, internally true, introspectively sincere manner." By means of association and suggestion—that is, deliberate discontinuous composition and alogical devices of poetic language—the poet must "express the complex feelings and perceptions of a contemporary person." Verslibrisme, as Leyeles puts it, is not just an innovation in form but an expression of a new content: "The new content is the modern life of the modern man, who is breaking away from the old idyllic world, from the old provincialism and small-town atmosphere."[23] When, like Eliot and Pound, the Introspectivists stressed that poetry should use the spoken language, it is "the spoken language of the more intelligent, more conscious part of the Jewish people" that they had in mind.[24]

Thus the poetic theory of the Introspectivists is based on several antinomies: introspection—but reflection of the social and political world; individual poetic language—but expression of "modern man." We may add a third pair: art for art's sake—but art as an "authentic" expression of "life." Answering the critic Nigger's demands for a "Jewish art," Leyeles claims: "Literature is *art*. And art has its own laws, the highest of which is—art itself." But he continues immediately: "Art is *only* an expression of life."[25] In another context, Leyeles explains the formula, "art for art's sake": "Armed with his intuition, the modern artist does not want to know any tasks or goals other than art," but here, too, he adds, "because he knows that, for him, art is the only road to arrive at the truth, to see the world in its real light and to understand his own relation to the world."[26]

These antinomies catch some of the central contradictions and polemics of Modernist poetry since Symbolism. They do not offer an uneasy marriage of opposites but a conjunction of two poles, making the one stronger when it is expressed through the other, and vice versa. Value judgment seems to require that both poles be expressed in each of the dilemmas.

23   See "Chronicle," No. 10.
24   See "Chronicle," No. 7.
25   See "Chronicle," No. 5.
26   See "Chronicle," No. 15.

From this conception, several additional antinomies can be derived. The Introspectivists did not impose on poetry any "Jewish" or other social mission but, "because it is art, it is Jewish anyway."[27] In their most experimental poetry, the Introspectivists invested "Jewish" elements; the Jewish experience was always part of their personal, "universal" experience. For them, Jewishness was a language rather than a mission: "A Jew will write about an Indian fertility temple and Japanese Shinto shrines as a Jew" ("Introspectivism"). Not just as human beings, but *as poets, as an essential aspect of their poetics*, they developed antennae sensitive to the political climate surrounding them and wrote about it rather than about conventional poetic topics. This was as true for their intense Americanness as for their deeply felt Jewishness. The Introspectivists were the first Yiddish poets who enthusiastically accepted the magnificence of the big American city, "the relation to the big city, to the Woolworth [Tower]'s, the Empire State's, the total gigantic rhythm of the Metropolis New York or the Metropolis Chicago" (A. Leyeles, *In Zikh*, October 1935). Yet even before the Holocaust, they shifted their emphasis to Jewish topics as part of their personal experience: "The same writers who perceived America and expressed it in poem, novel, drama, turned to Jewish history and sought characters and situations there for their contemporary and even 'American' ideas," Leyeles wrote in 1935.[28] That is why they were prepared to face the oncoming Holocaust and respond to it in the language of poetry.

Similar antinomies obtain in the perception of poetic form. The Introspectivists paid attention to the details of form and language. The individual image, the right word in the right place, no superfluous similes or adjectives, and the liberation of the word as the material of art from the conventional ballast of centuries—all these seem to have been influenced by Italian and Russian Futurism. At the same time, for them, enhancing the art of language meant enhancing true expression. For example, on the one hand Leyeles keeps emphasizing that "rhythm is what actually makes the poem," that "words, ideas, content, images by themselves have no independent meaning in the poem. They exist only to serve. They help to create rhythm." On the other hand, rhythm has no value when it is rhythm only, rather than the "soul" of the poem, its metaphysical "essence," something that transcends the trivial and accidental "content."

27   See "Chronicle," No. 5.
28   See "Chronicle," No. 22.

Free verse was a central principle of most modernist trends in poetry: Imagism, Futurism, Expressionism, Acmeism—all felt it to be a crucial issue for the nature of the new art in language. Though free verse appeared as a conscious tendency in French Symbolism in the last third of the nineteenth century and can be traced back to Goethe, Novalis, and Coleridge, it was moved from the periphery to the center of poetic theory at the beginning of this century. In 1905, F.T. Marinetti launched an international referendum on free verse, in which many prominent European poets participated. Published in 1909 in book form (together with the Italian Futurist Manifesto), the *Enquête internationale sur le vers libre* may be considered a landmark that transformed one late French Symbolist technique into a central hallmark of Modernism. However, the rationalizations of the theory of free verse as well as the actual forms it assumed differed widely.

Only a few free-verse poems appeared in Yiddish before World War I. The Introspectivists were the first to make this a cardinal issue dividing the new from the old. It was a genuine revolution, since it is not easy for a poet raised on metrical verse to free himself from the automatized habit of falling into scansion. The Introspectivists may have received the green light for this move from Anglo-American Imagism, but they had a different conception of the problem. They emphasized not so much the aspect of freedom from tradition as that of individual expression and deliberate orchestration of a richer, rather than a more prosaic, rhythm. For them, free verse demands "an intense effort" in coordinating and subordinating all aspects of sound patterning in the poetic texture. Free verse is to be an expression of individuality on all levels: of the poet, of the poem, and of the individual line. It is to express both "the natural rise and fall of a mood" and "the new music that stirs the world," the irregular tempo of the big city and the "disharmony" of the "contemporary psychic experience." Hence the emphasis not on uniformity or prosaic tone but on the interaction of many shifting rhythmical devices and the symphonic nature of a free rhythmic poem. Since individuality of rhythm, rather than freedom of verse, was the issue, this could be accomplished in regular meters as well, provided the variety of selected forms guaranteed the uniqueness of each poem. In sum, free verse was a departure from the dominant, conventional form of a symmetrical, four-line, rhymed strophe, and it went in two opposite directions: of less and more structured texts.

Monotony was death to poetry. Glatshteyn understood this in his own way when he denied the musicality of Edgar Allan Poe's "The Raven" (arguing against Leyeles, who translated it twice, in 1918 and in 1945 [!]). He used the term again when he exposed the danger of a whole literature becoming "monotonic and monothematic" in "wailing together" after the Holocaust. Glatshteyn himself tried to save the individuality of the poem, even in that age of "collective stammer." As he put it: "Our word is our weapon and we must not let ourselves become primitive [in wailing over the destruction]." Glatshteyn cites as an example the prophet Jeremiah who, when a whole people was enslaved, "played" with the art of language and sought perfection in his "Jeremiads" ("May one Enjoy Elegies?" *Sum and Substance*, pp. 428–434).

The poets themselves were aware that their poetics was part of an international trend: "Certainly, there is a more direct relation between an Introspectivist and a German Expressionist or English Vorticist than between us and most Yiddish poets of the previous periods."[29] For the outside world, however, the Yiddish poets were isolated in a sealed ghetto. A telling example was the answer of the editors of the English-language *Poetry*, asking whether the language of *In Zikh* was Chinese.[30] In the Jewish domain itself, there was a chronic scarcity of readers.[31] Of course, English poets, too, had only small circles of readers at the time, before Modernist poetry was introduced into college curricula, but Yiddish poets never enjoyed that canonization. Only the common national tragedy brought them back to the center of Jewish society and made them into social bards, sometimes at the expense of poetic quality. Then it became clear what immense work had been done in the development of a new poetic language in Yiddish in New York between 1919 and 1950.

FORMS OF YIDDISH POETRY

Meter and sound orchestration were central to Yiddish verse to an extent that a reader of contemporary English poetry may not be prepared to sense. The magic of repeated metrical patterns, symmetry, and parallelism, reinforced by sound play and rhythmical variation, does to the simplest words what music does to the elementary words of good songs. As in a song, the "magic" is not in the sound patterns themselves but in their interaction with a few, perhaps quite elementary words and suggested themes, which give the

29 See "Chronicle," No. 14.
30 See *In Zikh*'s reply in "Chronicle," No. 18, and also Nos. 24, 26.
31 See "Chronicle," Nos. 8, 13, 23.

sound patterns certain emotive and thematic directions and which are, in turn, reinforced by them.

This central, poetry-making function of meter and sound can be seen in the role they play in Russian poetry to this day. Russian Modernist poets—Mandelshtam, Mayakovsky, Pasternak, Tsvetaeva—molded their futurist metaphors and surrealist compositions in consciously metrical rhythms (or variations of them), dense sound patterning, and conspicuous rhyme inventions. This was also true for German Modernist poets at the beginning of the century, such as Rilke or George. In Yiddish this remains a strong tendency, as can be seen in the "Neo-Classical Modernism" of the greatest living Yiddish poet, A. Sutzkever.

After World War I, Yiddish poetry developed various deviations from this metrical tradition, at first in ways still close to it but deforming its effects of regularity. For example, in Halpern's "Our Garden," each strophe establishes a perfect meter of four trochees, which is repeated in four rhymed couplets in an almost folksong tone (though once interrupted by an exclamation, in the fifth, unrhymed line):

> What a garden, where the tree is
> Bare, but for its seven leaves,
> And it seems it is amazed:
> "Who has set me in this place?"
> What a garden, what a garden—
> It takes a magnifying glass
> Just to see a little grass.
> Is this garden here our own,
> As it is, in light of dawn?

This regularity is then suddenly subverted by an additional, unrhymed, non-metrical long line, in a provocative, "Jewish" conversational manner:

> Sure, it's our garden. What, not our garden?

A more radical departure was effected in the "free rhythms," as advocated by the Introspectivists. The main directions of their free verse may be called "dynamic" and "conversational" rhythms.[32] "Dynamic" rhythms are irregu-

---

32 See my paper of 1952, Benjamin Hrushovski, "On Free Rhythms in Modern Yiddish Poetry," in Weinreich, Uriel, ed., *The Field of Yiddish*, New York, 1954, pp. 219–266, where I suggested a typology for some of those free rhythms.

lar too—that is, they have no overall metrical pattern for a whole poem, but are more rather than less rhythmically structured, using rhythmical configurations strongly deviating from prose or an interplay of changing metrical segments, heightened sound effects, and internally inverted rhymes, all of which serve the local shifts of mood in the text. (An English example for one kind of dynamic rhythm can be seen in T.S. Eliot's "Ash Wednesday.") Leyeles claimed that Yiddish free verse, though influenced by the principle raised in Anglo-American Imagism, developed a richer gamut of rhythmical expression. Indeed, Yiddish poets combined the Russian sensibility for heightened sound-patterning in poetry with the Anglo-American "battle cry for freedom," as Eliot called it—that is, for the individuality of the artist, the single poem, and the particular line.

At the other pole, "conversational" rhythms were developed, especially by Halpern, Glatshteyn, and Leyeles. These introduce the intonations and interjections of a speech situation, suppressing meter as well as any tendency of parallelism between adjacent lines. The continuity of an advancing monologue rather than equivalences of verse lines determine their rhythmical impact. They are convenient for bringing out the full flavor of Yiddish conversation, verbal gesture, and characterization in poetry.

At the same time, however, there was a tendency to enrich the gamut of poetic rhythms through mastering difficult strophic forms, both as found in the European tradition and as originally constructed by the poet (as in Leyeles's "Herod," analyzed below).

Leyeles's sonnet garland, "Autumn," may serve as an example of a European form re-created in Yiddish. It has fifteen sonnets, written in iambic pentameter. The sonnets are concatenated: the last line of each sonnet is repeated as the first line of the next sonnet (often with subtle syntactic variations). The fifteenth sonnet is composed of the first lines of the fourteen preceding sonnets.

Each sonnet employs the difficult Italian rhyme-pattern, binding the first eight lines with only two rhymes, though in an inverted order: *abba baab cdcd ee* (with an English-type closing couplet). Since the sonnets are concatenated, a dense rhyme grid embraces the whole structure, creating innumerable echoes between the various sonnets and their key words. Two key rhymes occur twenty-eight and twenty-six times, respectively, and others occur fourteen times (with no rhyming word repeated)—a musical magic impossible to reproduce in translation.

FORMAL CONFINEMENT OF EVIL—THREE POEMS

> The horrors of Dante's *Inferno* would remain unalleviated horrors, the raptures
> of his *Paradiso* would be visionary dreams were they not molded into a new
> shape by the magic of Dante's diction and verse.
> —Ernst Cassirer, *An Essay on Man*

> [prose translation:]
> Through your searching, suffering, frenzy, hear my word
> In restrained and measured octaves.
>
> .   .   .
>
> When there is no limit to your anguish,
> Build your pain into a fence of rigorous form.
> —A. Leyeles, "To You, Yiddish Poets,"
>   in "A Dream Among Skyscrapers"

At about the same time, A. Leyeles wrote three poems with a surprisingly
similar perception of the soul as a battlefield of madness, of irrational drives
that possess a person. The points of view, however, are cardinally different—
and so, appropriately, are the rhythmical conceptions of the poems.

Herod is the brutal, paranoid madman slaughtering everyone in sight,
a Stalin out of Jewish history, breeding hatred and fear and himself a "slave
to a curse," moved by powerful internal forces he cannot control. "Shlomo
Molkho Sings on the Eve of His Burning" presents an intriguing historical
figure who preoccupied Leyeles because of his mixture of messianic vision
and daring arrogance, his stance as a redeemer in dark times of Jewish history, a leader who carries the masses with him in a utopian vision, only to
pay for it with his own isolation and inevitable destruction. (Molkho, 1500–
1532, was burned at the stake after an attempt to enlist the Pope in his cause
failed.) Not surprisingly, Leyeles's drama on this topic had its world premiere
in the Vilna Ghetto before its annihilation. In the poem, Molkho has the
Stalinist streak. He is the Messiah, the Redeemer, enjoying the blind submis-
sion of the crowd; he, too, is gripped by vanity, by the narcissistic aggrandiz-
ing of his "I," which breeds loneliness and fear of himself. But historically,
Molkho is a positive hero, and Leyeles presents his tortured self-understanding from within. Night, "the metamorphoser of forms," piles doubts on him
in its darkness, on the eve of his execution, and extorts his real, personal confession; Molkho's transformation makes him "humble and silent with joy,"

relieved to exchange the "redeemer's poison" within him for the pure breath of the flame of the auto-da-fé.

Shlomo Molkho Sings on the Eve of His Burning[33]

Night, metamorphoser of forms,
You who pile up doubts in your darknesses,
Who weaken a weak and weary soul—
Be now the witness of my truth.
Night, awakener of hidden fears,
You who magnify dangers,
Who extort unwanted confessions from split lives—
Now, put your black seal
On the joyful, liberated will
Of my confession.
Soon it will be here—my most truthful hour,
Ash and nothingness will remain of my proud fame.

Soon the fire will strip me
Of the false plight that deluded me with sweetness.
Soon the great silence will be here.
Oh, sweeter than all lusts of the body
Was the belief of the crowds:
Redeemer! Leader!
I clung to them with passion,
Each throb of blood in me rejoiced:
Redeemer. Leader. I.

In sinful clandestine silence
I sang a song of my I.

And while, like multitudes of sand,
My faithful gathered around me,
While I selected words to match their heavy anguish,
I built a sparkling throne

---

33 Molkho or Molcho, Solomon. Born Diego Pires in 1500 in Portugal of Marrano parents. Announced the coming of the Messiah, obtained the protection of the Pope and aroused the expectations of European Jews. In 1532, was burned at the stake by the Inquisition in Mantua.

For myself.
Frivolously, my arrogance embraced my faith.
Their belief grew, and with it
My haughty head.
And my loneliness too, and the fear—
Of myself.
I saw their faith become a heart with no eyes,
I saw their blind pain spread
Like a carpet
Before the treading, fondled feet
Of the redeemer;
And like stairs—
For the climbing, insolent steps
Of the leader.
Appalled, I saw
A forest of wills, tall as cedars,
Fall under the axe of falsehood:
The hewer sinks in indignity,
And the great bright goal—
The estranged wonder-bird—
Flies back, abashed,
To his distant, hidden nest.

Now Shlomo Molkho is humble and silent with joy.
He sensed in time the redeemer's poison
And exchanged it
For the good, free, pure breath
Of the flame.

In "Herod," though revealing the king's internal psychotic drama, he is seen from the outside—incorporating, however, Herod's own point of view in Free Indirect Style. Herod's position is formulated in rhetorical, aphoristic summaries. The tone is a solemn, concise, and nervous recitation, underlined by the formal strophic structure and declamatory rhetoric. In contrast, Molkho's is the internal monologue of a mystic transformed and liberated by embracing the exalted vision of his own burning. The poem's rhythm is as free as his liberated mood. It is not a prosaic free verse, however, but conveys the festive tone of an ode to the night, gradually transformed into a passionate confession leading up to the dramatic gesture.

The third poem, "Foreign Fencers," presents the sleepless nights of Leyeles's own arrogant and lone "I"—a resigned, latter-day Fabius Lind in sophisticated introspection, in the grip of overpowering drives and contradictions. No leader, redeemer, or slaughterer, he too is a "battlefield of madness"; within him, too, there are "masters of evil," devious demons descending "from a spiderwebbed attic" and devastating his "authentic image." (Is the attic his subconscious? Or should we say "superconscious"? Or is it a collective subconscious like a "*boydem*," an attic filled with antiques?) But he manages to externalize the battlefields, the whole "foreign fencing" that goes on inside him and from which he has no escape; he stands like an observer outside himself and smiles. The rhythm is free, too, following his fluctuating observations yet emphasizing their ironies almost from the beginning, and lacking the long, periodic sentences and exclamation points of Molkho's ode.

Foreign Fencers

His sleepless nights are battlefields of madness
For angry Nos, for graying Yesses,
For gloomy Heres, for twisted Nevers—
He can hardly see his connection with them.
He would like to escape,
He'd let the fencers die weird deaths,
He'd shed them like scabby skins,
And he himself would begin from the very beginning.
What would he have to do with the foreign fencers?
What is his business with hunters and beaters?
It is all their fault—the masters of evil,
The devious demons who descend from a spiderwebbed attic
And devastate his authentic image.

The sleepless man smiles.
Weary, he throws up his hands.
Burn in hell! You, brothers, do what you want.
You come anyway uninvited.
And there is no escape for me.

The evil inside the most individual Introspectivist and the introspection in the most evil figure of the century—transposed into the repetition of history—are two poles of one scale. There is an affinity between messiah and tyrant, between inhuman history and the frail humanity of the poet himself. The different conceptions, however, are reflected in the changing forms of the poems. According to Leyeles's theory of "bipolarity,"[34] "the most dedicated verslibriste will suddenly turn to the most confined, classical forms." I shall not analyze the rhythms of the two free poems, but will concentrate on the formal principles of "Herod." (The English translation preserved the exact meter but not all the rhymes.)

Herod[35]

Herod is old. His face, anointed with ointments,
Balsams and makeup from Egypt, looks young. But his gaze—
Restlessness, fear, and grim clouds in the darkening folds,
Monstrous two halves side by side in abyss:
Roman—and Semite; despair—and good fortune;
Patron of strange little swallows,
Breaker of nation's neck;
Slave on a throne,
King in the yoke
Of unsated desires, of sickly and stealthy suspicions.

Herod raced early to fortress of lust and desire,
Groomed in his youth for the golden scepter of might.
Lucky was he. Yet, are all things just hollowed-out vessels?
Could the old sages be right, that all pain is
Nothingness, wind, a mere human invention?
He—he will harness the tempest,
He is the scion of strength!
Pain—not for him.
The heart of the voice
That engulfs in laments of account and repentance—destroy it!

---

34 See "Chronicle of a Movement," No. 22.

35 Herod the Great (73–4 B.C.), an Edomite who became king of Judea under the Roman Empire. His reign was marked by extensive construction and his own mental instability and cruelty.

Herod gets grayer and ever unsettled. With age,
Choked by a craving to get what's forbidden to him.
Love! King wants love. If only he could, he would order—
Just like an exquisite wine from his cellars—
Barrels of smiles, fermented on kindness.
Maybe it will then be brighter
There where the darkness is heavy,
Blackness torments.
Is, then, his soul
Condemned to be ever a battlefield hosting the storm?

Herod's great love erects temples and Golems of marble,
Cities and baths. Yet the people curl up in their silence.
Mutely they measure the buildings—and count all the graveyards.
Stifled, entangled in riddles, the people
Stand there, refusing to sip from his wine.
Glowing hot coals to the ruler.
"Rabble will not—let it be!"
Fiercer his anger.
Wild is his hatred,
Stamping out the last sparks of the aging king's conscience.

Sometimes: he would lose himself in the arms of his wife.
Her he adores, she is good to his mouth and his touch.
"Fondle, Miriamne,[36] the king!" But suddenly hordes of
Demons, intruding their snouts, come together,
Whisper and sting and point at Miriamne:
Sweet is her flesh—you must kill it!
False and betraying it is!
He—heeds the voices.
Murder dyes crimson
His couch, and the mood of the king is a madhouse in drowning.

Still lies the land under Herod's hatred and hammer.
Hatred feeds hammer and hammer feeds fear—in a circle.
All who are close to him, flesh of his flesh—in a vise.

---

36 Miriamne—Herod's wife. She was of the Judean royal family, the Hasmoneans, thus lend-
ing legitimacy to his claim to the throne and, at the same time, threatening it. Herod mur-
dered Miriamne, her two sons, and her relatives.

All of them destined for dungeons of hangmen.
Herod counts clearly: so many of them
Died and were buried like dogs.
Yet the rebellious, like fleas,
Multiply still.
Heavy his yoke.
And he scribbles fresh notes with names hateful to him—for the morrow.

Ever more lonely, secluded the king, day by day.
Herod won't trust an assistant, a slave or a eunuch.
Sun is his foe, the earth and the stones are insurgents,
All of them traitors, and he—only one.
Yet, though the words of the Book bear a warning:
Stop—yourself and the mourners!—
He is the slave to a curse.
His world is asleep;
Waking, he dreams
But of ruins and corpses, kneeling and singing his praise.

Bedlam—the soul of the ruler. Mad spiderwebs
Spread, crawl thickly from under the villainous throne,
Cover, enfold every breath, so that no one will find
Even a crack for escape from the bedlam.
Now the last fear grips the king,
Strikes like a legion of vengeance:
Soon will the crowd
Trample your crown
And embrace, and rejoice, when your reign and yourself die together.

Herod plans carefully. If in his lifetime the joys of
Love are forbidden—let mourning surround him in death!
He will command: Take the best, in purple or tatters,
All who still live, as in spite of his will—
Kill them—as soon as his wick has burnt out.
Quacks will lament on that day,
Women will tear at their skin.
Oh, on that day!
Wailing will rule!
Triumphantly raves the mad tyrant—and night dies in fear.

"Herod" has fixed, rigorous strophic structures, enriched by free sound-orchestration and rhythmical variation. There are nine strophes of nine rhyming lines each, with a tenth line as an unrhymed defiant closure. The original reads (stressed syllables are in upper case):

> HORdos is ALT shoyn. zayn POnim, geRIbn mit ZALbn
> MITSrishe SHMIrekhtsn, KUKT nokh oys YUNG, nor zayn BLIK—
> UMru un PAkhad un KHMAres in TUNkele FALbn,
> OPgrunt vu S'LOyern MONstrishe HALbn;
> ROYmer—seMIT; halb farTSVEYflung, halb GLIK;
> ZORger far VILD-fremde SHVALbn
> BREkher fun Umes geNIK,
> KNEKHT oyf a TRON,
> KINig in KON
> bay umLESHbarer DORSHT, bay farDAKHtn geHEYme un KRANke.

Meter	*Rhyme*	*Ending*
— ⏑ ⏑ — ⏑ ⏑ — ⏑ ⏑ — ⏑ ⏑ — ⏑	a	f
— ⏑ ⏑ — ⏑ ⏑ — ⏑ ⏑ — ⏑ ⏑ —	b	m
— ⏑ ⏑ — ⏑ ⏑ — ⏑ ⏑ — ⏑ ⏑ — ⏑	a	f
— ⏑ ⏑ — ⏑ ⏑ — ⏑ ⏑ — ⏑	a	f
— ⏑ ⏑ — ⏑ ⏑ — ⏑ ⏑ —	b	m
— ⏑ ⏑ — ⏑ ⏑ — ⏑	a	f
— ⏑ ⏑ — ⏑ ⏑ —	b	m
— ⏑ ⏑ —	c	m
— ⏑ ⏑ —	c	m
⏑ ⏑ — ⏑ ⏑ — ⏑ ⏑ — ⏑ ⏑ — ⏑ ⏑ — ⏑	x	f

(f = feminine, m = masculine)

The meter begins with the solemnity of a dactylic, almost epic line. Unlike the iamb, the dactyl is a very pronounced meter in Yiddish, with its stress at the opening of each line and foot. The length of the lines systematically recedes, from five dactyls to two, the rhythmical units becoming more and more concise and tense.

The rhyme patterning does not coincide with the patterns of length; rather, it creates a counterpoint to them until the last couplet, where they fall together. In the couplet, each of the short lines creates a bow, leaning on two strong stressed syllables at its two ends, reinforced by rhyme and often by alliteration as well:

KNEKHT oyf a TRON,
KINig in KON

Against this background of the long-winded, forward-pulling, ever-narrowing dactylic rhythm, there is the unexpected break of the last line. Its meter is opposite: an anapest, it has no rhyme and, after the couplet of short-breathing exclamatory verses, sounds like an endlessly long line, a cry of madness breaking out of confinement.

This long-winded forward movement, too, is filled with obstacles and broken up into small autonomous segments, marked by the rhymes and by rhetorical pairs of oppositions ("Roman—and Semite; despair—and good fortune"), though never permitting a final stop until all rhymes are completed and the flow issues into the final long, unrhymed phrase. The tension between the ever-continuing, ruthless forward drive, in ever shorter and tenser units, and the stalling, local dams, constitutes the rhythmical character of this poem. The original strophic structure is its indispensable base.

A great deal of what was going on in Yiddish poetry in this period was invested with such intensive attention to the texture of sound and language.

THE END OF A LANGUAGE

> Night. In the darkest places sparkle traces
> Of words. Loaded ships with ideo-glyphs
> Sail away. And you, armored in silence and wisdom,
> Unwrap word from sense.
>   —J. Glatshteyn, "We the Wordproletariat"

The young Introspectivist Jacob Glatshteyn felt that one could not make sense of the *velt-plonter* ("tangle of the world") when shiploads of ideas sail away incomprehensibly. The Introspectivist poet wears the armor of silence toward politicized society, he retreats into personal wisdom, observes his own consciousness ironically, and tries to liberate words from the burden of sense. In the poetry of the early Glatshteyn, there is no denial of his Jewishness, but it is actually irrelevant for the human condition he represents. Jewish traces are simply part of his "impulses of memory," flashing suddenly in his field of consciousness like the strange word *tirtle-toyben* from his early childhood, in the poem "Turtledoves." Glatshteyn's first book opens with the poem "1919":

Lately, there's no trace left
Of Yankl, son of Yitskhok,
But for a tiny round dot
That rolls crazily through the streets
With hooked-on, clumsy limbs.
The lord-above surrounded
The whole world with heaven-blue
And there is no escape.
Everywhere "Extras!" fall from above
And squash my watery head.
And someone's long tongue
Has stained my glasses for good with a smear of red,
And red, red, red.
You see:
One of these days something will explode in my head,
Ignite there with a dull crash
And leave behind a heat of dirty ashes.
And I,
The tiny dot,
Will spin in ether for eternities,
Wrapped in red veils.

In "1919," a date in history filled with red headlines of the Red Revolution and rivers of blood from pogroms in Ukraine as well as the Red Scare in the U.S., he is running around in New York, a latter-day Jacob the son of Isaac, comically reduced to the familiar and mundane "Yankl, son of Yitskhok," a tiny round dot that rolls crazily through the streets with hooked-on, clumsy limbs. There once was "The Jewish Dot," the most elementary, irreducible point of identity of a Jew ("*dos pintele yid*," referring both to the smallest Hebrew letter and the smallest vowel, represented by a dot, as well as to the name "Jew" and the initial letters of God, Isaac, and Jacob). Now only the dot remains, a hard core, the tiniest visible existence, rolling in the streets. (These are two anti-allusions—allusions evoked to cancel the validity of the allusion.) His limbs do not belong to him but are somehow hooked on, haphazardly attached to his body, clumsily irrelevant, as the stylistically outstanding two long words (6 and 5 syllables) expressively convey: *a-ROYF-*

ge-tshe-pe-te, um-ge-lum-per-te ("hooked-on, clumsy," like those words themselves). "Extras!" (special editions of newspapers) fall everywhere from above, presumably from the El running above the streets of New York; but he cannot comprehend a thing, and they squash his dumb, "watery head."

There is no single specific reference in the poem to any political event, though the time was filled with them; only the character's myopic eyeglasses get smeared with red and he is condemned to spin, lost in ether for eternities, with red before his eyes. Of course, this is New York. Glatshteyn's contemporaries in Europe filled their Expressionist poems with direct descriptions of the horrors of World War I and the pogroms of 1919. His experience is only a reflection of the European world, of news reports about it that fall absurdly in rapid succession onto his uncomprehending head. But the chaos of the modern world and the noisy metropolis are expressed just as strongly in indirection and understatement.

Glatshteyn's "1919" is a self-ironic, kaleidoscopic poem and, at the same time, an inverted statement about the political world and the mess it is in. The direct, coarse, juicy, rich, spoken language, with its diminutives, allusions, stylistic clashes, and ironic twists, is as Jewish as Yiddish lyrical poetry never was before, even though thematically "1919" is a cosmopolitan poem, smelling of New York confusion. The conversational markers and precise sensibility for the effects of spoken intonations and sound relations in free verse demonstrate what the "Young Generation" missed with their exact meters and Symbolist poeticalness. There is also a direct jibe at Neo-Romantic poetics in proclaiming that there is "no escape," not from politics, its "Extras!" and red colors, but from the color "heaven-blue," a poetic cliché externalized in nature: "The lord-above surrounded / The whole world with heaven-blue / And there is no escape."

Two poems from *Credos* (1929), "Autobiography" and "Jewish Kingdoms," again exhibit Glatshteyn's rich Jewish language of situations, coupled with an ironic distancing from a Jewish world.

Autobiography

Yesterday I dumped on my son the following story:
That my father was a Cyclops and, of course, had one eye,
That my fifteen brothers wanted to devour me,
So, I barely got myself out of their clutches
And started rolling all over the world.
Rolling, I grew up in two days,

But I wouldn't go back to my father's house.
So, I went to Tsefania and learned *sprechen* Jewish,
I got myself circumcised and became a Yid.
So, I started selling flax, wax, esrogs with bitten-off tips,
And earned water for kasha.
Till I met an old princess
Who willed me an estate and died.
So, I became a landowner
And began guzzling and gorging.
And when I saw I was getting fat,
I made up my mind and got married.
After the marriage, my estate burned down.
So, I became a poor newspaper writer.

To my father, the Cyclops, I sometimes write a letter,
But to my fifteen brothers—the finger.

Jewish Kingdoms

Konskiwolie, Mazelbożec, Korznice,
Liewertow, Pulawe, Bechewe,
Glisk, Piusk, Szabeszin—
Names of Polish towns, the devil knows why
They float up in my memory like dry leaves in a bath.
When I was a fat little brat
I knew that a voyage there
Smelled of a coach, a carriage, a squeaking wagon,
Carrying warm maids to new places.
I saw all the towns as Jewish kingdoms,
Where Yom Kippur lays its fear
Even on goyish huts,
Where crosses hang on the walls
As amulets against the Jewish god.
I would give a wealth of poverty
If I could still long for that.

Like the Austrian Jewish novelist Joseph Roth, Glatshteyn suspects in "Autobiography," that he is a lapsed Gentile and grotesquely demystifies the whole issue of history and roots. "Autobiography" may not be as coarse or inwardly "anti-Semitic" as some of Halpern's poems about the old country (e.g., "Zlochov"), but it is as antinostalgic and cut off from it. In "Jewish King-doms," strange names of Polish towns float up in Glatshteyn's memory like dry leaves in a bath, but he is incapable of longing for them.

Gradually but persistently, the rhyme *erter—verter* ("places"—"words") emerges in Glatshteyn's poetry, as in the motto of this chapter. As the rhyme itself suggests, words contain places. The names of Polish towns are mere names, but they also recall a warm, early-erotic, childhood experience. In the poetics of the early Glatshteyn, places occupy a central position. Though a master of the kaleidoscopic technique, he is uneasy about it. Glatshteyn is a talker, a narrator, and he prefers to locate his speakers in dramatized fictional situations. The narration is presented mostly in the third person but repre-sents the point of view of the central character of the poem. A poem is cen-tered on a re-created human experience that is located in a fictional, fantastic situation. In the early poetry, the situations are mostly antirealistic, historical, or legendary: Gaggie the bear-trainer with his five wives, the poet's two-hun-dredth birthday, the Proud King or Abishag. The Baron, an incorrigible liar, invents places with his words. Only in *Credos* does a more political realism enter the book, and even so, the basic technique is neither kaleidoscope nor metaphor but re-created fictional situations. Poems are anchored in places where characters are situated and enact their desentimentalized behavior.

At least since Glatshteyn's poems of Nakhman from Bratslav, the connec-tion is thematized: on the way to heaven, Nakhman becomes "everythingless in the world" and loses all his places and all his words, because there are no words ("*verter*") without the places ("*erter*"). Glatshteyn keeps repeating his persistent pair; in itself, it is a trite, obvious rhyme, but it becomes the focus of a central theme, underlined by the spare and sporadic use of rhymes in his poetry. The theme is central even when the rhyme itself is absent. "Wagons" or "On the Butcher Block" are fictional places in which individual characters are located, expressing the horror of the impending Holocaust (rather than talking about it or attempting direct, realistic descriptions). In the chilling poem, "A Hunger Fell Upon Us," the speaker may be in the same suburban home and garden as in the poem on his "Two-Hundredth Birthday," though there are also indications of a panhistorical space: "You touch your fig tree / Stroke the bricks of your house." The safety of well-built bricks and of the biblical allusion ("everyone under his fig tree") are both undermined in the beautiful understatement: "Maybe nobody's come yet, / But my bones already ache / With the dampness of the Jewish weather." Hence, when the first news of the Holocaust arrives, he places the experience in space: "Here I have never been" (coupled with an anti-déjà vu: "This I have never seen"). The metaphor of space, embodying a "world" of experience and meaning, is central to Glatshteyn's thematics, poetic language, and fictional constructs.

But now the relation is inverted as well: in Glatshteyn's early poetics, places carried words; now, the words are the carriers of a lost world. When they lose their meaning, we lose our world:

> All the existing words, / The expressed, / The understood, / Lie in their dumbfounded clarity. / Their sucked-dry meanings dozing off. / It is our world, / Soon it will lower the curtain. ("We, Of the Singing Swords")

When Glatshteyn tries to understand the Holocaust, he conjures up a place, a tiny dot from which he re-creates a lost world:

> I shall stubborn myself, / Plant myself / In a private, intimate night / That I totally invented / And wondered-in on all sides. / I shall find a spot in space / As big as a fly, / And there I shall impose, / For all time, / A cradle, a child, / I shall sing into it a voice / Of a dozing father, / With a face in the voice, / With love in the voice [. . .] And around the cradle I shall build a Jewish town [. . .] ("I Shall Transport Myself." See also the poem "I Shall Remember.")

Those were words that carried in themselves the memory of places; you could conjure up whole Jewish worlds from them. (Did these worlds ever exist? Is he inventing them now?) But when the immediate pain of the Holocaust was somewhat subdued, a new pain arose, the pain of losing hold of the words themselves. The rhyme *erter—verter* ("words"—"places") is back, and so is their overlapping:

> As to sad synagogues,
> To doorsteps of belief—
> How hard to come back
> To old words.
> I know well their places.
> I hear their humming.
> At times I get close, I look longingly
> Through the windowpanes.
>
> ("Without Offerings")

Can we imagine the tragedy of writers—H. Leyvik, Jacob Glatshteyn, A. Leyeles, others—who felt such a mission of beginning in their own lifetime and stood before the abyss of the end, losing first their readership, then their source, their people in Europe (along with their own parents), and finally the very language that they had made into such a fine instrument?

Here stands the aging Glatshteyn, holding a handful of water in his palm:

> A few trembling lines on the palm of my hand.
> I held them long
> And let them flow through my fingers,
> Word by word.
>
> ("A Few Lines")

And again:

> Soon we'll have lost all the words.
> The stammer-mouths are growing silent.
> The heritage-sack is empty. Where can we get
> The holy prattle of promised
> Joy? A child's grimaces
> Are an alien spite-language.
> In the dark we compose
> Lightning words, fast extinguished.
>> And ash becomes their meaning.
>> And ash becomes their meaning.
>
> ("Soon")

This is a very private, a very final Holocaust, for someone who was not there, who lived through it here, in America.

AMERICAN ARTISTS

The artists selected in *American Yiddish Poetry* are part of the history of American art in the twentieth century. Large bodies of their work have nothing specifically Jewish about them. They were concerned with problems of the language of art and with personal expression. They were enmeshed in the context of the development of American art and its responses both to the new trends in Europe and to the phenomena of American life. At the same time, their work exhibits striking parallels to the work of the Yiddish poets, who also tried to express the experiences of a modern individual in an American metropolis, alert to Western culture and to the political world of the twentieth century. To the extent that these poets and the visual artists turned to "Jewish" themes, especially in their later years, it was from the achieved position of their art and in response to historical events, from the point of view of contemporary Americans with Jewish memories. The difference in their fate, nevertheless, is astounding, albeit understandable: since the language of art is universal, the graphic artists are part of the histories of American art, just as citizens of Jewish origin are part of American society in general, whereas the Yiddish poets have remained enclosed in the ruins of their unapproachable language.

As with the poets, *American Yiddish Poetry* concentrated primarily on several artists, all of them more or less figurative Modernists, preceding Abstract Expressionism. Most were born in Eastern Europe or grew up in the Jewish ghettos of New York City and were contemporaries of the poets in this volume (the middle date indicates the year of immigration to the United States): Max Weber (1881–1891–1961), Abraham Walkowitz (1878–1893–1965), Louis Lozowick (1892–1906–1973), Ben Shahn (1898–1906–1969), Raphael Soyer (1899–1912–1987), Chaim Gross (1904–1921–1991), William Gropper (born in New York, 1897–1977). For a while they were eclipsed by the New York School of the 1950s and the predominance of abstraction in art. This trend, too, contained many Jews. But in recent years, the figurative artists have been gaining public recognition, and with it, comprehensive exhibits in major museums and galleries and a prominent place in histories of American art.

Most of these artists went to Europe at one time or another and were profoundly impressed by the Modernist trends there. Max Weber went to Paris in 1905, studied with Matisse, was friendly with Derain, Vlaminck, and Picasso, organized the first Rousseau exhibition in the United States in Alfred Stieglitz's Gallery "291," and was the first to introduce Cubism into American painting. His friend Abraham Walkowitz, in Paris in 1906–1907, came under similar influences. Both exhibited their work in New York in Stieglitz's gallery and in the famous Armory Show of 1913. Chaim Gross studied art in Budapest and absorbed some principles of German Expressionist sculpture. When Ben Shahn came to Paris in the mid-1920s, the excitement of Cubism was over and Picasso himself was groping between deformation and figurative forms. But Shahn learned an important lesson and, though remaining figurative, employed forms of stylized simplification and abstraction, giving expressive force to his socially engaged paintings.

Louis Lozowick, born in Russia, immigrated to the United States by himself as a boy of fourteen, studied at the National Academy of Design, and received a B.A. from Ohio State University in 1918. When he traveled in Russia, France, and Germany in 1919–1924, he was a representative of American art and American industrial optimism in the eyes of his European colleagues. " 'Ah, America,' they say, 'wonderful machinery, wonderful factories, wonderful buildings' " (as he recalled in "The Americanization of Art," 1927). Indeed, his geometrically precise and imposing paintings of American cities and industry, of majestic buildings, ports, and factories, were close to the Constructivist spirit and were first painted in Berlin (though based on sketches from his earlier tour of the U.S.). In Europe, Lozowick befriended El Lissitzky, a major figure in Soviet abstract art and Constructivism, who organized the famous Soviet exhibition in Germany and introduced new methods in graphic art and book production. Both Lozowick and Lissitzky were Yiddish-speaking and Yiddish-writing Russian Jews, but in Berlin they represented Russian and American art, respectively, just as Gertrude Stein represented American avant-garde literature in Paris.[37]

Indeed, after spending only thirteen years in the United States, Lozowick felt profoundly "American" and recalled proudly that "all the references to my work stressed its Americanism." In his essay, "The Americanization of Art," written for a catalogue of the international Machine Age Exposition held in 1927 in New York, he wrote:[38]

> The dominant trend in America of today, beneath all the apparent chaos and confusion is towards order and organization which find their outward sign and symbol in the rigid geometry of the American city. [. . .] The artist cannot and should not [. . .] attempt a literal soulless transcription of the American scene but rather give a penetrating creative interpretation of it. [. . .] The intrinsic importance of the contemporary theme may thus be immensely enhanced by the formal significance of the treatment. In this manner the flowing rhythm of modern America may be gripped and stayed and its synthesis eloquently rendered in the native idiom.

These are motifs echoed in the paintings of Walkowitz and Weber in the early 1920s and in the poetry of Leyeles and others in Yiddish.

---

37   On Lozowick, see Janet Flint, *The Prints of Louis Lozowick*, Hudson Hills Press, 1982.

38   Flint, *Ibid.*, p. 19. See also the chapter on "The Image of Urban Optimism" in Joshua C. Taylor, *America as Art*, Smithsonian Institution Press, 1976.

To a large extent, this is true of the other artists as well. They felt they were first of all "Artists." They were attached to modern Western culture in its latest developments, were intellectually part of it, and felt free to participate in creating its art. The extent to which they drew on personal experience or national memories depended on the nature of their art at any particular moment. The Introspectivist conception of "Jewish" topics as only a possible part of a modern person's consciousness, reflected in the kaleidoscope of his response to the world, is valid for these artists as well. In Marc Chagall's statement quoted earlier, he expressed pride and optimism in the future contribution of Jews to art; it was, however, not "Jewish art" he was speaking about but "Art" in general, though it may be achieved, as in his case, through the use of Jewish materials. Whether such materials were used or not was immaterial to the value of the art.

Thus, in the 1920s, Lozowick was a spokesman of American industrial optimism and geometrical construction. Ben Shahn, in his paintings and photographs of the 1930s, was a major artist of American symbolic realism and social protest, whether portraying conditions in the South or the trial of Sacco and Vanzetti. William Gropper was an effective political caricaturist and social painter of the left. Raphael Soyer depicted the alienation and internal stress and emotions of individuals in the city. One critic wrote of Soyer's "office girls": "Hemmed in by the crowd, whose presence they do not acknowledge, they are absorbed in coping with life in the city. . . . His people [Soyer's]—appealing, even noble—are marked by the frailties, anxieties and emotional traumas inflicted on them by their environment."[39] Soyer's characters could have walked out of Glatshteyn's *Credos*, Leyeles's *Fabius Lind*, or Halpern's city poems.

This was a response to America by people who could observe its social context "from below" and with fresh eyes. There was nothing Jewish about the subjects of their work. And thus they were perceived by their contemporaries. The influential New York critic, H. McBride, wrote of Max Weber: "At last we have an artist who is not afraid of this big great city of New York." Similarly the vitriolic attacks against these artists as intruding foreigners stressed their "assault on the fortresses of academic culture" and the abominable introduction of Cubism and Modernism by those distasteful immigrants, the perpetrators of "Ellis Island Art," rather than any specifically Jewish content.[40]

---

39   Abraham A. Davidson, *The Story of American Painting*, New York: Abrams, 1974, p. 126.
40   See Cynthia Jaffe McCabe, *The Golden Door: Artist-Immigrants of America, 1876–1976*. Smithsonian Institution Press, 1976.

Yet, as the Yiddish saying goes: "A guest for a while can see for a mile." They looked and they saw.

Many painters of Jewish origin seem consciously to have avoided overtly "Jewish" topics for a long time. Like Kafka, whose interest in Jewish subjects is reflected in his correspondence, whereas almost any overt trace of it was excluded from his fiction, these artists were universal in their iconography. This is certainly true of Ben Shahn in the period of his fame in the thirties. It is also true of a painter like Abraham Walkowitz, who has no Jewish themes in his drawings of "Metropolis"; in his book, *100 Drawings and Paintings* (1925); in his hundreds of drawings of Isadora Duncan; or in his *Barns and Coal Mines*. Even when Walkowitz did turn to drawing Jewish religious types, he called his book *Ghetto Motifs*—that is, motifs painted from the distance of one who has left the ghetto. Max Weber, the most consciously Jewish among his contemporaries, painted his first major painting on a Jewish theme, "Sabbath," at the age of thirty-eight, and he, too, distanced himself from his intensely, fatally Jewish types through almost grotesque deformations. Similarly, Chaim Gross's biographer notes:

> On the whole, the religious theme is rare in his work, and this is odd; although, like many artists, somewhere in the transition between adolescence and young manhood he left his traditional, family religion behind, Gross, unlike many others, returned to the faith of his fathers. [41]

Breaking out into the modern world meant breaking away from the Jewish fictional world, its symbols and typology, and it was not easy to find artistic means with which to confront it again when returning in older age to its faith or identity. Gross drew many Jewish types and symbols throughout the years, when illustrating his brother's retelling of Jewish folklore in Yiddish, or other books of Yiddish literature. It is only into his own, original sculpture that Jewish symbolism found its way hesitantly and rather late. Only occasionally can we see in one of Soyer's paintings an element such as a Yiddish newspaper (read by the parents, with a picture of the grandparents of the old country on the wall, in "The Dance Lesson"). In the moving title of "Reading from Left to Right," Soyer's usual, apparently unemployed characters stand with their backs to the hand-lettered signs announcing food in English, alienated by the very direction of its writing (Jews read from right to left). But even this is not

---

41 Frank Getlein, *Chaim Gross*, New York: Abrams, 1974, p. 57.

a "Jewish" painting in any substantial sense; it merely draws on the experiences of immigrant Jews.

As artists, the sculptors and painters represented here were all consciously American, but in daily life many of them did maintain Jewish contacts, both because their social environment was largely Jewish and because Yiddish, the language of their childhood, was still a viable force in New York. A typical case was the Educational Alliance Art School on the Lower East Side of New York. A community center built by uptown German Jews for Eastern-European Jewish immigrants at the end of the nineteenth century, it became an important art school in the twentieth century. Indeed, "the initial attraction of the Alliance was that the language of instruction was Yiddish."[42] Among its students were Jacob Epstein, Jo Davidson, Chaim Gross, Peter Blume, Adolph Gotlieb, Moses Soyer, Ben Shahn, Saul Beizerman, Leonard Baskin, Louise Nevelson, Barnett Newman, and Mark Rothko, several of whom later became teachers there.

Several artists maintained contact with Yiddish literature. Abraham Walkowitz, Max Weber, Louis Lozowick, William Gropper, and others published paintings, lithographs, drawings, and essays in Yiddish literary and social journals. Moses Soyer wrote a weekly column, "In the World of Art," for a Yiddish newspaper. Abraham Shauer, the father of painters Raphael, Moses and Isaac Soyer, was a Hebrew teacher and later a professor of Talmud at Yeshiva University, where Yiddish poet J. L. Teller studied with him. Naftoli Gross, the elder brother of the sculptor Chaim Gross, was a well-known Yiddish poet and writer. Chaim Gross, Ben Shahn, Max Weber, Abraham Walkowitz, and others illustrated books of Yiddish literature. Louis Lozowick edited a book in Yiddish and English, *100 Contemporary American Jewish Painters and Sculptors*, published by the leftist Yiddish Cultural Association (YKUF).

Max Weber's woodcuts and linoleum blocks were originally published in the years 1919–1926 in the Yiddish literary journal *Shriftn*, which was dominated by the writers of the Young Generation. As Weber's biographer noted: "the reproductions in *Shriftn*, printed in black ink on off-white paper, were the exact size of the original prints and were characterized by a delicacy and fine clarity of line and form, particularly evident when compared with the later, flatter, and more heavily inked reproductions in *Primitives* (1926)." (Daryl R. Rubenstein, *Max Weber; A Catalogue Raisonné of his Graphic Work*, University of Chicago Press, 1980). As Rubenstein points out, "there is no record that

42 *Ibid.*, p. 15.

Weber titled any of his relief prints." Subsequent identifying titles were of two kinds; A "Jewish" and a cosmopolitan label, sometimes attached to the same figure (e.g., Rabbi Reading/Pensioned, or Rabbi/Face with a Beard).

Max Weber wrote and published poetry in Yiddish in the style of impressionist primitivism, describing the snow as a land of pure white nymphs or evoking "the big city of Cubist forms—New York." All of a sudden, in a poem entitled "Chanukah Candles" (*Shriftn*, 1920), we read:

> I was seeking the miracle of Chanukah / and instead, I found our eternal miracle. / Here, in a tiny store, far from Zion, / Where the old, grey, pious Jew stands / like a sign, an echo of bygone times, / He stands for the whole Jewish people. Eternal, eternal, eternal is the Jewish people! / Eternal—/ The eternal Chanukah miracle among peoples of the world.

Yiddish poets did it in a more sophisticated way.

Little by little, with age, recollections of childhood, and perhaps the need to join a social "tribe," some of the artists returned to memories of the world of their fathers and tried their hand at "Jewish" themes. Artificially tied to Orthodox religious iconography and Eastern-European stereotypes—and unavoidably so, because there were no separate visual signs for modern Jews or Jewish concerns—these paintings could not really express the artist's contemporary personality (as poems could) and often fell below the same artist's highest standards. As in Yiddish poetry, a wave of return to Jewish topics came in the wake of the Holocaust and the creation of the State of Israel. One solution was found by Ben Shahn. Reliving in his later work the world of Hebrew learning of his early childhood in Lithuania, Shahn made graphic art of the letters of the Hebrew alphabet, in their mystical apotheosis as God's tools in the creation of the world. He also turned to biblical proverbs, types, and motifs, rather than to the usual Eastern-European religious figures. Hebrew letters, the elementary vestiges of a culture, also appeared in the work of other artists, such as Louis Lozowick, Chaim Gross, and Leonard Baskin.

The tension between Jewish and universal iconography is subordinated to another tension—that between various demands of artistic form or, more specifically, the language of Modernism, on the one hand, and the challenges of confronting the real or mythological America on the other. Though most of these artists were highly aware both of Modernism and of the centrality of the language of art, they rarely represented an extreme artistic dogma; rather, they compromised under the pressures of an American expressive realism. This may have been due to a combination of their Jewish condition, the immediacy of social problems in America, the Socialist trends of Jewish New York (especially in the 1930s), and the lack of an aristocratic, isolated stance of high culture in American art as compared to Paris. Lozowick formulated this tension in the form of an ideal solution: "A composition is most effective when its elements are used in a double function: associative, establishing contact with concrete objects of the real world and aesthetic, serving to create plastic values." Indeed, Lozowick's own art was much closer to the first function than was Lissitzky's.

The uneasy compromise between the language of art and the demands of a message, between Modernism and realism, between being Jewish and creating human art was common to these artists and to the Yiddish poets. In both groups, it caused a hesitation between short periods of fully committed Modernist experimentation and the return to more eclectic responses—responses that were more "literary" in art and more "conversational" in poetry, and perhaps more human and emotional as well. This prevented the formation of a clear-cut Modernist "school" in American art until World War II.

When the dominant trend in America became abstract art, the Jewish topic all but disappeared, not only because there were more American-born artists among the Abstract Expressionists but because there were no more recognizable mimetic themes in their paintings. The participation of Jews in this new wave was even greater than it had been in previous movements. Thus, in 1935, when Mark Rothko joined a group of artists, "The Ten" ("The Ten Who are Nine") they were, apparently, all Jews. Indeed, in some comments by Newman or Rothko, one can detect allusions to Jewish mysticism. (And who would deny that abstraction is a Jewish tendency in this theoretical and scientific age?) But this was part of their wider cultural background, as was the case of most Yiddish poets.

Comparing various tendencies in the two domains of poetry and art, their historical unfolding in the context of American society, and even individual items, one is struck by many parallels, despite the radical difference between the two media and the lack of real contact between the poets and artists themselves. Max Weber's Cubist-inspired "Rush Hour" was described by a critic as "conveying the maddening unrest and visual diversity by means of a fuguelike composition in which fierce verticals alternate with vigorous diagonals."[43] The fugue is a central theme in Leyeles's theory of free rhythms;

43   Alfred Werner, *Max Weber*, New York: Abrams, 1975.

the interest in rhythm and in geometrical forms was shared both by several painters of the early 1920s and by Leyeles (see, e.g., his "Symmetry"). "Rush Hour" evoked many Yiddish poems, both because Jews had to use the subways and because their poetry was alert to the myth of the big city, which they brought from Europe and fully confronted in New York. The same mood is expressed in Walkowitz's geometrical paintings of the "Metropolis" and in Leyeles's hymns to big-city architecture.

This adoration of technology did not last long, however. A more inward, introspective, and individualistic conception ensued, as seen in Leyeles's *Fabius Lind*, in Teller's *Miniatures*, and in Soyer's paintings. A striking parallel can be seen in the defiant, unsentimental, independent look of Gross's "East Side Girl" of 1928 and Glatsheyn's "Girl of My Generation," published in *Credos* in the same year. At the same time, a poetry of the proletarian, harsh, ugly side of the city evolved, as exemplified by Halpern and Berysh Vaynshteyn and by some of the painting of the 1930s.

Both in the sculpture and paintings by Jewish artists and in American Yiddish poetry, Jewish elements were subdued and, if present at all, were used as a language to describe the human condition. But with the awareness of what was happening to the Jews in Europe, especially after the Holocaust, poets and artists of Jewish origin naturally felt the need to respond to the theme and to meditate on problems of Jewish history, identity, and symbolism. An interesting parallel can be seen in the return to the basic atoms of Jewishness, the letters of the Hebrew alphabet: for Lozowick, they became the material for a new constructive edifice; for Ben Shahn, they were the elements of creation, molded in a hieroglyphic-like organically unified body that became his artist's logo; and for Leyeles, they were a divine provocation for a people of texts and interpretations. All of these evolved at about the same time.

There was, however, a radical difference between the two domains that are brought together here for the first time. Both reflected similar problems of art in the twentieth century and may have been influenced by the same American ambience. But their social existence was profoundly different. While some of the artists occasionally maintained their ties with Yiddish literature, their natural allegiance was to the realm of American art, created and received by all Americans regardless of origin. As Raphael Soyer put it:

> I came to the United States at the age of twelve and have lived here ever since.
> I have benefited by all the advantages it has to offer one: schools, museums, art

galleries and libraries. My work has been influenced by the multi-ethnical character and the pluralistic culture of this country.

An artist, born to Jewish parents or not, could choose whether to demonstrate his origins or to bypass them altogether. Some of the Yiddish poets would have liked to do the same; indeed, one of the fascinations that the communist ambience held for them lay precisely in the possibility of freedom from being Jewish without, however, having to deny it. But the ghetto of their language (as Glatshteyn dubbed it) cast the Yiddish poets back into the isolated magic circle of a Yiddish newspaper culture and steeped them in Jewish problems—perhaps more than some of them had wanted to be in their youth.

The parallels between the graphic art and the Yiddish poetry of Jewish Americans is not intended to obliterate their obvious differences. Rather, it is meant to shed new light on the Americanism of Yiddish poetry and its va-lidity as an expression of American art. Yiddish poetry was one mode of the great trend of Jews to join general Western culture and contribute to it. The obsession of Yiddish poets with poetic form, though a legacy of Russian Sym-bolism, was part of a wider move to embrace the beautiful, to join the aes-thetic domain as one way out of the ghetto. The hunger of young Jews for real art emanated from the same impulse, though it obviously had specific causes in each particular biography.

5 THE LAST DAYS OF THE JERUSALEM OF LITHUANIA[1]

In September 1943, the Vilna Ghetto was liquidated and several thousand remaining Jews, including Herman Kruk, were transported to camps in Estonia, notably to Klooga, near Tallinn. Kruk continued writing his chronicles—in the form of diaries, narratives, and poems—up to the last day. He was killed and burned with most of the surviving Jews just hours before the Red Army liberated the area on September 19, 1944. The following poem, written in Yiddish in precise amphibrachic meter, was found among his writings from this last period and is presented here in a literal translation.

For Future Generations

Neighbors in Camp Klooga often ask me
Why do you write in such hard times?—
Why and for whom? . . .
. . . For we won't live to see it anyway.

I know I am condemned and awaiting my turn,
Although deep inside me burrows a hope for a miracle.
Drunk on the pen trembling in my hand,
I record everything for future generations:
A day will come when someone will find

---

1   Introduction to Herman Kruk, *The Last Days of the Jerusalem of Lithuania, Chronicles from the Vilna Ghetto and the Camps, 1939–1944*, edited by Benjamin Harshav, 2002.

The leaves of horror I write and record.

People will tear their hair in anguish,

Eyes will plunge into the sky

Unwilling to believe the horror of our times.

And then these lines will be a consolation

For future generations, which I, a prisoner,

Kept in my sight, things

I recorded, fixed faithfully. . . .

For me it is superfluous,

For future generations I leave it as a trace.

And let it remain though I must die here

And let it show what I could not live to tell.

And I answer my neighbors:

Maybe a miracle will liberate me.

But if I must die, it must not die with me—

The time of horrors I leave for future worlds.

I write because I must write—a consolation in my time of horror.

For future generations I leave it as a trace.

—*March 24, 1944*

HERMAN KRUK'S DIARY

Herman Kruk's monumental diary of the Vilna Ghetto is a major classic of Holocaust literature. The YIVO, "Yiddish Scientific Institute," a Yiddish research academy for the humanities and social sciences, founded in Vilna in 1925, shifted its center during the war to New York, where YIVO's founder, Dr. Max Weinreich, succeeded in escaping. When the diary, documenting the demise of Jewish Vilna and the death of the Jewish nation and culture in Europe, was brought to New York in 1947, its publication was obviously an urgent task of the YIVO. Nevertheless, Kruk's book was published only thirteen years later, in 1961, meticulously edited and annotated by Mordkhe Bernstein and introduced by Pinkhes Schwartz, Herman Kruk's brother. The hundreds of names mentioned by Kruk had to be identified and described, the facts and stories checked out against other sources, and the incomplete and damaged manuscript read and supplemented with missing information. Six hundred and seventy-two large pages of the published Yiddish book included almost five hundred long footnotes and dozens of editor's inserts in tiny letters.

The scope of this book, and the extensive knowledge of Vilna personalities and institutions required to understand it, certainly made any translation difficult and contributed to the fact that the book is still unknown in any language outside Yiddish.[2] Yet the main cause seems to be that at the time, the world was little interested in the Holocaust (except for heroism, perhaps), and it was practically impossible to publish translations of such books in English. As the Yiddish poet Jacob Glatshteyn wrote in 1938, before any ghettos were established by the Nazis: "I do not know if there is a better parallel to ghetto life than writing Yiddish."[3] Now Yiddish culture, in its last flourishing, embraced the Holocaust as its own: "A whole poetry has become monotonic and monothematic," wrote Glatshteyn.

With that background in mind, Barbara and I gladly accepted the invitation of the YIVO to translate the text and the footnotes into English, and to reedit the book for a new readership forty years after it was first published in Yiddish. It was an emotional experience for me in more than one sense. We tried to maintain precise scholarly standards in the translation and editing; yet in the preface, a few personal words are in order.

I was born in Vilna, "Jerusalem of Lithuania," as we proudly called it. My parents were Jewish secular intellectuals: my mother, Dvoyra Freidkes, was a mathematics teacher and principal of a Yiddish secular school (the Sofye Markovne Gurevitsh Gimnazye), and my father, Dr. Abraham Hrushovski (later, Dr. Agassi), taught history in Hebrew schools, the Hebrew Teachers' Seminar, and the Polish-Jewish Gymnasium of Dr. Epstein in Vilna. In 1940–41, under Soviet rule, they were both Pedagogic Directors of two of the four Vilna Yiddish Gymnazia (a Gymnazium, or academic high school, provided the highest level of Jewish education, and in its cultural status was equivalent to an American college).

At dawn of June 22, 1941, Soviet Vilna was bombarded by German airplanes, even before war was declared. After a day and night of bombardments, on the 23rd, my parents, my little sister, and I left our apartment with small rucksacks and hit the road. Only our tenant, old Pati Kremer, the veteran leader of the Bund, remained there. The neighbors were amazed: "You're

---

2 In the meantime, a Lithuanian translation was published: Herman Kruk, *Paskutinės Lietuvos Jeruzalės dienos, Vilniaus Geto Ir Stovyklų Kronnikos, 1939–1944*, edited and introduced by Benjamin Harshav, Lietuvos Gyventojų, Genocido Ir Rezistencijos, Tyrimo Centras, Vilnius, 2004.

3 See Benjamin and Barbara Harshav, *American Yiddish Poetry: A Bilingual Anthology* (Berkeley: University of California Press, 1986), pp. 802–4.

leaving everything just like that? The Germans are cultured people, they will not touch the city of the Vilna Gaon!" That was how people responded after Kristalnacht, the humiliation of Jews in Vienna and in Poland, and the establishment of crowded ghettos in Łódź and Warsaw. Although those things were unpleasant, no one suspected the "final solution." But my historian father said: "I read Hitler's *Mein Kampf* and I believe him." We went to the railroad station and barely squeezed into the hundred-wagon long train (*eshalon*), the only train that left Vilna before the Germans came, and which was crammed with families of Red Army officers and several thousand Jews. The next day, Vilna was empty of any power, and the Germans moved in. On the old Polish-Soviet border, however, all "Westerners," that is, people without Soviet passports, were forced to leave the train. As Kruk describes it, most of them were trapped, barred from crossing into Soviet Russia; many tried to go back to Vilna, and many of them perished on the way. We, however, my family of four, descended the train on the "wrong" side, and as soon as a German airplane began strafing us with machine guns and the train moved, we jumped back in. Later, we did walk for several days in Byelorussian forests, where I "celebrated" my bar-mitzvah; but eventually we boarded another *eshalon* and two weeks later arrived in the Urals. We were saved.

When I read Kruk's diary, I feel that I could have been on every page of it. I was thirteen when the war broke out. What would I have done when my whole street was taken to Ponar (as it was)? And I knew so many of the names in this book. My best childhood friend, Gabik Heller, worked in Kruk's library (after his father, the historian Dr. Moyshe Heller, died in the Ghetto). Our mutual friend and classmate Itsik Rudashevski wrote a memorable Ghetto diary.[4] Both perished. Boys a few years older went to the partisans (Avreml Zeleznikow, the Lubocki[5] brothers); their leader, Abba Kovner, was a friend of my father's, and we spent the summer before the war near his summer camp of Ha-Shomer ha-Tzair in the Carpathian Mountains. When Kruk mentions names of people who died in the Estonian camps, I see them before my eyes: my mother's students Zhozik Schreiber (and his father, the director of the Yiddish *Technikum*), the tall, thin Grisha Tsepelevitsh (commander of the Second Battalion of FPO, who perished in Estonia). And so many students, friends, and colleagues of

4   Published in Hebrew and English: Itsik Rudashevski, *The Diary of the Vilna Ghetto* (Tel Aviv: Lohamei ha-Getaot and Ha-Kibbutz ha-Meuhad, 1973).

5   The publisher of this book insisted that all Polish names be spelled in Polish. We left it here as in the book.

my parents appear here in their last journey: the doctor and cultural activist Pomerants; the teacher and principal of *Real-gimnazye* Mira Bernstein, who organized a Yiddish school in the Ghetto; the modest and splendid scholar Zelig Kalmanowicz (our neighbor in the house owned by the publisher B. Kletzkin); the music teacher Gerstein, who directed a famous choir; and many others. The medieval, narrow streets of the Ghetto were so familiar: I walked there every day on the way to *Real-gimnazye* on Rudnicka Street. And the pastoral, wooded hills of Ponar, which became the slaughterhouse of a hundred thousand Jews, were a frequent place of my family's Saturday outings.

There is a special place in my heart for the YIVO. Its founder, Dr. Max Weinreich, and his family were friends of our family. When I was one year old, I got a printed invitation to their home for the foundation of "Young Vilna" (Weinreich always understood that without a young generation Yiddish culture was doomed; he later used the same title for the budding group of modern Yiddish poets). On the tenth anniversary of the YIVO, in 1935, the historian Simon Dubnow and the artist Marc Chagall came to the conference (from Riga and Paris) and visited the summer colony for weak children, where my father was director. And at the age of 12, I had the honor of serving as a guide at the YIVO exhibition on the 25th anniversary of Y.L. Peretz's death. It was a small, poor wooden house on Wiwulski Street 18, just a few blocks from my home, but it exalted the pure principles of (humanistic) "science." In its poverty, it was a great research institute.

How could I work on Kruk's detailed descriptions without keeping all this before my eyes?

Yet when Barbara and I translated the book with all of its footnotes, new problems emerged. Indeed, it was important to keep the first editors' footnotes with minor editorial interference because they collected a great deal of information from Vilna people who survived and were still alive at the time (a large, international correspondence about it was conducted in the early 1950s); this oral history is something we no longer have access to. But at the same time it was imperative to overcome the limitations of that edition.

When the partisans returned from the forests to the ruins of Vilna Ghetto in July 1944, they went to find Kruk's diary in a ghetto cellar where it was buried. Yet the cellar had been broken into by robbers looking for "Jewish gold," and the pages of the diary had been scattered. Eventually, some of the pages (typed and numbered in the Ghetto by Kruk himself and his assistant) were recovered and sent to New York, and some of the pages were taken by Ruzhka

Korczak and others to Israel, and stored in Yad Vashem and in Kibbutz Givat Haviva.

The published book was not really Kruk's complete diary; it contained only two-thirds of the numbered pages. The first editors of the book interpolated their conjectures as to what Kruk wrote about in the missing pages, but they were often wrong. In an Israeli archive, I found Kruk's own detailed table of contents—101 pages in his own handwriting—often including ten or twenty topics recorded in one day. Kruk cherished it and saved it separately from his diary, and apparently carried it with him to the camps in Estonia. We deleted the first editor's wrong guesses and inserted all the recovered titles in the text; they read like a skeleton of a horror history.

We also inserted dozens of small pieces into the existing diary, using other copies of the typewritten pages or small fragments, glued together like a half-lost mosaic. This was a laborious job, though it will hardly be noticed by someone reading the integrated text.

Now the nature of the book had been transformed: instead of blindly translating the old Yiddish edition, we were trying to reproduce in English Kruk's original chronicle, insofar as it survived anywhere in the world (including a full translation of the first edition). Indeed, we found hundreds of pages of unpublished Kruk manuscripts, often fragmentary and hardly legible, in the Moreshet Institute in Israel, in the YIVO archives, and in Vilnius. Thus, the English edition is more precise and is 30 percent larger than the old one.

But in addition to corrections in the main part of the diary, there were also problems on a larger scale. The published book presented only two years of Kruk's life in Vilna under the Nazis, June 23, 1941–July 14, 1943. Kruk, however, wrote his chronicles during the five years of his Holocaust: from the collapse of Warsaw in September 1939 to one day before he was killed in Estonia on September 18, 1944. The YIVO was a Vilna institution and was naturally interested in the Vilna Ghetto. But Herman Kruk came from Warsaw, and we cannot properly understand his responses to events in Vilna without reading about the sudden collapse of Poland and the collapse of his own world in the fall of 1939, his six-weeks' flight from Warsaw and his life as a refugee in Vilna in the two subsequent years. We must also include the last stage of Kruk's life and the life of the remnants of Vilna Jewry—the year spent in Klooga and other camps in Estonia, right up to his death. This volume restores the full five-year scope (though, regrettably, not all surviving texts) of Herman Kruk's Holocaust.

Kruk was alert to the problems of genre and discourse in representing the Holocaust (for more about this, see the introduction): to his last day, he collected "objective" documents; recorded witness accounts; wrote diaries; reconstructed diaries in retrospect; wrote narrative chronicles and quasi-fictionalized historical representations; wrote "Ghetto Miniatures"—glimpses of typical, anecdotal situations; and crafted poems—reflecting an individual's experiences in the Estonian camps. He was constantly seeking the discourse most appropriate to the mode of representation befitting the particular situation—and all those genres were mobilized to the telling of the Holocaust. To select only the formal "diary," as the Yiddish edition did, is to misrepresent and impoverish Kruk's record.

And last but not least, when Kruk was taken from Vilna to the Estonian camps, where he survived for another year with 20,000 other Jews, he left his typist and typewriter behind. But he stubbornly continued to write his chronicles, often after 14 or 16 hours of hard labor. This is a direct continuation of his Vilna diaries. He clarifies some issues about the last days of Vilna Ghetto and the partisans, and describes the end of the last remnants of Jewish Vilna. The editors of the Yiddish edition included in their book only texts they found on typewritten and numbered pages, but our task was ten times as hard: the later texts are often scribbled on small pieces of paper, unfinished, and hardly legible. Still, it would be unconscionable if we had knowingly published the old, incomplete, and truncated edition of Kruk's diary while some of the later parts were recovered.

This is the terrible story of Kruk's Estonian chronicles: On September 17, 1944, one day before the liberation by the Red Army, Kruk buried his last diaries in Lagedi camp in the presence of six witnesses. The next day, he and most remaining Jews in Klooga and Lagedi were shot and burned on a pyre. One of the six, Nisan Anolik, hid and survived. He went back to the camp, uncovered the diaries, and brought them to Vilna, to the new "Jewish Museum" founded by A. Sutzkever and Sh. Kaczerginski, where other Kruk manuscripts were located. In 1947 the museum was closed by the Soviet authorities, and the papers were taken away by the NKVD, ostensibly for "recycling" in a paper factory. However, a righteous Lithuanian saved a great many confiscated Jewish books and manuscripts. They turned up half a century later, including hundreds of pages written by Herman Kruk. When Lithuania became independent of the Soviet Union, it became possible to recover Kruk's writings. Sam Norich (then director of YIVO) and the archivist Marek

Web acquired copies of the Vilnius Kruk manuscripts and brought them to me. The process of matching the pieces, deciphering them, rewriting them in a typed, standard Yiddish form, and translating them was as labor-intensive as translating the whole book.

From the beginning, I insisted on making every effort to recover all missing parts of Kruk's diary. That was my function as editor and our moral duty toward the *kadosh* Herman Kruk and the memory of the Holocaust. Indeed, we have succeeded in restoring some of the missing parts. The book now covers all five years of Kruk's Holocaust chronicles. Chapters 1, 9 and 10 are entirely new; a window was opened on Jewish life in the Estonian camps, including Kruk's suffering and tantalizing dreams of liberation; and dozens of corrections have been made in the earlier published parts.

In 2004, our edition of Kruk's chronicles was published in Vilnius in a Lithuanian translation.

TWO HOLOCAUSTS

The word *Holocaust* with its connotations of horror, outrage, and genocide, obstructs our view of the great variety of phenomena, stages, and experiences covered by this term.

In a sense, there were two Holocausts. One was the extermination of several million human beings—Germans, Frenchmen, Poles, Hungarians, Italians, and Russians of Jewish origin. Some of them (like Jean Amery) were Christians, some (like Primo Levi) were indifferent to their Jewishness, some belonged to a synagogue or participated in Jewish life, most were consumers of and contributors to another culture. As individuals, they were persecuted not for what they did or believed but for who their grandparents were. Six million individuals of Jewish origin[6] were slaughtered in the Nazi death machine. From this perspective, many millions of others were killed in World War II, and if you count the numbers of persons killed, there is no difference between them. The questions, however, still remain: What happened to them before they were killed? Why were their children condemned with them to death (unlike the children of German Communists and every other group except the Gypsies)? What did the Holocaust do to their hearts when they

6   This figure may be somewhat smaller in some accounts, but it may also be larger by 250,000 shot in the occupied Soviet territories that we did not account for before (as Yitzhak Arad argued).

were like hunted animals before they perished and to the hearts of thousands of other Jews—in Europe and elsewhere—who survived but experienced the horror and fear of their built-in, "genetic" destiny?

But there was also another Holocaust, the Holocaust of the modern Jewish nation and culture, especially as it had lived in Eastern Europe. There was a dense network of Jewish activities, competing ideologies and political parties, youth movements and sports clubs, literature in several languages, publishing and translations of world literature into Yiddish and Hebrew, newspapers and libraries, separate Jewish trade unions and educational systems—a secular, modern, European-type, autonomous Jewish nation—though without power over any territory—that emerged in the nineteenth and twentieth centuries and perished in the Holocaust. This was Kruk's world, and he recorded both those Holocausts.

When the German professor (of Jewish origin) Theodor Adorno asked how one could write poetry "after Auschwitz," it was the first kind of Holocaust he was referring to. "Auschwitz" was a death machine and is a symbol of total physical annihilation. The contemporary cult of the Holocaust deals with it as with a shipwreck we survived, without asking what continent the ship came from, what existed before that shipwreck. Why would the Holocaust be so horrible, why wouldn't it be just part of the general World War II, just 6 out of 50 million killed, if it were not a Holocaust of something, of a nation and a culture that disappeared with it? The Polish poet of Jewish origin Julian Tuwim expressed the problem succinctly: "I am a Pole when the blood is running in my veins, and a Jew when it is running out of my veins." Many people of Jewish origin have a Tuwim Complex. For them, the trauma begins and ends with the word *Auschwitz*.

Those two kinds of Holocaust are related to the two kinds of transformations that Jews underwent in the modern age. The "Modern Jewish Revolution"[7] responded to the criticism of the "medieval" Jewish existence and behavior, expressed both by anti-Semites and by the internal new Jewish literature. It produced a radical transformation of the Jews, their demographic situation, languages, education, professions, and conceptual world. The harbingers of those changes appeared in the nineteenth century, especially in Western Europe, but the great Jewish masses in Eastern Europe were involved in this process mainly after 1882. The Modern Jewish Revolution consisted of

---

7   I described this revolution in the first part of my book *Language in Time of Revolution* (Stanford, CA: Stanford University Press, 1999).

embracing the secular European world, its culture, genres and modes of discourse, and institutional frameworks. And it went in two directions: Intrinsic and Extrinsic. The "Extrinsic" trend brought millions of Jews into the general culture of the respective countries where they were living. The "Intrinsic" trend strove to create an equivalent Jewish culture, modeled on the European system. It was to be primarily in the Jewish languages, Yiddish and Hebrew, but also in the languages of the respective countries. And it was to create a trans-national Jewish cultural nation.

After 1882, all the new Jewish ideologies and parties, literature and art, a network of social and cultural organizations, several networks of Jewish schools in Hebrew, Yiddish, and other languages, all combined to achieve this goal. As it happened, however, the European idea of a nation based on language, culture, and history of an ethnic society did not succeed without territorial power. Only the small branch of the Modern Jewish Revolution that moved to Palestine, reinvented the Hebrew language, and established the state of Israel, survived the upheavals of the twentieth century in Europe.

Kruk, however, still lived with the ideals and culture of a politically autonomous, secular Jewish nation; in his case, as formulated by his own party, the Yiddishist and Socialist *Bund*. It was from this position, of a Jewish nation in the throes of death, that all the responses to the Holocaust emerged. Each person, naturally, fought for his or her own life; but in addition, they participated in finding responses to the state of the nation. It was a whole larger than their own life, embracing them and giving them some raison d'être. It was in the name of this Jewish nation with its proud history that the internal responses arose. Helpless as they were, no matter how little impact they made on the outcome of the war, in their own lives these responses were transforming moves of dignity and achievement. The two major directions of response were: joining the fight against the Germans, in the ghetto or in the partisan forests; or doing everything for "endurance" and "survival," as Kruk did. A few months before the liquidation of Ghetto Vilna, he expressed his opposition to the partisans because their acts might jeopardize the existence of "the last metropolis of the Bund in Poland," as he put it, that is, the Vilna Ghetto, which then numbered about 15,000 inmates.

In the eyes of the last Jews in Nazi-occupied Europe, this was the end of a nation, a millennia-old nation that had lived in Europe for a thousand years, about as long as the other European nation-states and languages. (They rarely considered the American Jewish community in this context, probably because it was not seen as a creative national center.) That is why the Holocaust was called in Yiddish by the Hebrew word *Khurban* (something like "total ruin, destruction"), which was the term for the Destruction of the First Temple and the first Jewish state in Palestine and the exile to Babylon, and for the Destruction of the Second Temple, which led to two thousand years of Diaspora around the world.[8] Now it meant the end of the Jewish nation in Europe, as final and as significant as the two destructions in biblical Palestine. It is not by accident that the Zionist establishment in Israel did not want to dignify the death of European Jewry with the term that denoted the end of a Jewish independent nation in the past. "Yad Vashem," the government institution established to commemorate the catastrophe, was called *Yad Vashem la-Gevurah ve-la-Shoah*, "Memorial to Heroism and Holocaust." "Heroism," of course, had the priority, but "Khurban," the name the survivors used, was not mentioned. "Shoah" (like the English "Holocaust") is a natural disaster, an external catastrophe rather than a pivotal historical event in the life of a nation. (With time, of course, "Holocaust" assumed that other meaning as well.)

And there is another sense in which two different Holocausts can be discerned (though not necessarily overlapping the previous division). It was one thing to be taken from your home to a concentration camp or a death camp, and quite another thing to live in the makeshift Jewish polity of a ghetto in your own city. The ghetto was drained of people almost daily, humiliated and terrorized; and yet, in the meantime, a social, cultural, and political Jewish life was carried on. Leon Bernstein, a Jew from East Prussia, said that he would never forgive the Germans for depriving him of his language and culture (German); but for the Yiddish and Hebrew intelligentsia in the Vilna Ghetto no such problems arose. A short time before the end, when the Bundist Grisha Yashunski was removed as director of the education department in the ghetto and the Zionist Leon Bernstein replaced him, Kruk lamented that now the Yiddish schools would be Hebraized! Yiddish or Hebrew—the pre-Holocaust "war of languages"; to live *here*, in the Yiddish Diaspora, or to emigrate to Hebrew Eretz-Israel—this is what really mattered in the long run, not the temporary rule of German cruelty.

The internal life of the ghetto community, in constant counterpoint to the incomprehensible chicanery of the Germans, is what is so outstanding in

---

8   The term *Khurban* was also used for the destructions of Jewish communities in times of persecution in the past (such as the "Khurban Ukraine" in 1919, which was the first great wave not of pogroms but of total extermination).

Kruk's chronicles. It is said that victims remember little of their trauma, yet here we have a richly detailed collective memory, because it is not the memory of an individual suffering unjustly, but that of a dignified nation; not of death, but of life in its shadow. That is why there are so many political parties, institutions, and individuals in this book, all of them remembered and valued, all of them symbols of prewar activity of one kind or another. It is not one death in so many repetitions, but many different and creative lives.

A similar book, Yitzhak Zuckerman's *Surplus of Memory*, written by the leader of the Warsaw Ghetto Uprising, displays the same wealth of social and political detail within a pluralistic Jewish nation in Poland, yet in this case not under the sign of survival, but under that of resistance.[9] An equivalent book, focusing on the growth of the resistance in the Vilna Ghetto and the struggle in the partisan forests, was written by Ruzhka Korczak but has not yet been translated into English. It would be a fitting counterpart to Kruk's very comprehensive book.

MODES OF DISCOURSE

In many ways, Kruk's diary is like Kafka's *Trial*. From the first sentence it is clear that Joseph K. is doomed; an inexplicable denunciation and strange arrest send him on a quest for any avenue that leads to justice, or at least to understanding, which only entangles him more and more in the web of the "system." K. is launched on an inexorable journey toward his own end, yet the end is ever postponed, thus giving us a whole book to explore the absurd rules of the game that is played against him. In the final analysis we don't understand a thing because "the incomprehensible is incomprehensible" (Kafka's parable "On Parables"). When the major aspects of the system are explored, the book is over, and K. is suddenly executed, as a non sequitur to the immediately preceding events and without the trial ever having taken place.

Herman K., too, is suddenly confronted with a total collapse of his world. Yet he lives through stages upon stages of total entanglement in a system that determines his every breath, and Herman tries to confront it with past habits, feverish activity, and attempts at recording and understanding. In a diary, each day is taken in brackets and autonomous explorations of life borrowed

9   Yitzhak Zuckerman, *A Surplus of Memory*, ed. and trans. Barbara Harshav (Los Angeles: University of California Press), 1993. See Barbara Harshav's survey of Jewish parties and youth movements in the introduction to that book.

for a while are inserted, exposing little human joys and frailties, called "survival," "politics," and "culture." His death is postponed to the very last moment, thus making it possible to describe all faces and stages of hell. And Herman K.'s end, too, comes out of the blue, apparently unconnected to the immediate context, as if a transcendental fictional hand closed the book when its story had already explored so many unthinkable possibilities.

Herman Kruk was executed by the Germans on September 18, 1944, one day before the first units of the Red Army arrived. He was not in a death camp, but in a German labor camp in Estonia. He was building fortifications for the German defense. Indeed, his German guards told him they were jealous of their Jewish prisoners, for they were surrounded and helpless, the Red Army would liberate the Jews and kill the Germans. Paris was saved by a German general, but Kruk could not be saved.

We have very few detailed diaries actually written in ghettos and concentration camps. One of the values of Kruk's diary is that it was written during the events themselves, from an internal point of view, without any knowledge of German intentions or plans, without the hindsight of the "final solution," and without the stereotypes and ideologies of the postwar period. In a diary, every delusion is an illusion in its own context, every horrifying event is horrible as it comes; in view of later events, of an immensely greater magnitude, those first impressions would have dwindled, one would be ashamed to even mention them. And this is precisely the value of beginning not from Ghetto Vilna (as the Yiddish edition did), but from the destruction of the narrator's normal life in Warsaw.

In August 1938, in an interview at his home in Riga, the great historian of "the eternal people," the octogenarian Simon Dubnow, said: "The tomorrow of the Jews is tied in with the tomorrow of all of Europe and all of humanity [. . .] The present is indeed very sad, in all the four thousand years of Jewish history there never were such horrifying moments as now." "But," he added, "*Jewish history will go on and continue.*"[10] Three years later, Dubnow was brutally killed by a German soldier on his way to the Riga Ghetto. Jewish history did continue, but it was impossible to see it from inside the "New Europe."

Herman Kruk lived in Warsaw, in the capital of the cultural, Westernizing Polish state, and the world center of Jewish life. He was both a consumer of Polish culture and a leader of the modern culture in Yiddish. Nazi-inspired

---

10 "'Di yidishe geshikhte geyt foroys un vayter!'—a sho mit prof. Shimen Dubnov," *Idishe bilder* 34, no. 66, Riga, August 26, 1938.

anti-Semitism raged through Poland in the late 1930s, but Herman was in his own words a "perennial optimist"; he believed in Bundist "*doikeyt*" ("here-ness"), in the necessity and feasibility of building a Jewish autonomous culture here, in Poland, as Polish citizens. If dark forces were menacing, culture and democratic Socialism would bring equality to everyone, including the Jews.

Therefore, when Poland was attacked on September 1, 1939, and the ostensibly strong Polish army was overwhelmed in a few days by the first German *Blitzkrieg*, his world collapsed on him. From September 5, 1939, when he left Warsaw and his wife behind, until October 10, when he reached Vilna, he wandered in a daze through defeated Poland, along with everybody else, it seemed. In an article "On the Ruins of Poland" (see Chapter 1 in the book), written a few months later, he writes: "Where is the enormously extensive Yiddish press? Yiddish publishing? Not to mention the political movements?! [. . .]" "The Jewish school system ceased to exist [. . .] Everything is now turned into ruins." By "everything," he means the glorious polyphony of Jewish culture; yet he does not single out the fate of the Jews: "In the Polish world as in the Jewish world—the destruction is horrible." Everything is in ruins, yet the Jewish Holocaust has not yet begun.

And later, when he compiles statistics about the extensive aid to refugees in peaceful Lithuanian Vilnius in 1940 (there were about 20,000 Jewish refugees from Poland added to the 60,000 Vilna Jews, most of whom lived in great poverty), he writes: "A sea of numbers, a terror of anguish and suffering. How terrible it is to tell about it. How anguished and painful are the horror stories."

Yet the first months of the German occupation of Vilna, between June and September 1941—when Jews are snatched in the streets by hired "snatchers," are humiliated, beaten, terrorized, extorted, and when some forty thousand disappear in the still unknown meat grinder of Ponar—are of an entirely different dimension of horror. Perhaps the senses were dulled in those few months, but even later, in the ghetto, there was no such emotionally draining experience as this. And this was only the prelude to the ghetto. And the ghetto was only the waiting room for the dark end.

From the point of view of the final annihilation, all those stages are irrelevant. But if we want to comprehend how it felt when the horrors grew on you, a forward-moving diary is the closest imitation of reality. Especially when it was written "naively," with no knowledge of tomorrow.

Furthermore, Kruk's diary is not just a personal journal, but is in many ways the journal of a community. His entries included three concentric circles: his private life and personal responses to events; the life of his party and extended family, the "Bund" and the Bundists; and the world of the ghetto as a whole. He consciously wanted to record not just his own life, but every angle and event in Jewish existence and annihilation under the Nazi occupation. And he was well placed to do so. He built a large library in the ghetto, which became a center for clandestine activities. Here every day he dictated his notes to a secretary who typed them in three copies. The ghetto knew of his mission and he got help from all sides. He was given the news heard on a clandestine radio and the information of the FPO (*Fareynikte partizaner-organizatsye*—the United Partisan Organization in the ghetto), as well as the inside information from the authorities, the Judenrat. Kruk was not a member of the partisan organization; he admired their wish for heroism, but was also afraid they might provoke the liquidation of all Jews in the ghetto. Yet he had highplaced informants through those Bundists who were in the partisans. Similarly, Kruk's first impulse was to oppose the Judenrat, but eventually he got close to the head of the ghetto, Jacob Gens, and received information directly from him. In addition, he was active in the "Aid Society" in the ghetto and in the Literary-Artistic Association. And he headed the brigade of scholars and writers who day after day went out of the ghetto, to the building of the former YIVO, to sort out the book treasures collected from all over Vilna, which gave him free access to move around the city.

Thus, entries in the diary are daily, as events unfolded, but much of the information is summaries, as reported by various witnesses (for example, about the end of Oszmiana or Święciany), hence not simply forward-moving. In several cases, it is a reconstructed diary, thus, on September 6, 1941, all Jews were taken to the ghetto, but only on the 20th can Kruk go back and write his diary from September 5 on.

Herman Kruk was neither a philosopher nor a literary critic. His culture, the Yiddish culture of the Bund, was populist, suffused with political rhetoric and folklore. There is no profound meditation here about history, culture, or human nature, making it more valuable as a voice from within, expressed in the language of emotions felt by the common victim. In his text, he mixed the reporting of facts with rumors and anecdotes, and added his own emotional outbursts; and he did not spare emotions or criticism in any direction. Yet he was aware of the subjective aspect of his writings and those of various witnesses, and wanted to bolster the objective side of his chronicle.

Thus, the second form of his records was a huge collection of documents of all kinds. Often, his diary reacts to things exhibited in the documentation and is unclear without the documents themselves. But the editors of the Yiddish edition gave up on including the documents, many of which are preserved in the YIVO and other archives.

The third mode of recording was witness accounts, which Kruk himself recorded in a concise, stenographic manner. We have here the first witness accounts about the slaughter at Ponar, told by escapees at a time when many serious people in the ghetto did not believe it. He has a series of recordings about the liquidation of Jewish communities in small towns all around Vilna. In the Youth Club, he organized students to collect evidence and witness accounts—and in his archives we have several accounts written in a childish hand in Soviet Yiddish spelling. And even in the camps of Estonia, he gathered information about the last days of the Vilna Ghetto and the capture of the Second Battalion of the FPO by the Germans. In Klooga, he collected witness accounts about other camps in Estonia and even about the fate of French and Belgian Jewry.

The fourth mode of discourse was Kruk's narrative chronicles. Kruk realized early on that the diary did not fully reflect the situation. Though precise, it atomized the stories, on the one hand, and in time became repetitive, on the other. Instead of a day-by-day record of a criminal trial in the ghetto, for example, he tells a summary story, rich in background detail. There can be no doubt that his narratives strive toward maximum faithfulness to history, and yet are constructs made from Kruk's position. He himself indicates the constructed nature by talking about a fictional "Vilmen" rather than Vilna. In time, he developed ambitious plans to write large fictional "Books"—many notes and chapters or parts survived. Book 2 was called "Underground Ghetto" and surely inspired A. Sutzkever's long poem "Clandestine Ghetto"; and Book 6 was called "Liberation," describing the camps in Estonia, clearly under the sign of imminent liberation, which never came. Those are vivid pictures of camp life, told not as a narrative but in typical, synoptic scenes. As a Socialist, he was especially attuned to injustice, the exploitation of the weak inmates by the "Strong Ones" in the Jewish camp, and the grotesque yet boisterous Jewish penchant for commerce under any circumstances.

The more time passed and typical events were repeated again and again, the more he was looking for synoptic, quintessential modes of writing that would provide a flash, a glimpse into a basic situation or emotion. That became especially true in Klooga, where he both kept a diary and also described the basic social relations in narrative chapters, yet here nothing was happening or changing daily, as in the ghetto. The real world dwindled, and poetry seemed best suited to express his feelings and views of the world. Thus, toward the end he developed two short genres: the "Ghetto Miniatures," written in the Vilna Ghetto and continued as "Klooga Miniatures"; and the poems, written in Klooga in precise, highly rhetorical and symmetrical meters (without rhyme) and often touching on personal feelings or major existential questions, couched in the naïve language of the political propagandist he was. Close to a hundred poems in Yiddish survived, still unpublished.

Kruk did not decide between those genres and their rather diverse tones of discourse. He wrote them simultaneously, as complementary kinds of documentation. It seems that he had literary ambitions and wanted to write several volumes of fictionalized ghetto chronicles, based on the diaries—after the Liberation. Fortunately, his literary imagination was limited; his language, though sometimes florid, was rather poor; and precisely for that reason, even the fictionalized writings are authentic documents.

Kruk's chronicles are one of the most detailed documents of daily life, personal and public, written from within the Holocaust without the benefit of hindsight. It was a heroic effort to record the events, experiences, and emotions for posterity, interrupted by the death of its author at age 47. Scholars and readers will be able to compare Kruk's information with other sources and evaluate the details and the author's opinions and judgments. We shall let the diaries speak for themselves.

In the following sections we provide the general context in which the diary was written: What was Jerusalem of Lithuania? What is the importance of a city of 60,000 Jews, reduced to 16,000 enclosed in a tiny ghetto? What was the historical and cultural situation in which the described events took place? What were the Jewish political parties Kruk refers to? And who was Herman Kruk himself?

JERUSALEM OF LITHUANIA

Vilna, nicknamed "Jerusalem of Lithuania," was one of the cultural symbols of the Jewish Diaspora in Europe, where Jews lived for a millennium. Founded in 1323 by the Lithuanian Grand Duke Gediminas, Vilnius was the capital of the Grand Duchy of Lithuania that stretched through forests and rivers between the Baltic and the Black Sea, and from the Prussian frontier to the outskirts of Moscow. The Duke invited merchants and artisans from Germany and Poland, who constituted the core of the city dwellers. In the fifteenth and sixteen centuries, the Grand Duchy of Lithuania united with the Kingdom of Poland under one crown, with its capital in Warsaw, and ceded Ukraine to Poland. The Lithuanian aristocracy was culturally Polonized and the city was called Wilno. Its famous university attracted such Polish poets as Adam Mickiewicz in the nineteenth century and Czesław Miłosz in the twentieth, who came from their Lithuanian estates to study here.

The capital of an immense and diffuse Lithuanian domain separating the Polish aristocratic "Republic" from the emerging Muscovite power, Vilna was a major junction on the highway from Poland and the Baltic to Moscow, later Russia. Napoleon stopped here on his way to Moscow in his Russian campaign of 1812 and on his flight back. Impenetrable forests and swamps supplied wood and furs, trades in which Jews were engaged at different times. Easy access by river to the Baltic sea created a window to the west and linked up with the north-south road, going down to Volhynia and Ukraine.

The medieval Grand Duchy covered a territory at least six times the present-day Lithuanian state, encompassing all of today's Belarus, parts of Russia, Poland, and Latvia, and Lithuania proper. Ironically, these vast boundaries are honored to this day only by the Jews: the whole area with its capital in Vilna is called in Yiddish *Lite (Litah)*, and its Jews, the *Litvaks*, are marked by a distinct Yiddish dialect and mentality, a penchant for learning, different customs of cooking, and a sense of cultural superiority.

Although few documents are extant, we may assume that the first Jews arrived in Eastern Europe at the beginnings of Christianity there and in the early centuries of the second millennium of the Common Era, coming up either from the Byzantine empire or from the West, via Prague and Germany. In the tenth century, a prominent Jew, Moses from Kiev, is mentioned, and in the fourteenth century, Jewish communities were established in such Lithuanian cities as Brisk, Grodno, and Troki (near Vilna). In Vilna proper, the Christian citizens were warding off a permanent Jewish presence (though the Jews lived in the suburbs), and a regular Jewish Community was legalized only in the second half of the sixteenth century. Individual Jews were lessees of the customs, coined money for the Polish kings, engaged in money-lending and commerce. A Polish king sent a Vilna Jewish merchant to negotiate with the Moscow tsar Ivan the Terrible. And around them, many poor Jews crowded.

In the sixteenth through eighteenth centuries, about two-thirds of world Jewry lived in the Kingdom of Poland and Lithuania, the vastest state in Europe. Vilna—as it was called in Jewish documents from the earliest times—became a Jewish "Principal City" and one of the capitals of the Jewish autonomous governing body. One of the great Talmudic scholars, the "Gaon of Vilna" (the "Genius of Vilna," Elijah ben Solomon, or HaGRO, 1720–1797), dominated the religious establishment of his time and excommunicated the new "irrational" Hasidic movement that was sweeping Jewish areas to the south of Lithuania. Thus, the anti-Hasidic Judaism of the *Misnagdim* (the "opposing ones") was launched, stressing learning, precise interpretation of the literal meaning of the text, and building a network of talmudic academies ("yeshivas") throughout Lithuania. Indeed, in the nineteenth and twentieth centuries, the hundreds of small towns of Lithuania became a breeding ground for Hebrew knowledge, supplying rabbis and teachers to the far corners of the Jewish Diaspora, including Ukraine, Poland, Palestine, and the United States.[11] Here, secular Hebrew literature of the *Haskalah* (Enlightenment) flourished in the second half of the nineteenth century, as did Yiddish literature in the twentieth.

The nickname "Jerusalem of Lithuania" was based on this fortress of Jewish learning and the printing of the whole Babylonian Talmud in Vilna. Yet apparently it was the secular movement, which in Vilna perceived itself as heir to the religious tradition, that invented and promoted this name. In 1859, a Hebrew book by the Maskil (enlightened writer) and scholar Rashi Fin (Samuel Joseph Fuenn) was published, describing the history of Vilna and its Jewish community. The book was called *Kiryah Ne'emanah* (Faithful City), describing Vilna in biblical terms used for Jerusalem. Had the name "Jerusalem of Lithuania" existed, Fin would have used it. It is, rather, the opposite: from the name of the book, the nickname was derived. The Vilna Yiddishist and secular movements, as well as modern Hebrew poetry, adopted the name, proud to continue the tradition of the Vilna Gaon. The Kletzkin publishing house and the YIVO were heirs to the printing of the Talmud. And the widespread thirst for knowledge and education seemed to support that honorific title.

Toward the end of the eighteenth century, Poland was dismantled by its neighbors, Russia, Prussia, and Austria. In 1795, Vilna was incorporated into

11   For the most recent impact on modern French culture, see Judith Friedlander's book *Vilna on the Seine* (New Haven: Yale University Press, 1991).

Russia and became the capital of a Russian Province (*Guberniya*) included in the Jewish Pale of Settlement. The Pale was a huge geographical ghetto confined to the former Polish territories, beyond which the Jewish masses were not allowed to live. The Jews were outside the three legally defined estates in Russia: the gentry, the peasants, and the citizens; they had no voting or other civil rights, and no place in the Russian administration or police. Only a few thousand Jews, who were either merchants of the First Guild or professionals with a university degree, were gradually permitted to live inside Russia or in the capital of St. Petersburg. Since Jewish Lithuania stressed learning, many of its sons were among them: the sculptor Marc Antokolsky, the painter Leon Bakst, the choreographer of the Bolshoi Ballet Asaf Messerer, and the Hebrew poet Yehuda-Leyb Gordon (YaLaG) all lived in the Russian capital. Others went to nearby Prussia (the philosopher Solomon Maimon), Palestine (the standard-bearer of the revival of Hebrew, Eliezer Ben-Yehuda), Paris (Marc Chagall, Chaim Soutine, Emanual Levinas), or America (the founder of the New York Jewish daily *Forward*, Abe Cahan, and the head of RCA, David Sarnoff).

In the Pale of Settlement itself, the Jews constituted about fifteen percent of the population. Yet the demographic structure of their settlements was unusual: they were basically an urban society. In a few large cities, between a third and a half of the total population was Jewish, while in most small towns (the so-called *shtetls*), they constituted two-thirds of the population or more. The Jewish *shtetls* were surrounded by a sea of Christian villages, where only about one percent of the population was Jewish. The *shtetl* served as a marketplace and manufacturing center for the surrounding villages, and as a link between them and the city centers and, beyond them, the markets of Western Europe. It was dominated physically by one or several churches and politically by a Christian administration and police. A *shtetl* could count between 500 and 5,000 inhabitants and was administratively and professionally different from a village: its inhabitants did not belong to the class of peasants and did not work the land, nor did they possess any land, as the gentry and the Catholic Church did.

This network of hundreds of Jewish communities conducted its separate life in its own three languages: Hebrew of the Bible, the prayer book, the incessant flow of religious books, and official correspondence; Aramaic of the Talmud and Rabbinic knowledge; and Yiddish as the language of home and community life, folklore and modern literature, a language and culture that constituted a bridge between the European world and the traditional religious library.[12] The Jews had their own educational networks, religious institutions, publishing houses, professional organizations, health and philanthropic institutions, and, in modern times, literature, newspapers, libraries, ideologies, political parties, hospitals, and social organizations. Indeed, it was a densely connected social and cultural network, a veritable empire within an empire. Jewish religion had no formal hierarchical organization, and in principle, every rabbi in the smallest community was sovereign. Yet an intense ideological-cultural discourse, conducted in their own private languages, and the authority of the books and of several charismatic scholars, bound them all in one extraterritorial society. In medieval times, the overall framework was religious and defined by law; in modern times, it was secular and voluntaristic. The spreading Hasidic sects, crossing the boundaries of individual communities, and the modern political parties and voluntary organizations cemented this unified network.

In the nineteenth century, European Jewry experienced an unusual population growth: in 1800 there were 2.2 million Jews in the world, and in 1880, 7.5 million. The burden of this growth lay in the confined *shtetls* of Eastern Europe, especially *Litah*, where poverty was rampant. In 1897, when a major census of the Russian population was conducted, there were 5.3 million Jews in an empire of 120 million. Between 1881 and 1914, about 2.5 million Jews emigrated from the Russian Empire, mostly to America; yet in 1914, on the eve of World War I, there were still 5.5 million Jews in Russia.

In 1897, Vilna had 63,831 Jewish inhabitants; in 1921, after World War I, their number declined to 46,000, then grew again to 60,000 in 1939. The influx of Jews from the provinces was compensated for by emigration. There were more Jews "from Vilna" around the globe than in Vilna proper; the reason is simple: "from Vilna" meant from Vilna Guberniya, or *Litah* as a whole. Like Jena and Weimar, Cambridge and Oxford, Vilna was a small city, a cultural center serving a large hinterland. The ties between Vilna and the network of small towns were very close, people traveled back and forth, the city served as a kind of "shopping center" and cultural focus for the whole area, and many small towns fulfilled important roles as well: famous yeshivas were located in small towns, such as Volozhin, Mir, Ponevezh; a major Hasidic sect, *Chabad*, that emerged in eastern Lithuania, had its capital in

12   See my book, Benjamin Harshav, *The Meaning of Yiddish* (Los Angeles: University of California Press, 1986).

Lubavitch, a town of 1,667 Jews. Indeed, most Vilna writers and intellectuals were born elsewhere, as for example, the Gaon of Vilna, Max Weinreich, Zelig Kalmanowicz, A. Sutzkever, and others. On the other hand, many young people from small towns came to the capital to study in its Rabbinical Seminary or in its Hebrew and Yiddish Teachers' Colleges, then to go back to teach in a small town or emigrate to Palestine or the West.

Hence, when a city of merely 60,000 Jews felt that it was a major center of a worldwide culture, it was because of its cultural institutions and the millions of Eastern European Jews they served and represented. When the intellectuals among only 16,000 remaining Jews in the Vilna Ghetto in 1942 went through the same motions of cultural creativity and competing ideologies, they no longer had that hinterland. Indeed, among the heart-rending parts of Kruk's records are the terse and terrifying chronicles of various liquidated *shtetl* communities.

In the mid-nineteenth century, when the tsarist censors forbade all Jewish printing except for two cities, Vilna was one of them. The publishing house of the Widow and Brothers Romm executed the extremely complex printing job of the whole Talmud with commentaries, and published Hebrew and Yiddish books for learning and entertainment. In the twentieth century, the publishing house of B. Kletzkin published many of the Yiddish classical and modern writers. Vilna was a center of the Modern Jewish Revolution: Jewish society was transformed from a religious to a national entity, and a new literature in Yiddish, Hebrew, and other languages, as well as a gamut of ideologies and political parties, sprang up almost overnight. In 1897, the year Kruk was born, the illegal Jewish Socialist party, Bund, which would have an enormous influence on the Jewish masses and intellectuals, was founded in Vilna. Half a year later, the Bundists were instrumental in organizing the Russian Social Democratic Workers' Party in Minsk. In the beginning of the twentieth century, Vilna was also the seat of the Zionist and Labor Zionist parties of Russia.

After the Bolshevik Revolution, the Russian borders rolled back. In 1918 both Poland and Lithuania regained independence, and in 1920 the Polish army occupied the city and the surrounding area against Lithuanian objections, and ruled it until September 1939. The majority population of the city was Polish-speaking, and so were the gentry in their estates in the countryside; yet the bulk of the population living in villages was Byelorussian to the north and east and Lithuanian to the west. Under the auspices of the Treaty of Versailles and the League of Nations, national minorities in Poland had autonomous rights to their own cultural activities and education in their own languages. In this framework, a whole rainbow of Jewish political parties and cultural institutions flourished in Vilna and its surroundings. Yiddish, the language spoken by the masses and intellectuals alike, and Hebrew, the language of tradition and of the revived Hebrew society in Palestine, were competing for dominance in the new Jewish national culture. On the other hand, Polish, the language of the state and the universities, exerted its powerful pull. Like Prague, at the crossroads of several cultures, Vilna had an ironic perspective on it all and fostered a modern Jewish culture. It had separate secular schools in Yiddish, other schools in the traditional Ashkenazi Hebrew, yet others in the "Sefardi" Hebrew as revived in Palestine, as well as Jewish schools in the Polish language, observing the Jewish Sabbath; it also had religious schools teaching in Hebrew or in Yiddish, either of a Zionist-and-liberal direction (Mizrahi) or of an ultra-Orthodox kind (Agudes Yisroel), as well as traditional Heders and Talmud Torahs. There were several *Gymnazia* in the different languages (ambitiously academic schools, with a cultural status equivalent to the American college today) and a Yiddish institute of technology, the *Technikum*. Many young Jews went to study in the Polish university, although the anti-Semitic pressures there were mounting; or in universities in France, Belgium, and elsewhere.

In the interwar period, Jewish Vilna had a dense network of social and cultural institutions and organizations: a Yiddish theater; several daily newspapers; scholarly and popular journals, including the prestigious YIVO-bleter; a literary monthly for children, *Grininke beymelekh* ("Green Trees"); a journal for public health, *Folksgezunt*; Jewish trade unions and professional organizations; sport clubs; public libraries; and so on. Now the Jews could vote both for the Jewish Community Council and for the Polish institutions of city and state. In 1934, several Yiddish writers and artists, including Abraham Sutzkever and Chaim Grade, formed the group of *Yung-Vilne* (Young Vilna), which made a considerable impact on Yiddish literature.

In 1925, the YIVO, Yiddish Scientific Institute, was founded in Vilna by a group of scholars headed by Dr. Max Weinreich and Zelig Kalmanowicz. Members of its governing body included the great Jewish historian Simon Dubnow and Sigmund Freud. The YIVO was a research institute in the Jewish humanities and social sciences, combining the functions of an academy of language and a center of cultural policy. The YIVO competed with the Jewish section of the Soviet Academy of Sciences in Kiev and the Hebrew University in Jerusalem, founded in the same year, yet it was poor in means and could not match a full-fledged university in Jerusalem. In 1939, when World War II broke out, Max Weinreich was at an international linguistics conference in Copenhagen and succeeded in getting to the United States, where he became the moving spirit of the New York branch of YIVO and wrote his monumental *History of the Yiddish Language*. Zelig Kalmanowicz was a spiritual force in the Vilna Ghetto and perished in Estonian camps. The Germans turned the building of the YIVO into a center for collecting and classifying Jewish books to be shipped to Germany for a future *Institute for the Study of Jewry Without Jews*. Herman Kruk, the author of this diary, was the leader of the brigade of Jewish scholars and writers who worked there.

POLITICAL PARTIES

To understand Kruk's diary, a brief description of the range of political parties among the Jews is necessary. With the Modern Jewish Revolution, it became imperative to reunderstand and reformulate the situation of the Jews in the modern world, as well as the human condition in general. After the consolidation of the big nation-states in Europe, the smaller nations also strove to achieve cultural autonomy or national independence. The Jews were an extraterritorial group spread throughout Europe with no majority in any specific territory. Hence they could either merge with the dominant languages and cultures or vie for cultural and political autonomy. At the beginning of the twentieth century it was impossible to foresee the direction and destinies of nationalism and socialism, to weigh the pros and cons of optimism and pessimism. The very existence of the Jews as a culture and as individuals was put in question, hence those ideas about the future deeply touched every person's life and emotions. A variety of diagnoses of the situation and prognoses for the future provided contradictory alternatives which were hotly debated. Hence the justification of a wide range of ideologies, some of which fermented in intellectual circles and crystallized into political parties. When such views and habits of thought and discourse were suddenly caged in a small ghetto, while most of European Jewry was already annihilated, they seemed all nostalgically correct and abysmally irrelevant.

All parties had their antecedents before World War I, and with few exceptions, constituted nationwide parties throughout Poland or even worldwide organizations. Between the two world wars, Poland was the world center of secular culture in Yiddish. Most parties had their own youth movements and cultural and social institutions affiliated with them. Belonging to a party was like belonging to an extended family that provided most of your cultural needs.

At the extreme left were the Communists. The proximity to the Soviet border, vicious anti-Semitism in Poland, the appalling poverty of the masses, the hopelessness facing young people in the stagnant economy of the Polish "margin lands" (*Kresy*)—all those, coupled with the closing of the American border and no road to immigration, made the utopia of universal equality an attractive proposition. The Communists were the only general Polish party where Jews were welcome and influential; here they could shed their Jewishness without feeling like traitors to their tribe. Communism also appealed to the idealism and penchant for abstraction widespread among young Jewish intellectuals. Poland, however, became independent in a cruel war with the Bolsheviks, when the Jew Trotsky's Red Army was stopped at the outskirts of Warsaw by "a miracle on the Vistula" in 1920, hence Communism was felt to be Poland's archenemy. Although Poland was legally a democracy, the Communist party was outlawed and its members were put in concentration camps, tortured and humiliated. Several thousand youths crossed the Soviet border illegally, to participate in the "world of tomorrow"; eventually they were all purged by Stalin and many perished, including the brilliant Yiddish writer Moyshe Kulbak. In conditions of conspiracy, the number of actual party members was small, but they were rigorously disciplined and had a wide periphery of sympathizers. The Polish Communist Party got its orders from the Communist International, and in 1938 it was dismantled for alleged "Trotskyism." Yet when the Soviet army took Vilna in September 1939 and again in May 1940, the former Communists were serving the new order, and in the ghetto they were the link to the Soviet partisans and to the only power that could liberate them from the Germans, the Red Army.

A much more popular Socialist party was the Bund, founded in 1897 in Vilna.[13] The Bund was influential in the Jewish trade unions, among the masses and intellectuals alike. It was theoretically Marxist, but anti-Soviet and anti-Communist. It was a pragmatic party, active in all areas of daily life and culture, and believed in a separate Yiddish national culture and in *doikeyt*

---

13   Its full name was *Algemeyner yidisher arbeter-bund in Lite, Poyln un Rusland* (General Jewish Workers' Union in Lithuania, Poland, and Russia).

("here-ness"), that is, in building a Jewish culture in Poland ("here") while simultaneously behaving as full-fledged Polish citizens. It supported Yiddish literature, the Yiddish secular ("worldly") schools, public libraries in the cities and *shtetls*, and other cultural activities. Not by accident was the first activity of the Bund in the Vilna Ghetto, the establishment of a Social Aid Committee. For the Bund, the Diaspora was a normal way of Jewish existence, if only justice could prevail and Poland could be made more democratic. Yet the non-Jewish Socialists saw the Bundists as hopelessly nationalistic, they were actually expelled from the Russian Social-Democratic Workers' Party in 1903 for nationalist separatism, and even the Russian Menshevik Plekhanov is said to have described them as "Zionists afraid of sea-sickness."

Among the non-Socialist and non-Zionist groups, we may mention the Folkists, populist liberals and Yiddishists, including the admired Vilna social activist Dr. Tsemakh Szabad. Another non-Socialist party was the General Zionists, a middle-class Zionist party with a liberal and a conservative wing, including the head of the Vilna Jewish Community, Dr. Jacob Wygodzki. All these parties were secular in outlook and form. Among the religious Jews, there was a national-Zionist party, Mizrahi, and the orthodox and anti-Zionist Agudah (Agudes Yisroel). As in most cities, the religious Jews were a rather small though respected minority; thus, the first Judenrat in Vilna, elected by a group of prominent Jews, had only one representative of the religious in a body of ten. All Zionist parties were affiliated with their counterparts in Eretz-Israel and elsewhere. The Zionists believed in a Jewish home in Palestine, but not many immigrated there.

On the other hand, the radical Zionist movements on both the left and the right educated the young to activism and immigration to Zion. On the far right were the Revisionists, a party founded by the brilliant Russian, Yiddish, and Hebrew writer Vladimir Zeev Jabotinsky (who died in New York in 1940), who organized the Jewish Legion in the British army in World War I. He split his movement off from Chaim Weizmann's general Zionist organization, accusing them of talk and inaction. In the late 1930s, Jabotinsky preached a "Catastrophic Aliya," a mass immigration of Jews to Palestine, rightly believing that the ground was burning under their feet. But he could not collect a fleet of ships or alarm Polish Jewry, the British mandatory power would not allow any mass immigration to Palestine, and the Zionist establishment ostracized him. His youth movement, Betar (Beytar), was a disciplined, para-military organization, whose members wore brown shirts and were hostile to both the Diaspora and all socialists. Furthermore, Jabotinsky had contacts with Mussolini's Italy. All that made the socialists (Zionists and anti-Zionists alike) see them as Fascists. The last commander of Betar in Poland was Menachem Begin, a trained Polish officer, who fled to Vilna in 1939, was arrested by the Bolsheviks, then reached Palestine to head the Revisionist underground there, and eventually became prime minister of Israel. When the police in the Vilna Ghetto, and eventually the head of the ghetto (Jacob Gens), were in the hands of former Revisionists, the left had a preconceived image of them.

At the opposite end of the spectrum were several Labor Zionist parties. The most influential was Poaley-Zion (Labor Zionists), a moderately Marxist social democratic party affiliated with Ben-Gurion's Labor party in Eretz-Israel and the largest Kibbutz movement. Poaley-Zion Left was a small party that had tried to enter the Comintern in 1921 but was rejected for its Zionism. Poaley-Zion, which became the larger party, supported Hebrew as the language of the new Zionist society in Israel, yet cherished Yiddish education and literature in the Diaspora; the Left Poalei-Zion, however, was for Yiddish in Eretz-Israel as well. In contrast, Ha-Shomer ha-Tzair (The Young Guard) fostered Hebrew. It was an influential youth organization with no adult political party, because they swore to immigrate to Eretz-Israel as soon as they became adults. They were a scout organization, including uniforms, parades, sport activities, summer camps, and so on; yet they combined it with intense intellectual activities, debating elitist literature, philosophy, and ideology. They also had a strong Kibbutz movement in Eretz-Israel and were perhaps the first intellectual group in the world to combine Marxism with Freud in communes in Palestine after World War I. All Labor Zionist parties had Kibbutz movements. Unfortunately, after the British White Paper of 1939, it was almost impossible to immigrate to Palestine, and several thousand *Halutzim*, refugees from Poland, got stuck in Vilna,

The Communists, the various Labor Zionists, and the Revisionists were all radical critics of the Jewish situation before the war, and therefore were better prepared to launch a resistance underground in the ghetto.

TWO WORLD WARS

Vilna suffered heavily during World War I. The city was flooded with Jewish refugees, who were expelled by the Russian army from the frontier areas.

Large-scale activities were developed to aid the refugees, although the war years were marked by poverty and food shortages. The German army occupied the city from September 1915 to November 1918. The Jewish leadership, headed by Dr. Jacob Wygodzki, maintained a dignified relationship with the Germans. The war was followed by the two Russian Revolutions of February and October 1917. When the Red Army occupied Vilna in January 1919, factions of the leftist parties expressed support for the Communist power, but most Jewish party activities were forbidden. In April, the Polish army took the city back and killed many Jews as "Bolsheviks." The city passed from hand to hand, again to the Bolsheviks, then to the Lithuanians, until Polish army rule was reestablished in October 1920. In March 1922, Vilna and its surrounding area were annexed to Poland and remained Polish until September 1939. The traumatic events of that period molded the attitudes and memories of the Vilna Jewish population and its leadership, and were remembered when they were faced with a new German occupation. But this was an altogether different Germany.

After more than a century of occupation by foreign powers, Poland regained its independence in 1918. It was a much smaller Poland than its medieval predecessor and only about half the Jewish population of the Pale of Settlement was included in it, while the rest remained in the Soviet Union and in the Baltic states. Still, with about 3.5 million Jews toward the end (10 percent of the population, while the Poles made up 70 percent), it was the second-largest Jewish community in the world (after the United States). In cities like Warsaw, Vilna, Lódź, and Lemberg, Jews constituted a third or more of the population. Independent Poland was the major Jewish cultural and political center in the world (Palestine had 80,000 Jews in 1922). Jewish life was bustling with all kinds of activities: political parties, social organizations, schools, literature, newspapers, a news media agency, and so on—if ever there was a secular Jewish nation and national autonomy, it was in Poland between the two world wars. The center of all those activities was naturally in the capital of the state, Warsaw, with its population of more than a million (among them, 353,000 Jews in 1931). The Central Committees of most Jewish parties and organizations had their offices in Warsaw. Vilna, with its 60,000 Jews, was a small town in comparison. Moreover, Jews played a key role in Polish industry, commerce, and literature, and the majority rapidly assimilated to the Polish language and culture.

Jews could vote and were represented in the Polish Sejm and Senat, although Poland was intermittently democratic and dictatorial; and in the late 1930s, Nazi influences rose and the air was increasingly anti-Semitic. Jewish merchants were pressured, Jewish students at Polish universities had to sit in special ghetto seats and preferred instead to stand at the back of the classrooms; they were often beaten by Polish nationalist students. In 1938, Dr. Max Weinreich went to the Vilna Governor (Wojewoda) and demanded that the pogrom against Jewish students be stopped; on his way home, he was attacked by Polish students and lost an eye.

World War II began with almost the same participants and in the same theater as the previous war, but this time both Germany and the Soviet Union were totalitarian states ruled by extremist ideologies. Barely a year after the appeasement in Munich, in March 1939, the Germans dismantled Czechoslovakia with impunity. At dawn of September 1, 1939, the German army launched a Blitzkrieg on Poland. On September 3, England and France declared war on Germany, and World War II began. It was the first German Blitzkrieg of the war: within a week, the Polish defense crumbled, the legendary Polish cavalry was no match for the German tanks, and Warsaw was surrounded. Pockets of the Polish army fought on for three more weeks, but the government, along with many of the Polish and Jewish political and intellectual leadership, fled abroad. Thousands of residents, especially young men, left Warsaw, marching toward the East. Herman Kruk was among them.

On September 17, 1939, implementing the Molotov-Ribbentrop secret pact, the Soviet army crossed the Polish border in the East, and Poland was again divided between its two neighboring powers. In the first days the Germans humiliated Jews, tortured and killed them, and eventually closed them in walled ghettos in Warsaw and a few other Polish cities. In eastern Poland, now annexed to Byelorussia and Ukraine, the Soviet authorities arrested and exiled or shot Polish officers, "bourgeois elements" (including many Jewish manufacturers and merchants), and activists of most Jewish parties. The leaders of the Bund, Henryk Erlich and Wiktor Alter, were arrested and eventually executed. Several Vilna intellectuals and political leaders were taken away and disappeared, among them Zalmen Reisen, author of a multivolume lexicon of Yiddish literature and editor of the highbrow Yiddish newspaper *Der Tog*, and the lawyer Joseph Czernichow, who had defended many Communists in Polish trials.

In October 1939, the Soviets turned Vilna over to Lithuania, at the time a semi-fascist state, which, however, maintained normal relations with the free world. The city was renamed Vilnius and became the capital of the small Lithuanian state. An influx of Lithuanians, including many Jews, filled important positions in the municipal administration and social institutions. Many Jewish refugees from Poland who were stuck in the Soviet zone, especially members of non-Communist parties, Zionist pioneers (Halutzim), writers and intellectuals—the elite of Polish Jewry—tried to cross the new Soviet-Lithuanian border illegally to get to Vilnius. Thousands of refugees filled the city; it was estimated that, in its heyday, Vilna had 80,000 Jews out of a total of 200,000 inhabitants. From independent Lithuania, people who got visas, aided by international organizations, could immigrate to America or Canada via Siberia and Japan, or to Palestine via Odessa. But visas were hard to come by, and only a few thousand were fortunate enough to reach their destinations; some got stuck in Japan and were interned in a ghetto in Shanghai during the war years.

In June 1940, the Soviet army occupied all the Baltic states, and Vilnius became the capital of Soviet Lithuania. All political parties were abolished, all former newspapers were closed, all Jewish schools became Soviet-Yiddish institutions. The immigration of refugees, especially to America, still went on, since the Soviets liked the heavy ransom money that was paid, and Kruk was active in sending comrades out. He himself could not make it, and was caught by the German occupation. In mid-June 1941, just a week before the treacherous and massive German attack on their Soviet allies, a new wave of arrests shook the city of Vilna. Many of those lucky "enemies of the people," who were sent in cattle cars to Siberia, survived the war and the Holocaust.

On June 22, 1941, the German armies crossed the Soviet border and moved east in a Blitzkrieg toward Moscow. World War II was in full rage. Several thousand Jews from Vilna tried to escape to the east, but most were stopped on the former Soviet border and not allowed into the Soviet Union. They turned back, were betrayed and massacred by peasants and the oncoming German army, and not many returned to Vilna to face the horrors there. Only a few succeeded in crossing the old Soviet border and fleeing deep into Russia. Herman Kruk, himself a refugee from occupied Warsaw, was in a resigned mood, decided not to renew his flight, and instead resolved to keep a diary of the impending events. Actually, it was a continuation of his earlier attempts to chronicle the collapse of Poland and its Jewry.

HERMAN KRUK

Hershl, or Herman, Kruk was born in the Polish city of Plock (read "Plotsk") on May 19, 1897, a crucial year in modern Jewish history.[14] Symbolically, several major political and cultural options were inaugurated in 1897: the first World Zionist Congress was held in Basel; the Bund was founded in Vilna; Simon Dubnow wrote his first "Letter on the Old and New Judaism" formulating the theory of Autonomism; the Yiddish newspaper *Forward* was inaugurated in New York; the Hebrew literary journal *Ha-Shiloah* was published by the spiritual Zionist Ahad Ha-Am. Thus all options of modern Jewish literature and ideologies came of age when Kruk was born. The year 1897 was also the year of the great census in the Russian Empire, which gives us a precise image of Jewish demography and settlement in Eastern Europe; it was the year in which a programmatically anti-Semitic ideologue was elected mayor of Vienna and Sigmund Freud joined the Jewish lodge of B'nai B'rith.

Kruk's father, a "scribe" in a vinegar factory, died at the age of 44. Of his six children, three died in infancy. Hershl, the eldest, was 17 years old when his father died and World War I broke out (his sister was 14 and his brother 12). Plock changed hands several times, and when the Russian army ordered the immediate evacuation of all Jews, the Germans marched into town. Herman was a trained photographer and moved around the neighboring towns to record events and support his family. When the German occupation powers made an appeal for workers to pave highways, many young Jews registered, both to become productive workers—as modern Jewish ideologies demanded—and to support their families. For the Jews, the German occupation meant freedom from persecution and oppression: Jewish clubs, unions, and libraries sprang up overnight. The German powers organized factories for preserving fruits and vegetables to be sent to Germany, and Herman Kruk was a supervisor in one of them.

At the same time, he immersed himself in reading and in the activities of the new political trends. At first he was active in Zionist circles and avidly read books he borrowed from the Ha-Zamir (Nightingale) library (founded during the revolution of 1905 and managed by a group of Bundists and Zionists). He was fascinated by modern Yiddish literature, and a circle of young people gathered for long evenings at his home, debating Yiddish literature and

14   The early biography of Herman Kruk in this chapter is derived from the essay written by his brother, Pinkhes Schwartz, published in the Yiddish edition of Kruk's diary.

current events. Political activities focused around the Ha-Zamir library and the new Yiddish political-cultural weeklies that arrived from nearby Warsaw. He was especially attracted by the figure of Vladimir Medem, the son of a Russian general, who returned to the Judaism of his ancestors, learned Yiddish, and became a fiery orator and influential ideologue of the Bund; and by Medem's theory of national-cultural autonomy for the Jews. At the same time, Kruk frequented a semi-clandestine Polish leftist circle affiliated with SDKPL (Social Democrats of the Kingdom of Poland and Lithuania), whose leaders included Rosa Luxemburg, and which soon joined the new Communist International. As a Communist, he participated in disarming German soldiers after the German Revolution of November 1918.

When Poland regained its independence, Kruk was drafted into the army, where he continued his clandestine Communist activities but became increasingly critical of Soviet terror and the Communist neglect of the Jewish question. He was attracted to the Yiddish cultural activities of the Bund in Warsaw and became an ardent critic of Communism. Although he had no formal education, he was always immersed in learning and believed in promoting education among the workers. At the National Committee of the Trade Unions in Warsaw he organized a Cultural Department, whose secretary and moving force was Kruk himself. Later, as secretary of the Cultural Department of Tsukunft (the youth organization of the Bund) he organized "traveling libraries." In 1930 Herman Kruk became the director of the Yiddishist Grosser Library at the Kultur-lige (Cultural League) in Warsaw, and headed its Library Center, which comprised some 400 libraries in towns around Poland. He edited its monthly library journal and published many articles and studies on library matters in Yiddish and Polish journals. In 1936 Kruk became secretary (that is, leader) of the Cultural League.

Herman Kruk's first wife died young, and their child died during labor. He remarried a few years before World War II. The war broke out on September 1, 1939, and on September 5 the Polish government left Warsaw. Kruk left at 4:00 p.m. with five others, without their wives, assuming that men were in greater danger and would be drafted into the Polish army anyway. In January 1940 he described his wanderings from Warsaw and sent the memoir piecemeal to his brother-in-law in Tel Aviv.

Kruk managed to cross the frontier to the Soviet occupied zone of Poland, where he met his brother and eventually joined a group of Yiddish writers that reached Vilna on October 10, just before it was turned over to independent

Lithuania. He attempted to bring over his wife, but she was arrested on the way by the Soviets and exiled to Russian camps. In the summer of 1940, the American Jewish Labor Committee got a number of U.S. visas for writers and political activists who were in danger of being arrested by the Soviets. Kruk's brother, Pinkhes Schwartz, and many others left for the United States via Siberia and Japan. According to his brother's conjecture, the hope of seeing his wife someday prevented Kruk from using an American visa and leaving the Soviet Union. He helped ship others to the United States but didn't make it himself. In Vilna, he researched the history of Jewish libraries there and sent the materials to his brother in New York for a future study.

Finally, Kruk also bought a ticket to Vladivostok in the Russian Far East, but it was too late: the Soviet authorities would not let him go unless he consented to join the Polish army in England and work as a spy for the Russians, which he refused. On June 24, 1941, the German army marched into Vilna.

KRUK IN THE GHETTO

Poland ruled Vilna from March 1921 until September 1939. The Soviets occupied Vilna in September–October 1939 and arrested a number of prominent Jewish intellectuals, politicians, and community leaders and shipped them off to the East. In October 1939 the Soviets transferred Vilna to independent Lithuania in return for military concessions. Vilna was renamed Vilnius and a process of Lithuanization began. The local Vilnaites, Poles and Jews alike, did not know the difficult Lithuanian language, and many functions were assumed by newcomers from Kovno (Kaunas). In June 1940, the Red Army took over all of the Baltic states and the Lithuanian Soviet Socialist Republic was established. The Reds were back in Vilna. A year later, in mid-June 1941, mass arrests were carried out in Vilnius; thousands of former political "enemies," "bourgeois" persons, refugees, and other "elements" were sent to Siberia. Many of them were freed from Soviet camps during the war, as former Polish citizens; many died in exile. But many didn't know how lucky they were, and survived the Holocaust in Russia; as former Polish citizens, they could return to Poland after the war, and from there, most left for Israel, the United States, and other countries.

Vilnius was still paralyzed from the great purge in mid-June 1941, when the Germans attacked their Communist allies and marched on Moscow. Vilnius was taken on June 24, 1941. The horrors of the first months under the Nazis are described in Kruk's diary, and we shall not preempt it here. On September 6, 1941, the surviving Jews were herded into the tiny ghetto, encompassing seven narrow streets in a former slum and medieval "ghetto" area (there had never been an official ghetto in medieval Vilna). Of an estimated 76,000–80,000 Jews before the war, about 40,000 were crammed into two ghettos. Forty thousand Jews were summarily executed in Ponar—it was the first mass execution of Jews the Germans undertook when they crossed into the territory of the Soviet Union. Soon, the smaller "Second Ghetto" was liquidated and most of its inhabitants were sent to Ponar.

When the underground in Warsaw Ghetto learned about Ponar, they concluded that this was the beginning of the extermination of all Jews in Europe, an ideological policy rather than a unique case.[15] The same conclusion was drawn by Abba Kovner, the leader of the Ha-Shomer ha-Tzsair youth movement in the Vilna Ghetto, who on New Year's Eve 1942 called for an end to delusions and for armed resistance.

The sense of a vibrant Jewish city between the two world wars, which lived in the memories of most Vilnaites, unique in its richness and vitality, was based on a multitude of cultural and political options, arguing and competing with each other. There was in Vilna a highly intelligent, alert, and erudite youth, oriented toward culture and ideas. Some of them left to study in Western Europe; others perished in the Soviet Union, in the partisans, and in the Holocaust. There was a "war of languages": between Yiddish and Hebrew, between traditional Ashkenazi Hebrew and the Zionist "Sephardi" Hebrew, and between all of them and the language of culture, Polish; and there was an uninterrupted argument between all the political trends. But all those were dialogues conducted on one stage; they hated each other, enriched each other, and yet needed each other.

Now a United Partisan Organization, FPO, was formed in the ghetto, with members of all youth movements sharing each clandestine cell of five. After all, they spoke one common language. Their story was tragic; the envisioned revolt in the ghetto did not sweep the masses and did not materialize. Nevertheless, several hundred of them reached the forests and fought in the Soviet partisan movement, and many of them survived. Kruk had contacts with the partisans;

---

15 Antek (Yitzhak Zuckerman), who was born in Vilna, heard about Ponar in November 1941 and concluded: "This was the beginning of the end. A total death sentence for the Jews." See his book *A Surplus of Memory*, pp. 154–155.

part of the Bund organization joined them, but he himself was reserved about them. Eventually, when the liquidation of the ghetto came, he accepted the next German lie and persuaded people to leave for the "work camps" in Estonia.

In the less than two years before the ghetto, Kruk was occupied in various social functions and refugee activities. Only in the ghetto did he become a visible figure in Vilna's cultural and social life. We must remember that Vilna was stripped of most of its Jewish leadership. Some were arrested by the Soviets in 1939 and in 1941; some emigrated during the window of independent Lithuania and even in the last Soviet year, especially to the United States and Palestine. And some were killed by the Germans in the first months of their occupation, among them the old leader of the community, Dr. Jacob Wygodzki. Thus, some central positions in the ghetto were occupied either by outsiders or by young people. The head of the ghetto, Jacob Gens, was a Lithuanian army captain; the director of the Youth Club, Leon Bernstein, was from Prussia; Kruk was from Warsaw; Abba Kovner was twenty-three years old and had to make crucial decisions concerning the life of the revolt and the lives of its soldiers, while all senior party leaders had left. Kruk was a Bundist and felt like a fish in water in the political and social life of the ghetto.

Kruk was a librarian and the builder of the library in the Vilna Ghetto. When the hundred thousandth book was borrowed, he made a special celebration. When abandoned secular and holy books were found in the liquidated "Second Ghetto," he organized an expedition to save them. For the sake of the Rosenberg Institute, he collected Jewish books from the Polish university and from around the city, for which he got German permission to move freely in the city. Kruk, Sutzkever, and others tried to save rare books and manuscripts from the YIVO collections, smuggle them into the ghetto, and hide them in cellars. The wise old man Zelig Kalmanowicz told them: "*Kinderlekh*, don't even try, the Germans will do it better than you ever could." For the YIVO workers, it seemed terrible that they had to pack the books in crates for shipment to Germany. But paradoxically, Kalmanowicz was right: those books were saved, found after the war, and shipped to YIVO in New York by Lucy Dawidowicz and others.

We may conclude this section with two vignettes (both quoted in Pinkhes Schwartz's "Biography of Herman Kruk" in the Yiddish edition of this book).

Dina Abramowicz tells about the "*Aktion* of the yellow permits" in October 1941, when those without such permits were sent to Ponar. "When the column of Judenrat employees began to move, we suddenly saw, to our amazement and fear, a strange couple: Herman Kruk walked in his short coat and beret, with firm strides and lifted head, and on his arm the ancient Pati Kremer, who, with her grey hair and wrinkled face, looked like his grandmother." Pati Kremer, 75 years old, widow of the founder of the Bund Arkady Kremer, was a veteran leader of the Bund and its moral authority in the ghetto. By a miracle, they passed German muster as husband and wife. Pati was saved for another year or two.

The Vilna University librarian Anna Šimaite, who often helped her Jewish colleagues, writes: "Like a little mouse, gathering grains one by one for its nest, Herman Kruk himself brought and encouraged others to collect books for the ghetto. . . . It was amazing to see the consistency and patience with which he dug into the materials. When he came to the [university] library, he was always restrained, calm, and polite. Some university employees said: 'When this little Jew with the yellow patches on his chest and his back comes to us—we want to stand up and bow our head to him.'"

Kruk was not the only one who wrote diaries in those days. Even before the war, writing autobiographies and diaries was cultivated by most intellectual circles. The experiences of World War I and the precarious situation of the Jews linked the present to its historical roots. The circle and the journal *Yunger historiker* (Young Historian) in the late 1930s heightened this awareness; Emanuel Ringelblum, the chronicler of the Warsaw Ghetto, was one of the young historians. Herman Kruk was a parallel figure in the Vilna Ghetto, and he was well positioned to collect information and documentation, and well known enough for many to bring him materials.

ESTONIA

The partisan movement in the ghetto was in a difficult dilemma: a real base for their anti-Nazi activities could be found in the Soviet partisan movement in the deep forests around Vilna. But they had decided to stay with their people in the ghetto and lead the masses in an uprising before the liquidation of the ghetto. The leadership of the FPO were young representatives of the major youth movements in the ghetto (except for the religious, who were negligible and didn't have such ideas). The Commander of FPO was the veteran Communist Itzik Wittenberg, an "elder statesman" in his mid-thirties, while the others were in their twenties. The Communists were a strong and disciplined group, experienced in underground work. It was also natural to have a Communist at the helm because he could establish contacts with the only resistance movement outside the ghetto, the Communist party in the city and the Soviet partisans who got orders and weapons from Moscow.

For more than a year there was a lull in the Vilna Ghetto (January 1942–March 1943), the mass persecutions seemed to be over, and the remaining Jews were so productive that they would be saved to contribute to the German war effort. Law and order and social and cultural activities dominated ghetto life. No one knew about the Nazi decision on the "final solution" of the Jewish question. But in March, the persecutions and deportations began again; the Jewish communities in the small towns were liquidated one by one, their remnants crowded into the Vilna Ghetto.

In April–May 1943, an uprising in the Warsaw Ghetto reverberated in the world media. It was crushed by the Germans but became a heroic page in the book of Jewish resistance. Suddenly, in July 1943, the Vilna Gestapo demanded the extradition of the FPO leader Itzik Wittenberg *alive*, or else they would destroy the whole ghetto. The head of the ghetto, Jacob Gens, incited the masses with the slogan: 1 or 20,000. Underworld characters and Jewish police as well as masses of ghetto Jews besieged partisan headquarters with screams: "We want to live!" The Germans were staying out of it. For the partisans, it made no sense to start the uprising then and there because that would mean fighting the Jews rather than the Germans. In a terrible bind, the partisan leadership decided to let Wittenberg go alone to the Gestapo. He apparently got hold of a cyanide capsule and committed suicide the same day.

This was the beginning of the end. "Wittenberg Day" changed the direction of the FPO, and they began sending people to the forests. The Germans learned about the existence of a partisan organization in the Vilna Ghetto and wanted to avoid the Warsaw experience. The new ruse was to send people to labor camps in Estonia.[16]

After the liquidation of the small Jewish community in Estonia in 1941, Jews from Theresienstadt and Germany were brought there in September 1942. Ninety percent of them were liquidated. Then, about 20,000 Jews from Vilna (and Kovno) were brought to work for the German war industry. They were taken from Vilna in four waves: on August 6, 1943; August 24; September

---

16   Most of the information on the camps in Estonia in this section is based on M. Dworzecki's book *Vayse nekht un shvartse teg (White Nights and Black Days: The Jewish Camps in Estonia* [Tel Aviv, 1970]). There were also a Hebrew and a shorter French version.

1–3; and September 23–26, at the final liquidation of the Vilna Ghetto. The first wave provoked a revolt of the Jews who were to be sent; they were fired on and many died or were wounded. To calm the atmosphere, the Germans sent several Jewish brigadiers to Estonia to see the situation for themselves, and organized personal letters from those in the Estonian labor camps. The purpose was to convince the Vilna Jews that, for a change, Estonia meant not extermination but work. Kruk, who did not opt for the partisans, walked from house to house in the Ghetto to convince the hiding Jews to go voluntarily. Hundreds of Jews were hiding in underground *melinas* (hiding bunkers, equipped with all necessary provisions). But the Estonian police and the Germans found the melinas, broke in, and took them out by the hundreds.

The background for the expulsions to Estonia was both the German decision to liquidate the Vilna Ghetto and Himmler's order of June 21, 1943, ordering all able-bodied Jews transferred from the ghettos of "Ostland" to the concentration camps, and all "unnecessary" ones liquidated. Estonia was close to the Leningrad front, and Hitler's ambition to take that city was thwarted. On August 11, 1943, Hitler ordered the construction of an "Eastern Wall," a defense line stretching from near Leningrad to the south. The Jews were to help in building that wall in the north.

The inmates were constantly shifted from one camp to another, both to fill various needed works and to confuse the prisoners. Kruk himself was apparently sent to Estonia in September (23?), 1943. He wrote a diary from September 1943 in the main camp, Klooga, and continued in camp Lagedi, where he was taken on August 22, 1944, until his death on September 18, 1944.

In the summer of 1944, the Red Army pushed into Estonia, first cutting it off in a cauldron. The final offensive began on September 15. On September 16, the German army was allowed to retreat from Estonia. On September 18, Obersturmfuehrer Otto Brenneisen, Commandant of all Estonian camps, arrived in Lagedi, promised to transfer the Jews to a warmer camp, gave them food, and loaded them on trucks. That was the usual German lie. They were taken to a place 40 kilometers from Lagedi, where a big pyre of wooden logs was prepared. The Germans tied 10–12 Jews with ropes and ordered them to lie on top of the logs, where they were shot. The others were kept at a distance. The process lasted from 11:00 a.m. until dark. In the end, the Germans set fire to the pyre. On the 19th, a mass slaughter finished the largest Estonian camp in Klooga. Soon, the Soviet army marched in and found the pyres with the burned bodies. Only a very few survived.

The day before, on the 17th, Kruk wrote his last sentences and buried his diaries in the presence of six friends; only one of them, Nisan Anolik, survived, went back to Lagedi, retrieved the diaries, and brought them to Vilna. From there, some of Kruk's manuscripts were taken to Israel and preserved in the Moreshet Institute, and others were confiscated by the Soviets and kept for half a century. Some of them miraculously survived.

EPILOGUE: THE END OF JERUSALEM IN EUROPE

We called this book *The Last Days of the Jerusalem of Lithuania*. "Lithuania" is not the small Baltic country that carries the name today, but the vast area between Poland and Moscow that was the multilingual Grand Duchy of Lithuania in medieval Europe, whose official language was Byelorussian, later Polish, and whose towns and markets resounded with Yiddish, and whose spaces were eulogized by Czeslaw Milosz and preserved in Jewish popular myth.

The Jewish religion and national consciousness are symbolized not by a person but by a place. The longing for Jerusalem throughout two thousand years of Diaspora provided the pivotal axis for the self-perception of the Jews as a nation in Exile, waiting for Redemption. The last two terms are often used as an ideological pun: *GoLA-GeuLA*, as if the two concepts of Exile and Redemption were inseparable twins. Indeed, from the very beginning of Jewish mythology, the moral image of man hinges on a two-place axis: one you were exiled to and one you are yearning for. Adam and Eve are banned from the Garden of Eden, which remains forever their measure of ideal values; the first father of the nation, Abraham, is exiled "from your country and from your homeland and from your father's house" in Aram of the Two Rivers (Mesopotamia)—and sent to the Promised Land; the Exodus from Egypt and the return to the Promised Land, celebrated every Passover, is the great parable of Jewish existence. The modern return to the Holy Land is used as a response to the Holocaust.

By calling their city "Jerusalem of Lithuania," Vilna Jews stressed this bipolar existence. On the one hand, it means "wherever we are, we are longing for Jerusalem"; on the other hand, it implies "whatever we have here is a substitute for Jerusalem"—if not in power, at least in spirit. There were other communities that called themselves "Jerusalem": Frankfurt am Main; Charleston, South Carolina. But Vilna was embraced as such by the whole modern Jewish culture.

By calling this book *The Last Days of the Jerusalem of Lithuania*, we indicate that it is not just about the sufferings of one person, the refugee Herman Kruk who was stranded in Vilna; or about the monstrous, stupid, and sadistic liquidation of a town of 60,000 Jews; but about the end of the Second Jerusalem. For more than a millennium, dating from the beginning of the Christian era, Jews lived and created in Europe, longer than they had been sovereign in their original independent state in Palestine.

Jews have always remembered the first Jerusalem as the utopian home of their dignity as a nation. The recent *Khurban*, as the survivors called it, the Destruction of European Jewry, is of the same magnitude as the two Destructions of the Temple and the state in the ancient Land of Israel. Now that a worldly third Jerusalem has been built in its original place, we must not forget the Second Jerusalem in Jewish history.

ART AND POETRY

6 ON THE BEGINNINGS OF ISRAELI POETRY AND YEHUDA AMICHAI'S QUATRAINS

A Memoir[1]

In the fall of 1949, the War of Independence was over. The short periods of "ceasefires" interrupted by outbreaks of fierce fighting, resulted in a consolidation of the disparate islands of Jewish settlements into a contiguous territory of the fledgling Jewish state, including part of Jerusalem and the road to it from the Jewish mainland at the seashore. A generation of young people fell in the war. The Palmakh brigades, the active military force trained in Kibbutzim in the underground under British rule, which were the spearhead of most Jewish conquests in the War of Independence, were now considered politically incorrect (left of center) and were dissolved by Ben-Gurion. Yehuda Amichai was demobilized from the Negev Brigade and I came out of the Harel Brigade. The drawing point was the Hebrew University in Jerusalem.

It was a time for poetry. If you read the poetry of that time, you cannot find any break between Hebrew poetry of the ages and the poetry of the state of Israel. They were one continuum.

Amichai grew up in Jerusalem; it was his city. He was only four years older than I but seemed a generation apart: he had been a soldier in the British army in World War II and thus was older by one major war. Unlike anybody else in our circles, Amichai was already married and wrote what were rumored to be large quantities of poetry; but he did not publish with his contemporaries,

---

1   1996.

the poets of the Palmakh Generation (like Chaim Guri or Amir Gilboa) and gravitated to us, the student-poets of the young generation.

I, too, had been in Europe during World War II (though on the Soviet side) and came to Palestine on the last illegal boat in May 1948, to join the Palmakh the same night I landed. But I had read a great deal of Russian poetry and had the advantage of two free years in devastated Germany, where I devoured German, French, American, and even Yiddish Modernist poetry. I knew Mayakovsky, Blok and Lorca by heart, and had read T.S. Eliot in Curtius's German translation and Rilke in the original. Thus, when I was released from the army in October 1949, I went to study Hebrew Literature at the Hebrew University in Jerusalem and was as dissatisfied as many with a teaching that emphasized ideology and history rather than reading the actual poetry of the recent generations of Hebrew Modernism.

I lived in a small room adjacent to a wide roof on the fifth floor of an old walk-up across from the first Knesset. The country was poor, and so were we. There were neither any natural resources in Israel nor an agriculture that could provide vegetables and food for the population. Floods of immigrants, first from Europe and then from North Africa, had quadrupled the population of the country in the course of several years. A rigid regimen of austerity and food rationing (*tsena*) was imposed by the Socialist government. And after the exhilaration of independence, the young generation experienced an anti-climactic mood of weariness of any ideological discourse, of great causes and greater slogans, and a need for the autonomy of an individual's life and experience. The saying went: "when 'Zionism' was put in quotation marks" (meaning not just Zionism but Socialism as well).

From an uncle in New York I got that precious invention, Nestle's "Nescafé," and a Hermes Baby Hebrew typewriter. Several young poets gathered in my room in the evenings, walked in the streets and came back, often until the early morning. Beyond the thin partition, the poet Yosef Lichtenboym, to us a relic from another age, was making Hebrew rhymes of the interminable epics of the Polish national bard Adam Mickiewicz; and on this side of the partition we argued about modern poetry, about Stalin, the betrayal of Communism, the danger of a Soviet takeover of the Near East, and what not, shyly read each other's first writings, and began to publish here and there. Israel was a much less tolerant and less pluralistic place then. As the country was dominated by Ben-Gurion and his Social-Democratic Mapai party, so literature was dominated by A. Shlonsky and the literary empire supported by the leftist Mapam party.

In 1951, several young poets, initially Arye Sivan (Bumshteyn), Moshe Dor (Klebanov), Nathan Zach (Seitelbach), and I (Hrushovski), launched our own literary journal, *Likrat* ("Towards"), to which several dozen young poets and writers gravitated. At the age of twenty-three, barely three years in the country, I had read most modern Hebrew poetry and wondered where Hebrew poetry should go (three years later, I started teaching poetry at the Hebrew University). I was two or three years older than my friends and some kind of authority on European poetry (in collaboration with Sivan or Dor, I translated poems by Blok, Lorca, Moyshe-Leyb Halpern, and published them in various places). I was actually the editor, proofreader and typist of the mimeographed journal *Likrat*; yet I was attentive to the authoritative value judgments of the young Nathan Zach. I typed it all on stencils on my Hebrew Hermes Baby and ran it off in our friend Chaim Hagiti's Jewish Agency youth office in 40 copies. (The operation cost 10 Lirot, which we had a hard time collecting.) We sent copies to all literary supplements of the newspapers; they all attacked us furiously, as if we were undermining the Jewish nation and Hebrew and World Culture; we were especially ostracized in the name of "Socialist Realism"—and *Likrat* became famous overnight. It brought to Hebrew literature such names as Nathan Zach, Yehuda Amichai, David Avidan, or Itshak Livni, who subsequently shaped the military radio station as the most intelligent, interesting and open-minded station in Israel.

Likrat and its cultural spirit and direction launched the great shift in Hebrew literature from ideological engagement to individualist poetry (and in the next generation of Yehoshua, Oz, and others—to significant prose, influenced by the poetics of this poetry). It shifted Hebrew verse overnight from the bathos and exuberant imagery of the Russian tradition to the ironies and understatements of Anglo-Saxon modernist poetry. Yet Europe was not far away, Existentialism and Kafka deeply impressed us, Mayakovsky and Russian Futurism, Rilke and German Expressionism were hovering options in our world. Whereas the dominant Hebrew poets, such as Shlonsky, Alterman, or Leah Goldberg, were still steeped in the language of the Bible and even used Biblical tenses, the poets of *Likrat* wrote their poems as a matter of course in the spoken language of the new Israeli society with its European tense-system—and the basic three times: past, present and future—accommodating selective allusions to the Bible within the framework of the spoken discourse.

I typed and published in *Likrat* the first published poems of Yehuda Amichai, at least the first poems of the new, the "real" Amichai. Years later, he himself, in an autobiographical note to me, wrote that his first publication was in 1955, but I published his first poems in *Likrat* in 1952. We edited and published his first book, *Now and In Other Days* ("Akhshav u-be-yamim akherim," 1956), which established the shape of a poem, the style, thematics, and poetic personality of Amichai for the world and for himself. Amichai started with regular meters, rhymes and sonnets, but soon shifted to free verse in the Israeli idiom, casual and nonchalant. We sensed in him a true representative of the new Hebrew poetry and drew him to us; in time, the small difference in age became negligible. Amichai was an anti-political political poet, he praised the intensity of the moment, the temporary experiences of love "now," with no certainty about any past or future, the mundane values of just living and loving: "I saw you open the refrigerator, my girl, / Illuminated in the light of another world"—a far cry from Ben-Gurion's Biblical "Light for the Nations." Or that Amichai line memorized by a generation: "But I want to die in my own bed." After eight or nine years in uniform, he detested war, sloganeering, even history itself—and constantly engaged them in his poetry. Amichai's early books became the most popular books of poetry in the history of Hebrew literature, many were set to music, many were memorized by thousands of readers, and raised generations to admire the significance of poetry as a privileged mode of discourse and as a force in their own lives.

We were all identified with the Socialist-Zionist left, though we distrusted the structures of political power. Outside of the small group of "Canaanites," radicals in their own right, there were hardly any young intellectuals who would openly not be on the left. Yet, unlike most of us, Amichai had graduated from a religious high school in Jerusalem, which made him more explicitly anti-religious, on the one hand, and steeped in the language and imagery of Hebrew religious texts, on the other. The framework of Amichai's discourse was blunt, straightforward, spoken Palestinian Hebrew, including many new idioms of the modern, secular, quotidian Hebrew reality; and in that frame he set many phrases from the prayerbook (beside the ubiquitous Bible everyone alluded to). This made him attuned to the double meanings of Hebrew words and expressions, often contradictory when placed in a secular or religious context, and the ironies of reterritorialized language. The clash of the two large universes, the secular and the religious, that occurred within the same grammar and vocabulary, and within the same biographical persona, provided Amichai with an inexhaustible wealth of metaphors and existential themes throughout his poetic career. God is one of the major protagonists of Amichai's fictional world, yet introduced into the secular domain, he is a regular schlemiel garage mechanic:

> God lies on His back under the world. There,
> Something's always breaking down, needs repair.
> I wanted to see him, but I keep
> Seeing only the soles of his shoes, and I weep.
> *And this is his glory.*[2]

The last phrase, repeated after every strophe as a refrain, is a quotation from a prayer on the Days of Awe, thus both imbued with religious authority and ironized by the secular distance: it is not the poet's language but a quotation, confronting the lofty hymn with the scene of the humble but practical garage mechanic.

In spite of his ostensibly simple discourse, Amichai's cultural horizons were broad. Like Nathan Zach, Amichai was born in Germany and had access to its language and literature; and, having served in the British army, he discovered in the desert an anthology of English poetry and was receptive to the intonations of Eliot and Auden. But he grew into that culture of world poetry gradually. The impact of Rilke's "Duino Elegies," for example, was stronger in his second decade as a poet than in his beginning. Amichai had such a strong individual world of images, situations, personal relations, encounters, and interacting Hebrew discourses, that he molded his own voice from the very beginning, and only gradually reached out for the so-called "influences," which were not so much influences as selected appropriations of different sources.

And then there was Hebrew poetry. Either mild by nature, or a bit too old to be rebellious, Amichai did not discard the internal tradition altogether. He learned slowly and reached out to selected moments in Hebrew poetry beyond the idol of the day, Nathan Alterman, with his Futurist imagery and exuberant metaphors, rhymes, rhythms, and sound patterns. There was a great deal of poetry in Amichai's upbringing, notably, the poetry of the Jewish liturgy and the poets that were taught in school, such as YaLaG (Gordon), Bialik and Chernikhovski, who were all very formal poets in their own time and genres, written in Ashkenazi Hebrew, but they did not sound as regularly metrical when read in Israeli Hebrew: the richly-rhyming poets of the liturgy counted

---

2   "And This is Your Glory," in: Yehuda Amichai, *A Life of Poetry: 1948–1994*, translated from the Hebrew by Benjamin and Barbara Harshav, Harper Collins, 1994, p. 32.

the number of words, irrespective of any rhythmic articulation. The poets of the nineteenth and twentieth centuries wrote in Ashkenazi Hebrew, and their precise, European meters were lost when taught in the "Sefardi" dialect spoken in Israel. What remained was the impact of rich rhymes and verse lines similar in size. Indeed, in his early published poetry, Amichai wrote in a kind of free verse with balanced groups of stresses. He wrote either rhymeless poems or in strophic shapes using couplets of rhymes, a deviation from Hebrew poetry of the last centuries. He also liked the refrain of many liturgical poems.

As a young poet, Amichai became acquainted with the learned poet, translator and professor of comparative literature Leah Goldberg, who wrote many sonnets, terzinas, and other Russian Symbolist forms of Italian or Provençal origin and translated all of Petrarch's sonnets into Hebrew in precise meters and rhymes. About the same time he learned the use of regular meters and some of his early sonnets do indeed sound like Leah Goldberg's.

And here I come back to the role of the Hebrew University. Unhappy and revolutionary as young people could be, especially in a time of crisis of ideology, culture and discourse, we learned a great deal about Hebrew literature in the last millennium—from medieval Spain through the Haskala and beyond. The great revelation was, of course, the Hebrew poetry of medieval Spain. It was taught by the evidently boring, dry and monotonous, but descriptive and precise Professor Chaim Shirman, who was free of any phraseology or ideology, a lifelong bachelor and a somewhat comical figure with a crooked head, whom we eventually came to love. It was not just the historical depth of a secular Hebrew poetic tradition that we acquired but a colorful, fascinating world in its own right and a Hebrew poetic language different from anything we knew. Our heroes were not so much the "Zionist" Yehuda Halevi as the sickly and tortured, profoundly individualist and proto-Existential Shlomo Ibn Gabirol, and the Prime Minister and Commander of Granada's army and wise poet, Shmuel HaNagid, whose war poetry is perhaps unsurpassed in Hebrew poetry to this day.

The kindred spirit Amichai found in Hebrew Spanish poetry is manifest in the fact that, among his early poems, two are devoted to Yehuda HaLevi and Ibn Gabirol, and Shmuel HaNagid is often evoked. But a link to the poetics of Spanish poetry is a different matter. The language and poetics of modern Hebrew poetry, written in the post-Renaissance European tradition, is cardinally different from Spanish Hebrew poetry, written in the tradition of Arabic poetics.

Amichai introduced, or reinvented, the medieval quatrain written in Spain, marked by its rigorous rhyme frame, thus making a statement of a revived connection to the Hebrew poetic tradition. The most salient, indeed the defining feature of the quatrain is rhyme, and it is not just a formal element but a crucial factor in determining the composition and nature of the poem. Like many European poetries, Modern Hebrew poetry almost exclusively favored alternating rhymes and the interplay between them (e.g., abab or aabccb), and this is what Amichai learned from the sonnet tradition and from the modern Hebrew and German poets. But Spanish Hebrew poetry, in the Arabic tradition, employed one rhyme, endlessly repeated, stringing together dozens of lines of a long poem by their ends, like a long string of beads (*haruz*, "rhyme" in Hebrew, means "bead," and "to rhyme" is "to string"). Already in Spain, both in Arabic and in Hebrew, there was a strong move to overcome this monotonous concatenation, both through the creation of strophic poetry with alternating rhymes, invented in Spain (the *muwashahat*), and in the use of the quatrain. A similar liberation from the endless rhyming chain occurred at the other end of the Islamic world, in Persia, notably by the twelfth-century mathematician and poet Omar Khayyam.[3]

The quatrain was first employed in Hebrew poetry by Dunash Ben Labrat, who lived two centuries before Omar Khayyam. Raised in Baghdad and creative in Spain in the tenth century, Dunash was the first major Hebrew poet to introduce Arabic meters in Hebrew. He and his followers' quatrains were still linked to the long string of beads: aaaR bbbR cccR, and so on (where R symbolizes the string rhyme). Yet, by its very internal rhyme, the quatrain formed an autonomous unit and eventually became an independent poem.

Yehuda Amichai wrote several cycles of quatrains. He linked up to the "Spanish" tradition, but gave it his own form. Instead of the medieval Hebrew aaaR rhyme scheme, or Omar Khayyam's aaxa (where the third line is unrhymed), he created a strophe with one fourfold rhyme: aaaa. Thus, the playful European alternation of rhymes was avoided, all verse lines are really parallel to each other, they form a cube "at right angles," as Amichai called it, yet the monotonous long string of Arabic poetry is absent.

This tight form, emphasizing formal composition, gave Amichai the internal freedom from meter (as he would experience Spanish poetry when read

---

3   As known to English readers from the Edward Fitzgerald adaptation, "The Rubáiyát of Omar Khayyám."

in Israeli Hebrew). Thus the poem conveys the feeling that it is the weighty voice of contemplation rather than any preprogrammed meter that dictates the rhythm of the text. There is, however, an internal balance in each line, usually of six stresses per line, sometimes more or less.

Following Spanish Hebrew poetics, Amichai's rhymes in the "quatrains" are richer (including more rhyming sounds) than required in modern Hebrew poetry, thus even more conspicuous. The rhyming words he selected are often either surprising or accidental, for the rhyme pattern is the most important structural element, overruling any thematic purity or careful diction. The difficulty of finding four words conjoined with one rich rhyme brought together quite disparate images and often disjointed lines, thus creating an effect of elliptic, even surrealist composition, which enriches the resonance chamber of the poem. In our translations, we have followed the same principles.

The compact, closed cube of the quatrain is conducive to poetry of wisdom, combining striking and sensuous imagery with epigrammatic statements, summarizing the existential situation and flirting with the metaphysical. Amichai has to restrain his narrative impulse for the sake of an enigmatic gem. The reader has to feed his understanding from the rest of Amichai's poetry.

Yehuda Amichai
Hebrew Quatrains[4]

1

In the sands of his prayers, my father saw traces of angels at heaven's gates.
He bequeathed me a road, but on many roads his son procrastinates.
Hence his face was bright. Mine is scorched and abdicates.
Like an old office calendar, I'm covered with dates.

2

Once I knew answers. "Sit down!" said God. And didn't blink.
The world calm, the wind at rest. I must, and I blow at the brink.
Trees will sprout buds, not caring if I flourish or shrink.
The world is covered with answers and flowers. I must think.

---

4   This is an English version of the complete cycle of quatrains, "In a Right Angle," first published in Amichai's book, *Two Hopes Away* (1960). Several fragments from this cycle were published in an earlier translation in our comprehensive selection of Amichai's poetry, *Yehuda Amichai: A Life of Poetry, 1948–1994*, translated from the Hebrew by Benjamin and Barbara Harshav, Harper Collins Publishers, 1994, 480 pp.

3

Sign of Gemini, lucky star, Capricorn, my star again.
Who will love the things that are naught and in vain?
I, who stand in my days like water in the rain,
I love the things that are naught and in vain.

4

Now I know where they live, like the night owls,
But I shall never feel my hands as a stranger's hand that growls.
God left me only consonants, took away all the vowels.
That's why my life's in a hurry. That's why my life howls.

5

I must think many stones till I have my true home.
I invent whole new seasons, till my hour will come.
I am writing long scrolls and don't have my signature yet. The earth
Will forget all the layers. Only my mother remembers my birth.

6

Streets have names, pains have names, ships have names on their prow.
Already spring. Already negotiations. But the document is signed anyhow.
My father, harnessed in Tefillin, and I in dreams, in the sweat of my brow.
The world is plowed in us, for them. For us, it is undecipherable now.

7

Be calm, oh rose in the blood of the other, and wait.
Your blossoming was slow. My head too is heavy and late.
If there was a verb from "tomorrow," I would tomorrow at the gate.
Be calm. Like you, I love to blossom in the other's blood, and wait.

8

The greatest wandering is of a heart that stopped wandering.
The greatest loss is something lost returned, wondering.
The greatest weeping is of a mouth that laughed between stone
And cypress trees, yesterday afternoon, laughed alone.

9

My parents made a fate of many colors fit for me.
I grew up, and my bare arm sticks out for all to see.
My fate hasn't grown with me, my body is filled with history
Like the Book of Genesis, up to the brim, like a sea.

10

Now my love explains me as the commentators in their prime.
Spring translates the world in all languages, for all time.
Our bread, prophecy on the table. All words ring beautiful, as a chime.
But inside us, destiny works overtime.

11

Great orators hold their microphones to their mouths.
I, your head to my lips. Oh, lift my love to north and south
And to all the winds. We have nothing to hide in our stammer.
We are simple, easy to learn, as words in an elementary grammar.

12

At the end of green spring, God begins His steps
Like a smoking, terrible factory. Perhaps
To transform us like iron. Therefore, I shall place my profile to languish
Between Him and the world: perhaps to link, certainly to distinguish.

13

Electrical strings are taut over all. The world is my oud.
I sing: Lo and behold. My food grows cold. Nothing is lost for good.
No more excuses of doors and locks, all is destiny, inscribed in stone.
The angel will descend. I am ready, stretched like an airfield, and alone.

14

I once fled, I don't recall from what god, for what wish.
Hence I travel in life like Jonah inside his dark fish.
In the world's guts, my fish and I get along quite devilish:
I will not abandon Him. He won't digest me as a dish.

15

I live now inside an abandoned love, like a guest.
When did the tenants leave? Did they find what is best?
I discovered it at a hard time of unrest.
I live in it now. So far, I have no request.

16

I passed by the place where I once was a lover.
I had hopes as sharp as fingernails, as lamb's eyes. It's all over.
Now the sky covers me. And I just cover
The ground under my feet. It's my whole endeavor.

17

Take my picture in the sand, by the broken tank, leaning.
Take my picture for a moment against the gleaning
Of words not repeated. With no hope, in a festive screening.
My arm on the girl and my free arm with no commentary or meaning.

18

Two hopes away from the battlefield, I had a vision of peace.
My tired head must go, my feet dream, do not cease.
The scorched man said: I'm the bush that burned with no trace.
Approach, you may. Leave your shoes on your feet. This is the place.

19

A young soldier lies in spring, cut off from his name.
His body sprouts and blossoms. The blood of every vein
Is little and ignorant, chattering with no rein.
God cooks the kid in its mother's pain.

20

At the right angle between a corpse and his mourner
Now will be the place of my life, my corner.
The woman sits with me, the little girl went up in the cloud
Of her burning, and into my heart as a shroud.

21

In the end, we too will be winds from beyond the rim
Of window, of east, of hope. We shall be the glim
Of a beautiful horse power and flower power. We shall be the pseudonym
Of the world and of the other sea, where we didn't learn to swim.

7 THE MODERN HEBREW POEM ITSELF

Nathan Alterman, Abba Kovner[1]

NATHAN ALTERMAN

A Summer Night

לֵיל קַיִץ

דּוּמִיָּה בַּמֶּרְחָבִים שׁוֹרֶקֶת.
בֹּהַק הַסַּכִּין בְּעֵין הַחֲתוּלִים.
לַיְלָה. כַּמָּה לַיְלָה! בַּשָּׁמַיִם שֶׁקֶט.
כּוֹכָבִים בְּחִתּוּלִים.

זְמַן רָחָב, רָחָב. הַלֵּב צִלְצֵל אַלְפַּיִם.
טַל, כְּמוֹ פְּגִישָׁה, אֶת הָרִיסִים הִצְעִיף.
בְּמַגְלֵב זָהָב פָּנָס מַפִּיל אַפַּיִם
עֲבָדִים שְׁחוֹרִים לִרְחַב הָרָצִיף.

רוּחַ קַיִץ שָׁטָה. עֲמוּמָה. רוֹגֶשֶׁת.
עַל כִּתְפֵי גַנִּים שְׂפָתֶיהָ נִשְׁפָּכוֹת.
רֵעַ יְרַקְרַק. תְּסִיסַת אוֹרוֹת וָחֶשֶׁד.
רְתִיחַת מַטְמוֹן בְּקֶצֶף הַשָּׁחֹר.

---

1   This reading is from *The Modern Hebrew Poem Itself* (1965) and follows the editors'
    instructions.

וְהַרְחֵק לַגֹּבַהּ, בִּנְהִימָה מָרְעֶבֶת,
עִיר אֲשֶׁר עֵינֶיהָ זְהַב מְצֻפּוֹת,
מִתְאַדָּה בְזַעַם, בְּתִמְרוֹת הָאֶבֶן,
שֶׁל הַמִּגְדָּלִים וְהַכִּיפּוֹת.

Nathan Alterman, for a time the most influential Hebrew poet since Bialik, was born in Warsaw in 1910. The son of a Hebrew educator, he was reared in Kishinev, arriving in Palestine in 1925 where he completed his studies at a Tel Aviv *gymnasium.* Somewhat later he went to France to study agronomy.

A disciple of Shlonsky, Pasternak, and of French Symbolism, he became the most prominent exponent of the "imagistic" trend in Hebrew poetry. His brilliant wit and fantastic imagery, his mastery of language and meter, the seemingly "spoken" flavor of his charged rhetoric, brought him two generations of admirers and imitators. It was only natural, then, for his "line" to become the main target of attack in the 1950s when a new trend, influenced by Anglo-American poetry, proclaimed the virtues of understatement, irony, prosaic diction, and free verse.

Alterman's writing is extremely rich and varied. Besides his four volumes of lyric poetry, he is the author of a large collection of satirical, topical verse and songs, two plays (one in verse), children's books, and translations from English, French, Yiddish, and Russian. (Shakespeare's *Othello, Julius Caesar, The Merry Wives of Windsor, Antony and Cleopatra*; a collection of *Ballads and Songs of England and Scotland*; Racine's *Phaedre*; Molière's *Le Misanthrope, Le Malade Imaginaire,* etc.).

Almost from its beginnings, Alterman's work was marked by two distinct strains which occasionally intermingle. On the one hand—his often brilliant, ballad-like topical verse published weekly under the heading "The Seventh Column"; these became a running "poetic" commentary on the turbulent thirties and forties and played a remarkable role in expressing and shaping the mood of a people caught up in the birth of a country and the death of its European communities. On the other hand—his lyrical, hermetic, and "literary" poetry, which made no overt references to actual events or to personal biography. His first book, *Kohavim Bahúts* (*The Stars Outside*, 1938), with its neo-romantic themes, highly charged texture, and metrical virtuosity, immediately established him as a major force in Hebrew poetry.

Our selection from his first volume is a poem characteristic in mood and technique. A mysterious atmosphere surrounds the speaker who waits as if lost in time and space. No other people, no specific events, yet something is happening around him in the warm summer night. The setting of the poem spreads out between two fields of light: the "innocent" stars far above in the quiet sky (stanza 1) and the fuming stones of a distant city evaporating in the "rage" of its illuminated towers and cupolas (stanza 4).

(1) *Silence whistles in the (wide) spaces.* (2) *Glitter of a knife in the eye of cats.* (3) *Night. How much night! In the skies: quiet.* (4) *Stars in swaddling clothes.*

(5) *Wide, wide time. The heart rang two thousand.* (6) *Dew, like an encounter, veiled the eyelashes,* (7) *With a golden whip a street-lantern throws down (prostrate)* (8) *Black slaves across the width of the platform.*

(9) *A summer wind roams (floats). Muted. Agitated.* (10) *Her* [the wind's] *lips are poured out upon shoulders of gardens.* (11) *[A] greenish malice. Fermentation of light and of suspicion.* (12) *Boiling of a treasure in the black foam.*

(13) *And far, toward the height, with famished growl,* (14) *A city whose eyes are plated with gold,* (15) *Evaporates in rage, in the stone billows* (16) *Of the towers and the cupolas.*

Dimensions of time and of space overlap. The lone speaker feels that time is motionless and almost unreal. It is a matter of "How much night!" (3) and of "wide, wide time" (5)—*raháv* ("wide") repeats the root of *merhavim* ("spaces," 1), literally meaning "wide spaces."

The silence is so overpowering that one can hear it. *Dumiyá* (patterned on the stock oxymoron *hadmamá zoéket*, "silence shrieks") is a more unusual word for "silence"; and *soréket* ("whistles") suggests a silence roaming like a wind whistling over the plains.

Line 2 is a typical Alterman device: creating abstract qualities by manipulating concrete elements. The cats—a traditional accessory in magical circumstances—are not individualized; they are endowed with one collective, menacing eye. The "glitter of a knife"—later echoed by "greenish evil" (11)—is at once contrasted with the "quietude" of the skies.

This quiet is almost idyllic, so that the stars are seen as innocent, sleeping babies swaddled in diapers (4). The concrete image of a hazy halo surrounding the stars on a hot southern night is presented by its implication for the speaker: the stars, traditionally a symbol of eternity, appear as new-born.

Time is not old but "large" (5). Only the heart marks the passage of time by its fateful "ringing." The number "two thousand," which refers to the span of the Diaspora, is a hackneyed phrase in Israel—linked with *keórekh hagalút* ("as long as the Diaspora"), a proverbial expression for interminable duration. Hence, for the heart, the length of time seems unreal, immeasurable.

The sudden "encounter" (6), answering as it were the heart's expectancy (5), is introduced by an inverted simile—a method often found in Alterman's verse: instead of comparing the less known to the better known, he does the reverse. Thus even the encounter is not explicitly embedded in the setting but merely hinted at by means of a simile. With line 9, the emotional tone intensifies, as the detached adjectives body forth the feeling. But the erotic element (10) is not individualized: the lips (feminine in Hebrew) pour out upon the gardens (masculine). The entire setting is suffused with wind and with unreal imagery: greenish malice, seething of lights and suspicion, foam that is black, a boiling treasure. The strangeness is reinforced in Hebrew by the use of a neologism (*hésed*, "suspicion") and less common forms *róa* ("evil") and *yerakrák* ("greenish"). Moreover, the sonal effect of lines 11–12 is remarkable for its onomatopoeic quality and for its intricate orchestration of groups of consonants in changing orders which are echoed in neighboring lines. The closely related sounds of *r, kh,* and of *t, k* occur 18 times in obvious interplay with 5 sibilants.

Though the setting in the first 3 stanzas is specific, there are hardly any concrete details. Everything around the man on the platform is caught in motion, yet there is neither succession nor development. This effect of "timelessness" is emphasized by the predicateless sentences (2–5, 11–12) and the preponderance of nouns (almost five times as many as verbs or adjectives). Though the sensuous elements are present, they are generally divorced from their normal environments. Thus each introduces a realm of its own, rich with overtones, but the resulting images are vague in outline, emphasizing the diffused haziness of this summer night and the unexplicated feeling of something vague, strange, ominous.

The traditional quatrains, rhyming *abab* and alternating feminine with masculine rhymes, have a slow movement of trochaic hexameter (with the exception of lines 1, 4, 12) but only line 5, where time is being "measured," has all 6 stresses. The final stanza, with its single inverted sentence and the caesuras after unstressed syllables, is in strong contrast to the segmented movement of the preceding lines—as though one breathless sweep were carrying the strong finale of the poem. The last line is the only one where two consecutive stresses are skipped; the whole line is reduced to two major stresses.

The rhymes, when not identical, are compensated for by the equivalences of preceding sounds. Thus in *mur'évet-haéven* (13–15) the identical sound is *éve* but the sounds *m*, *r*, *t* of the first rhyme-word appear in the word preceding the second rhyme: *betimrót*; and the *h*, *n* sounds of the second rhyme-word are present in the word preceding the first: *binhimá* (*binhimá mur'évet—betimrót heaven*). Actually all consonants of both pairs are involved in the rhyming, but in changed order. The identical sounds are in CAPITAL letters:

BINHIMa MuREVET
BeTIMRoT HaEVEN

Such sonal patterns linked to rhyme often run though entire stanzas in Alterman's first book.

This Night

לַיְלָה הַזֶּה

הַלַּיְלָה הַזֶּה.
הִתְנַכְּרוּת הַקִּירוֹת הָאֵלֶּה.
מִלְחֶמֶת שְׁתִיקוֹת בְּחָזֶה מוּל חָזֶה.
חַיָּיו הַזְּהִירִים
שֶׁל נֵר הַחָלָב.

רַק שְׁמוּעָה שֶׁל אֵין־נֹחַם, כְּרוּחַ קְרִירָה,
פֹּה הֶחֱלִיקָה לְאֹרֶךְ גְּדֵרוֹת הָרוּסוֹת
וְלִטְּפָה רְצִיפִים נְטוּלֵי הַכָּרָה
וְהֵנִיעָה גְּשָׁרִים כְּשׁוּרַת עֲרִיסוֹת.

בַּכִּכָּר הָרֵיקָה צֵל עוֹבֵר. נֶעְלָם.
הֶמְלַת צְעָדָיו לְבַדָּהּ עוֹד הוֹלֶכֶת.
אַל תִּשְׁכַּח, אַל תִּשְׁכַּח־נָא, עֲפַר הָעוֹלָם,
אֶת רַגְלֵי הָאָדָם שֶׁדָּרְכוּ עָלֶיךָ.

הַלַּיְלָה הַזֶּה.

מְתִיחוּת הַקִּירוֹת הָאֵלֶּה.

קוֹל נֵעוֹר וְשׁוֹאֵל. קוֹל מֵשִׁיב וּמְהַסֶּה.

לְטִיפָה מוּזָרָה. אוֹר חִיּוּךְ מְעֻשֶּׂה.

חַיָּיו וּמוֹתוֹ

שֶׁל נֵר הַחֵלֶב.

אָז יָרֵחַ מַלְבִּישׁ מַסְכוֹת שַׁעֲוָה

עַל חַלּוֹן, עַל עֵינַיִם קָרוֹת, עַל נוֹפִים,

עַל הַשּׁוּק הָעוֹמֵד מְאֻבָּן בַּשֶּׁבֶץ,

בִּידֵי גֹלֶם שְׁלוּחוֹת שֶׁל קְרוֹנוֹת וּמְנוֹפִים.

"This Night," from Alterman's first volume, brings us into a world of metonymy in which man is expressed by the objects surrounding him, without
any direct defining of his feelings:

(1) *This night.* (2) *The estrangement of these walls.* (3) *War of silences in
chest (breast) confronting chest (breast).* (4) *The cautious life* (5) *Of the tallow
candle.*

(6) *Only a rumor of non-consolation, like a cool wind,* (7) *Glided here along
ruined fences* (8) *And caressed unconscious quays* [lit. *which fainted*] (9) *And
rocked bridges as [though they were] a line of cradles.*

(10) *A shadow passes in the empty square. Disappears.* (11) *The tumult of its*
[lit. *his*] *steps still walks on by itself.* (12) *Don't forget, please don't forget, dust of
the world,* (13) *The feet of the man that trod on you.*

(14) *This night.* (15) *The tenseness of these walls.* (16) *A voice awakes and asks.*
A voice answers and hushes. (17) *A strange caress. Light of an artificial smile.* (18)
The life and death (19) *Of the tallow candle.*

(20) *Then the moon clothes in masks of wax* (21) *A window, cold eyes, landscapes,* (22) *[And] the market that stands petrified in a stroke* (23) *[Closed] in the
extended hands of a monster (golem), [hands] of wagons and levers.*

The objects that "fix" the emotions of the participants are introduced by
means of demonstrative pronouns and definite articles (literally "The night
this one," "The estrangement of the walls these ones"). It is a specific night
with specific walls and a specific candle yet the total effect is indefiniteness,
estrangement, mystery.

As in the preceding poem, the unidentified voice does not describe the setting directly. It is the non-material objects and spiritual qualities that hold the stage: alienation, silence fighting silence, the cautious breath of a candle (stanza 1); rumor roaming like a cool wind, an anonymous shadow, the independent noise of steps (stanzas 2–3); tension, a disembodied voice, a weird caress, the unspecified light of a deceptive smile (stanza 4). Such non-material things, or rather the relations between them (the silences of a heart, the ghost-like steps and voice), populate Alterman's poetic world. As Leo Spitzer pointed out, the grotesque effect of Christian Morgenstern's verse is dependent on the relational nouns detached from their normal relational framework—e.g., *Ein Knie geht einsam durch die Welt*, "A knee walks lonely through the world." Alterman uses this same device, much as Rilke does, to elevate spiritual and non-material elements above specific events and objects—which are seen as adventitious. Moreover, there is often a pronounced element of horror in these non-material nouns, detached from their normal framework, and from any chain of events. The noise of steps (11–12) lives on after the shadow of a man has disappeared from the square—and perhaps from life.

The emotional appeal to "the dust of the world" (*afár haolám*, 12) after the disappearance of the footsteps, is rich with connotations; for *shohén afár* ("the dweller in the dust") is a traditional figure for the dead, but *olám* ("world") also means "eternity."

The fourth stanza is patterned on the first. The "estrangement" becomes "tenseness"; the "silences" are replaced by detached voices; and the "cautious life of the tallow candle" is now the "life and death" of the candle. The candle is "cautious" because the winds of tension are about to break out. The menace is ever-present and the talk (16), the strange caress, and the artificial smile usher in its death. A recurrent symbol in Alterman's poetry, the candle bears overtones of a poor and simple setting, folk superstitions, fatal circumstances. Here the death of the candle is an omen for the death of whatever lived between the opposed personae in the scene.

The poem moves from the "interior" (stanza 1) to images of weird motion in the "exterior" (stanzas 2–3) and back again to the room (stanza 4) where the "strange caress" echoes the "caress" of "despair" (6–8). Though the poem has come full circle with the repetition of its initial pattern, it does not end at this point. The fifth stanza now "freezes" the external world. Even the "marketplace"—which in Alterman's poetry represents colorful, dynamic life—is here petrified (like the quays of line 8); the "cold eyes" become but another item in a list of external objects. Thus, though the point of departure was intimate, and the external setting (stanzas 2–3) seemed to be an extension of the human situation, the finale reverses the point of view, placing the poem in the larger context of "nature." Both domains, the human and the natural, the internal and the external, echo each other and *both* are frozen in "masks of wax" (20)—recalling death and the eternity of a wax museum.

The anapestic flow of the poem is constantly interrupted in stanzas 1 and 4 by frequent full stops, feminine rhymes, and missing unstressed syllables (thus line 1 is amphibrachic; *shel ner hahélev*—"of the tallow candle," 5—lacks an unstressed syllable after *ner*, which slows down the reading).

The halting movement of stanzas 1 and 4 is counterpointed by the stanzas that follow them (2 and 5): here the 4–beat anapestic line is intact, running through the stanza in one complex sentence without interruption of missing syllables or feminine rhymes.

Stanza 3, at the poem's center, is a kind of mediate member. It begins with the curt, factual tone of the first stanza, then passes to a longer 2–line sentence which suddenly introduces the direct appeal of a human voice.

The Foundling

הָאֲסוּפִי

הִנִּיחַתְנִי אִמִּי לְרַגְלֵי הַגָּדֵר,
קָמוּט פָּנִים וְשׁוֹקֵט. עַל גַּב.
וָאַבִּיט בָּה מִלְּמַטָּה, כְּמוֹ מִן הַבְּאֵר, -
עַד נוֹסָה כְּהַנֵּס מִן הַקְּרָב.
וָאַבִּיט בָּה מִלְּמַטָּה, כְּמוֹ מִן הַבְּאֵר,
וְיָרֵחַ עָלֵינוּ הוּרַם כְּמוֹ נֵר.

אַךְ בְּטֶרֶם הַשַּׁחַר הֵאִיר, אוֹתוֹ לֵיל,
קַמְתִּי אַט כִּי הִגִּיעָה עֵת
וְאָשׁוּב בֵּית אִמִּי כְּכַדּוּר מִתְגַּלְגֵּל,
הַחוֹזֵר אֶל רַגְלֵי הַבּוֹעֵט.
וְאָשׁוּב בֵּית אִמִּי כְּכַדּוּר מִתְגַּלְגֵּל
וְאֶחֱבֹּק צַוָּארָהּ בְּיָדַיִם שֶׁל צֵל.

מֵעֲלֵי צַוָּארָהּ, לְעֵינַי כֹּל יָכוֹל,
הִיא קְרַעְתַּנִי כְּמוֹ עֲלוּקָה.
אַךְ שָׁב לַיְלָה וְשַׁבְתִּי אֵלֶיהָ כִּתְמוֹל,
וַתְּהִי־לָנוּ זֹאת לְחֻקָּה:
בְּשׁוּב לַיְלָה וְשַׁבְתִּי אֵלֶיהָ כִּתְמוֹל
וְהִיא לַיְלָה כּוֹרַעַת לִגְמוּל וָלָעַל.

וְדַלְתוֹת חֲלוֹמָהּ לִי פְּתוּחוֹת לִרְוָחָה
וְאֵין אִישׁ בַּחֲלוֹם מִלְּבַדִּי.
כִּי נוֹתְרָה אַהֲבַת־נַפְשׁוֹתֵינוּ דְּרוּכָה
כְּמוֹ קֶשֶׁת, מִיּוֹם הֻלַּדִּי.
כִּי נוֹתְרָה אַהֲבַת נַפְשׁוֹתֵינוּ דְּרוּכָה
וְלָעַד לֹא נִתְּנָה וְלֹא לְקוּחָה.

וְעַל כֵּן עַד אַחֲרִית לֹא הֵסִיר אוֹתִי אֵל
מֵעַל לֵב הוֹרָתִי הַצּוֹעֵק.
וַאֲנִי - שֶׁנֻּתַּקְתִּי מִבְּלִי הִגָּמֵל -
לֹא נִגְמַלְתִּי וְלֹא אֶנָּתֵק.
וַאֲנִי שֶׁנֻּתַּקְתִּי מִבְּלִי הִגָּמֵל
נִכְנָס אֶל בֵּיתָהּ וְהַשַּׁעַר נוֹעֵל.

הִיא זָקְנָה בְּכִלְאִי וַתִּדַּל וַתִּקְטַן
וּפָנֶיהָ קָמְטוּ כְּפָנַי.
אָז יָדֵי הַקְּטַנּוֹת הִלְבִּישׁוּהָ לָבָן
כְּמוֹ אֵם אֶת הַיֶּלֶד הַחַי.
אָז יָדֵי הַקְּטַנּוֹת הִלְבִּישׁוּהָ לָבָן
וָאֶשָּׂא אוֹתָהּ בְּלִי לְהַגִּיד לָהּ לְאָן.

וָאַנִּיחַ אוֹתָהּ לְרַגְלֵי הַגָּדֵר
צוֹפִיָּה וְשׁוֹקֶטֶת, עַל גַּב.
וַתַּבִּיט בִּי שׂוֹחֶקֶת, כְּמוֹ מִן הַבְּאֵר,
וַנֵּדַע כִּי סִיַּמְנוּ הַקְּרָב.
וַתַּבִּיט בִּי שׂוֹחֶקֶת כְּמוֹ מִן הַבְּאֵר,
וַיֵּרַח עָלֵינוּ הוֹרֵם כְּמוֹ נֵר.

Each of Alterman's books marks a distinct phase in his poetic develop-ment. The overloaded imagery, rich dissonant rhymes, and leaping, elliptic composition of *The Stars Outside* (1938) were followed by the relatively con-trolled language and composition of the poems in *The Joy of the Poor* (1941), a cycle regarded by some as Alterman's major work. He achieved even greater simplicity of language and imagery in a series of ballad-like poems written in the early forties (subsequently published in *The City of the Dove*, 1958). The poems of this period are concerned with themes of enlarged scope, often of a moral or existential nature. They are less involved in complicated and un-realistic metaphors. The images are basic, often "universal"; the composition symmetrical; the rhymes exact. There is a folklore-like, semiballadic strain in the tone and in the symbolism of the verse.

The monologue of the dead "Foundling" is in many ways characteristic of Alterman's work at this period:

(1) *At the foot of the fence my mother placed me,* (2) *[My] face creased and still. On [my] back.* (3) *And I looked at her from below, as from a well,—* (4) *Un-til she fled as one flees from a battle.* (5) *And I looked at her from below, as from a well,* (6) *And a moon was raised over us like a candle.*

(7) *But before the dawn lighted, that same night,* (8) *I got up slowly, for the time had come* (9) *And I returned to my mother's home like a rolling ball* (10) *Which comes back to the feet of the one who kicked it.* (11) *And I returned to my mother's home like a rolling ball* (12) *And I embraced her neck with hands of shadow.*

(13–14) *In the sight of the Almighty she tore me off her neck like a leech.* (15) *But when night returned, I returned to her as on the day before,* (16) *And this became our custom (law):* (17) *When night returns I return to her as on the day before* (18) *And night after night she bows to the recompense (retaliation) and to the yoke.*

(19) *And the doors of her dream are wide open to me,* (20) *And there is no-body in that dream but me.* (21) *For the love of our souls has remained taut* (22) *As a bow, from the day of my birth.* (23) *For the love of our souls has remained taut* (24) *And it can never be given nor taken.*

(25) *And therefore until the (very) end, God did not remove me* (26) *From my parent's screaming heart.* (27) *And I—who had been pulled away without being weaned—* (28) *Have not (ever) been weaned (found release) and shall (ever) pull away.* (29) *And I who had been pulled away without being weaned* (30) *Enter her house and lock the gate.*

(31) She grew old in my prison and (grew) lean and (grew) small (32) And her face became creased as my face. (33) Then my small hands clothed her in white (34) Like a mother clothing her living child. (35) Then my small hands clothed her in white (36) And I carried her (off) without telling her where.

(37) And at the foot of the fence I placed her (38) Watchful and still, on (her) back. (39) And she looked at me laughing, as from a well, (40) And we knew that we ended the battle. (41) And she looked at me laughing, as from a well. (42) And a moon was raised over us like a candle.

There are immutable ties such as those between mother and child, which "can never be given nor taken" (24). A mother may abandon her infant, helpless, "on its back" (2), at the foot of a fence (1), but it will live on in her imagination and rule her dreams: so long as she is alive, she will carry her unweaned baby within her.

In Alterman's ballad, this basic psychological situation is dramatically inverted: it is the dead foundling who is the active participant in the relationship. He who was never weaned (28) imprisons her in his world, punishes her for having transgressed elementary, superhuman laws. He who was never a *gamúl*, "a weaned child," inflicts the *gmul*, the "punishment" or "recompense" (18).

The nightly "yoke" (18) is forcibly expressed in the unrelenting repetition of the infant's return, in simile after simile, stanza after stanza. And the "recompense" (18) is fully realized in the total reversal of roles (stanzas 6, 7): the mother becomes creased and small until she assumes the attributes of the infant of the first stanza—white shrouds instead of white swaddling clothes (33–34). Now she too is released: she looks at him "laughing" (39)—and the battle is ended.

The vocabulary of this forceful ballad is extremely simple. (In fact, most of the words appear in a list of basic Hebrew, and about half of them belong to the 400 words most commonly used in contemporary Hebrew.) Syntactic units and lines are parallel in each stanza. The anapestic pattern is unusually regular and it is emphasized by the absence of feminine rhymes. The variation usually achieved in Hebrew by alternating feminine and masculine rhymes is replaced here by alternating the length of the line: 4–3–4–3–(4–4) anapests— a common device of folk songs.

"The Foundling" relies upon direct, elementary similes (there are hardly any metaphors), simple diction, conventional meter and rhymes. But the fantastic realism of the framework and the paradox and fatality of the inverted dramatic situation endow the basic images with the value of symbols, in the best tradition of folk poetry.

The Mole   הַחֹלֶד

One of the major works of modern Hebrew poetry, *The Joy of the Poor* is a complex of 31 poems, loosely linked by a developing pattern of motifs, basic symbolic situations, and related elements of language and of imagery. Although the total effect is kaleidoscopic (recalling the genre of Eliot's *Waste Land* or Rilke's *Duino Elegies*), the settings are restrained in color and detail, the vocabulary simple and suggestive, often echoing familiar word-patterns in the Bible (especially Ecclesiastes and Lamentations) and in the Prayerbook. An almost imperceptible thread of plot runs through the work, which is extremely varied in strophic and metrical forms.

Though it would be of course impossible to give an idea of the impact of *The Joy of the Poor* as a whole, a few remarks may serve to outline the background of "The Mole," which is taken from the first sequence.

The book opens with a series of poems spoken by a dead lover to his living beloved. He is at first characterized as "the poor one who is like a dead one"— *ani kemét*, patterned on a well-known proverb: *ani hasúv Kemét*, "the poor are (as good) as dead." He is "poor" in his lack of materiality. The unreal setting, which endows the most conventional themes with remarkable resonance, establishes the book's central ideas: the indestructibleness of spiritual values, especially of those non-rational ties between lovers and friends, parents and children, that subsist beyond death.

As in "The Foundling," the metaphor of the dead being alive in the thoughts of the living is dramatically realized and the situation inverted: it is the dead, no longer destructible, who voice the "joy of the poor." In a later poem, when the city is besieged, the dead man is the only one who, in the guise of the "alien," can pass through the gates. He is "the witness" and he is the guardian of memory.

The Mole

לֹא לַהֶבֶל נִשְׁבַּעְתִּי לָךְ אֹמֶן.		Not for naught (for vanity) have I vowed to be faithful to you [lit. faithfulness].
לֹא לַשָּׁוְא עֲקֵבַיִךְ אָשׁוּף.		Not in vain do I assault your heels.
עִם הַחֹלֶד חָתַרְתִּי מֵעֹמֶק,	3	With the mole I burrowed (strove) from the deep,
וְכָמוֹהוּ עִקֵּשׁ וְכָשׁוּף.		And, like him, stubborn and charmed (enchanted).

אַתְּ עֶצֶב רָאשֵׁי הַמַּקְרִיחַ,

אַתְּ יְגוֹן צִפָּרְנַי הַגְּדוֹלוֹת,

אַתְּ שִׁמְעֵנִי בְּנֶפֶץ הַטִּיחַ,

בַּחֲרוֹק הָרִצְפָּה בַּלֵּילוֹת.

You are the sorrow of my balding head,

You are the grief of my big (finger) nails,

7   (You,) listen to me in the cracking of plaster,

(In) the creaking of the floor at night.

מוּל מַרְאָה מְשֻׁבֶּצֶת בִּנְחֹשֶׁת,

מִתְנוֹעֵעַ נֵרֵךְ הָאֶבְיוֹן.

הַהוֹלְכִים אֶל פָּנַיִךְ בַּחֹשֶׁךְ

בָּךְ צָפוּ מִכְּתָלִים וְחֶבְיוֹן.

Your poor (humble) candle sways

Facing a mirror inlaid with copper.

11   Those going toward your face in the dark

Watched you from walls and from hiding (-place).

וּבְצֵאתִי לְגָנְבֵךְ כְּשִׁבֹּלֶת,

סִנְוְרֵנִי הַנֵּר בְּהִלּוֹ,

וְנוֹתַרְנוּ אֲנִי וְהַחֹלֶד

חֲשֵׁכִים וְסְמוּרִים לְמוּלוֹ.

And when I went forth to steal you as [if you were] an ear of wheat

The candle blinded me with its brightness,

15   And we remained (alone), the mole and I,

Dark and bristling against it [the candle].

*   *   *   *

לֹא לַהֶבֶל נִשְׁבַּעְתִּי לָךְ אֵמֻן

וּבְצַר לִי גֵּו־אֶרֶץ אָשׁוּף.

אֶל חַיַּיִךְ כָּלִיתִי מֵעֹמֶק,

כִּי הַחַי הוּא כִּשּׁוּף עַל כִּשּׁוּף.

Not for naught (vanity) did I vow to be faithful to you

And in my distress I assault the body of the earth.

19   For I longed for your life from the deep,

For the living is (a) spell upon spell (charm upon charm).

תִּמְהוֹנִית אַתְּ! רְאִי מַה נִּלְעַגְתִּי

מַה שִׁנַּנְתִּי לֶכְתֵּךְ וְעָמְדֵךְ.

גַּם עַל קַט וְטָפֵל לֹא דִלַּגְתִּי,

גַּם חָרַדְתִּי מִגִּיל בַּעֲדֵךְ.

You are my amazement! See how ludicrous I became,

How I rehearsed (learned by heart) your walking and your standing.

23   Nor did I skip (even the) trifling and (the) paltry,

(And) I also trembled with joy for you.

מִסְּבִיבֵךְ מַחֲשַׁבְתִּי מְהַלֶּכֶת,

מַחֲשַׁבְתִּי מְסַמֶּרֶת הָעוֹר,

עַל נְזִיד־הַפָּרוּר וְהַלֶּחֶם

וְהַנֵּר שֶׁיַּסְפִּיק לְמָאוֹר.

Roundabout you my thought (concern) stalks,

My thought which bristles the skin,

27   [My thought of] the pottage of the pan and the bread [idiomatic for "a modest meal"],

And the candle that should suffice for light.

The relationship between the dead lover and his living beloved is radically complex. On the one hand, he urges her to join him, which means to die: the "Day of Joy," as he says in the opening poem, will be the day of her burial. On the other hand, he wants her to continue to live; it is he who "defends" her from hunger and poverty in the besieged city.

The image of the dead lover undergoes constant transformations. The persistent lover, who awaits her in death, becomes the "alien," the "foreigner"—the only one who can care for her in the besieged city, "for the living cannot save the living." The lover who swears to avenge her upon her enemies, as he listens to her sobbing through the window panes, becomes the "vulture," the "man of eyes," crazed with jealousy, forever shouting "My wife, my wife!" In "The Mole" he comes even closer: he is present in her room, blind but stubbornly striving to reach her from the depths:

(1) *Not for naught (for vanity) have I vowed to be faithful to you* [lit. *faithfulness*]. (2) *Not in vain do I assault your heels.* (3) *With the mole I burrowed (strove) from the deep,* (4) *And, like him, stubborn and charmed (enchanted).*

The opening words, *lo lahével,* link the first and last lines of the book, paraphrasing and insistently denying the dictum of Ecclesiastes: *havél havalím, hakól hével,* "Vanity of vanities; all is vanity." Obviously this denial, coming from the mouth of a dead speaker, is more than ambiguous. Moreover, the atmosphere of violence and destruction in which the book is steeped, and the lover's longing for a "joy of doom" and for her death, give his repeated negation a very special significance. The second line of "The Mole," using the rare verb *ashúf* ("I shall oppress [bruise])," reinforces the motifs of darkness-death, vigilance-vengeance, by alluding to God's curse upon the serpent, in Genesis 3:15 ("it shall bruise *[yeshufhá]* thy head, and thou shall bruise *[teshufénu]* his heel"), and to the verse in Psalms 139:11 ("surely the darkness shall cover me" *[yeshuféni]*).

The setting of the poem is now established and the major "characters" are introduced: the dead lover is like a mole (4) and he also burrows and strives with the mole (3). The two are interchangeable. The second stanza evokes both the changes taking place in the body of the dead and the physical appearance of a mole:

(5) *You are the sorrow of my balding head,* (6) *You are the grief of my big (finger) nails,* (7) *(You,) listen to me in the cracking of plaster,* (8) *(In) the creaking of the floor at night.*

The inverted reality of the poem is now supported by a scene from folklore and folk-belief: (10) *Your poor (humble) candle sways* (9) *Facing a mirror inlaid with copper.* (11) *Those going toward your face in the dark,* (12) *Watched you from walls and from hiding (-place).*

The woman is absorbed in an act of divination: she is summoning the dead. But the light of the candle defends her from the darkness and is also a symbol of her life. Elsewhere the lover, in the guise of the "alien," says: "And on the verge of doom, I shall extinguish you like a candle." This is the paradox underlying the image of the candle in the last stanza of the prelude to "The Mole":

(13) *And when I went forth to steal you as [if you were] an ear of wheat* (14) *The candle blinded me with its brightness,* (15) *And we remained (alone), the mole and I,* (16) *Dark and bristling against it [the candle].*

In the next section, the various motifs are developed and almost all the lines of the prelude are repeated, in different order and in contexts which transform their meaning:

וַאֲנִי הַגּוֹחֵן אֶל יָדַיִךְ,		And I (am the one) who stoops over your arms,
מְיֻגָּע וְזָקֵן כְּאִמֵּךְ.		Tired and old like your mother.
וְנוֹשֵׂא אֶת עָנְיֵךְ וּמְרוּרַיִךְ	31	And I [am the one] who carries your poverty and wretchedness
בְּלִי מִפְלָט וּמָנוֹחַ מִמֵּךְ.		Without refuge or respite from you.
אַתְּ עַצֶּבֶת רֹאשִׁי הַמַּקְרִיחַ,		You are the sorrow of my balding head,
אַתְּ יְגוֹן צִפָּרְנַי הַגְּדוֹלוֹת,		You are the grief of my big finger) nails,
טָרְדָתִי הַכְּבֵדָה מֵהִשָּׁכֵחַ,	35	My anxiety (burden)—too heavy to be forgotten,
מוּעֶקֶת הִרְהוּרַי בַּלֵּילוֹת.		The distress (oppression) of my mediations (thoughts) at night.
כִּי נִשְׁבֶּרֶת הִנָּךְ כְּשִׁבֹּלֶת		Because you break like an ear of wheat
וְצָרֵינוּ עוֹמְדִים עַל תִּלָּם,		And our enemies persist [lit. stand on their mound]
וְנוֹתַרְנוּ אֲנִי וְהַחֹלֶד	39	And (only) the mole and I remained
חֲשֵׁכִים וּסְמוּרִים לְמוּלָם.		Dark and bristling facing them.
וּבְמַרְאָה מְשֻׁבֶּצֶת בִּנְחֹשֶׁת		And in a mirror inlaid with copper
מִתְנוֹעֵעַ הַנֵּר הַלּוֹחֵךְ.		The flickering candle sways.
אַתְּ רוֹאָה אֶת פָּנֵינוּ מֵחֹשֶׁךְ,	43	You see our faces from the dark
וְיוֹדַעַת כִּי לֹא נִשְׁכָּחֵךְ.		And you know that we shall not forget you.

כִּי חֲצוּי הָעוֹלָם, כִּי הוּא שְׁנָיִם,

For the world is split, for it [the world] is two

וּכְפוּלָה הִיא הֶמְיַת מִסְפֵּדוֹ,

And the clamor of its lament is double,

כִּי אֵין בַּיִת בְּלִי מֵת עַל כַּפַּיִם,   47

For there is no home without a dead [one] on [its] arms,

וְאֵין מֵת שֶׁיִּשְׁכַּח אֶת בֵּיתוֹ.

And there is no dead [one] who forgets his home.

וּבְלִי קֵץ אֶל עָרֵי נְכָאֵינוּ

And endlessly, the dwellers of darkness and mound

יוֹשְׁבֵי חֹשֶׁךְ וְתֵל נִבָּטִים.

look out at the cities of our sorrows.

נִפְלָאִים, נִפְלָאִים הֵם חַיֵּינוּ,   51

Wonderful, wonderful are our lives,

הַמְּלֵאִים מַחֲשָׁבוֹת שֶׁל מֵתִים.

Which are full of the thoughts of the dead.

(17) *Not for naught (vanity) did I vow to be faithful to you* (18) *And in my distress I assault the body of the earth.* (19) *For I longed for your life from the deep,* (20) *For the living is (a) spell upon spell (charm upon charm).*

(21) *You are my amazement! See how ludicrous I became,* (22) *How I rehearsed (learned by heart) your walking and your standing.* (23) *Nor did I skip (even the) trifling and (the) paltry,* (24) *(And) I also trembled with joy for you.*

(25) *Roundabout you my thought (concern) stalks,* (26) *My thought which bristles the skin,* (27) *[My thought of] the pottage of the pan and the bread* [idiomatic for "a modest meal"], (28) *And the candle that should suffice for light.*

(29) *And I (am the one) who stoops over your arms,* (30) *Tired and old like your mother.* (31) *And I [am the one] who carries your poverty and wretchedness* (32) *Without refuge or respite from you.*

(33) *You are the sorrow of my balding head,* (34) *You are the grief of my big (finger) nails,* (35) *My anxiety (burden)—too heavy to be forgotten,* (36) *The distress (oppression) of my meditations (thoughts) at night.*

(37) *Because you break like an ear of wheat* (38) *And our enemies persist* [lit. *stand on their mound*] (39) *And (only) the mole and I remained* (40) *Dark and bristling facing them.*

(41) *And in a mirror inlaid with copper* (42) *The flickering candle sways.* (43) *You see our faces from the dark* (44) *And you know that we shall not forget you.*

The point of view has changed. Now it is not the dead (4) who is "enchanted" (*kasúf*) but the living who weaves an unbreakable spell (*kisúf*). The pursuer (2) becomes first a protector (21–30) and then one who is pursued (31–36). Whereas he was dark and bristling (16), now it is his unrelenting concern, his "thought," that makes the woman's flesh bristle (26). The lover-mole went forth to steal her as though she were a stalk of wheat (13); but the stalk of wheat is fragile and must now be protected from the powerful unnamed enemies (38).

The last two stanzas formulate one of Alterman's basic themes: (45) *For the world is split, for it [the world] is two* (46) *And the clamor of its lament is double,* (47) *For there is no home without a dead [one] on [its] arms,* (48) *And there is no dead [one] who forgets his home.*

(49–50) *And endlessly, the dwellers of darkness and mound look out at the cities of our sorrows.* (51) *Wonderful, wonderful are our lives,* (52) *Which are full of the thoughts of the dead.*

When *The Joy of the Poor* was written Europe was occupied by the Germans, the first signs of the approaching holocaust were reaching Palestine. The German army was on the threshold of Egypt. The book does not refer directly to these events, but their presence is clearly felt, especially in the second part, where the personal situation is enlarged and transformed into a social one. In "The Mole" there is only the barest intimation of the larger, perhaps national, ramifications of the theme: there is no force to oppose the "enemies" other than the imaginary forces of darkness—the dead lover and the mole. The seeds of the larger metaphor are, however, already present. "The Underground" that will defy the enemy later in the book is already hinted at in the attributes of the unreal figures here burrowing in the deep (the verb *határti*, "I burrowed, strove," [3] becomes the noun *mahtéret*, "underground," which serves as the title of a poem toward the climax of the volume).

ABBA KOVNER

Opening

פְּתִיחָה

בְּאֵרוֹת־קְדוּמִים נְקֻוּוֹת לִפְתַּע בָּעֵינַיִם
כָּל נַהֲרוֹת דָּמֵי עָרִים כְּפוּלֵי־אָפִיק.
וְלֵב נָעוּל אָז. מִצֵּאת. מָבוֹא. מִגֶּשֶׁת.
וְרַק שִׁכְשׁוּךְ שֶׁל מַיִם אַדִּירִים וְקוֹל עַתִּיק:

אַל תִּפְסַע, רֵעִי, מוּזָרוֹת רַגְלֵינוּ כָּאן

וְהוּא, רֵעִי, פּוֹסֵעַ. וְרַגְלֵינוּ - מְיֻתָּרוֹת.

הִנֵּה צְעָדֵינוּ כְּבִים. לֹא אַתָּה הוּא כָּאן

הַהֵלֶךְ־הַגָּדוֹל, רֵעִי -

פָּשַׁט רֵעִי חֲפָנָיו, רַכַּן, מַגַּע כַּפּוֹת

וְהָאֲדָמָה בָּאָה.

עֲדָרִים־עֲדָרִים מְהַמָּה הִיא אֶת רַגְלֶיךָ

בְּאוֹר בּוֹזֵז. וְרַגְלָיו נוֹתְבוֹת־וְלֹא־נוֹתְבוֹת.

"רֵעִי, נָפַל" – אוֹ־אָז כָּלָה תָּבוֹא

בְּגֵל אֶל זְרוֹעוֹתֶיךָ

הָאֲדָמָה הַזֹּאת.

Born in the Crimea in 1918, Abba Kovner grew up in Vilna, where he was graduated from a modern Hebrew *gymnasium* and became a student at a Polish university. He played a leading role in a Zionist youth movement, while also devoting himself to sculpture and to Hebrew poetry. In 1943 he assumed command of the United Partisan Organization of the Vilna ghetto, and when the ghetto fell and small groups broke through to the forests, he served as the commander of the Jewish "Vengeance" battalion. Not long after the defeat of Germany, he settled in a kibbutz in Palestine (1946), only to take up arms again, in the War of Independence.

As one would expect, Kovner's poetry is interwoven with his tragic and heroic experiences as a fighter in Europe and in Israel. His long modernist poems attempt a fusion of personal and historical materials in the broad genre of Alexander Blok's "The Twelve." "Until-No-Light" ("Ad-Lo-Or," 1947) recreates in lyric-dramatic narrative the life of the partisans in the forests and swamps. "The Key Drowned" ("*Ha-maftéah Tsalál*," 1951) gives symbolic expression to the tragedy of the ghetto fighters who knew they could not save the mass of the people then clinging to life and unwilling to believe they were doomed.

The War of Independence, however, provides the specific background for Kovner's prose trilogy *Face to Face (Panim el Panim*, 1953) and the verse sequence entitled *A Parting from the South (Pridá Mehadaróm*, 1949). Varied in tone and theme, the latter projects a complex vision of the Israeli War of Independence, unified by recurring images and leitmotifs, through the perspective of a soldier's experiences.

"Opening," the second poem in the section "Night March" in *A Parting from the South*, revolves on the double confrontation of the soldier: with death and with the strange desert. The antiquity of the landscape, echoing, as it does, a national past, suddenly overwhelms the intruder:

(1) *Wells of old gather suddenly in the eyes* (2) *All the rivers of my blood are alert in double [river] beds.* (3) *And the heart is then locked. Nothing shall go out of it, nothing come into it, nothing approach it. [lit. From leaving. From entering. From approaching].* (4) *And only the clamor of mighty waters and an ancient voice.*

The soldier's eyes are flooded by "wells of old"—*beerót kdumim*, an expression patterned on *náhal kdumim*, "rivers of mold," from Deborah's war song (Judges 5:21)—much as the dry desert rivers of the Negev are suddenly overrun by powerful streams from the mountains. By the use of the word *afík* ("river bed," 2) the image is placed in its traditional context, for it clearly recalls the simile of Psalm 126:4: "Turn again our captivity, O Lord, as the streams (*afikím*) in the Negev (South)."

The awakened "rivers of blood" (2) move in both directions: to and from the heart, but they are double in another sense also; they now stream here as once they streamed "there."

The sudden surge of "ancient wells," the alerted "rivers of blood," virtually place the heart in a state of siege: cut off from the outside world—within and without at the same time—belonging and not belonging—it can only listen to a warning voice from the past. The clamor of "mighty waters" (4)—again a biblical phrase; from Moses' victory song (Exodus 15:10)—and the "ancient voice" *both* seem to rise from within the depths of the speaker, addressing himself and at the same time describing his own reactions. (In the Hebrew, the poet speaks to himself in the second person and of himself in the third.)

(5) *Don't step, my friend, our feet are strange (alien) here* (6) *And he, my friend, steps. And our feet—[are] superfluous.* (7) *Here (now) our footsteps are being extinguished. You are not the one here [who is]* (8) *The great walker (wanderer), my friend—* (9) *My friend stretched forward the hollows of his hands, bent down, a touching of palms* (10) *AND THE EARTH CAME [toward him].*

The ancient voice, welling up from the individual and historical depths of the soldier-speaker, warns him that he is alien to this unchanging landscape that "extinguishes" his steps and those of his comrades as water extinguishes fire. This desert earth, in the image of the "great walker-wanderer," streams constantly under his ephemeral steps; he is transient and he is an intruder. In

an attempt to make the earth respond to him, to create actual, physical contact, he "stretches forth his palms" (9)—*pashát yad* also means "to beg"—to
the earth.

(11) *Herd upon herd, she* [the earth] *murmurs softly about your feet* (12)
With plundering light. And his feet [both] *trace and do not trace* [a path]. (13)
"My friend, we shall fall"—Oh then ALL OF HER [the earth] *shall come* (14) *In
a wave to your arms:* (15) *This earth.*

The moving "herds" of sand dunes, upon which the speaker is borne, enfold his steps with a constant soft rush of light. Kovner produces a striking
effect here (11) by using the intransitive verb *hamá* (denoting a soft, longing sound, as of pigeons) in a transitive manner—the sense is that the earth
enfolds, covers your feet with a soft noise, envelops them in soft sound. But
this is done with a "plundering light"—a light that overwhelms the speaker's
very existence, threatening him with extinction. In this light, his feet leave
hardly any imprint upon the ground (12)—and here, again, Kovner produces
an unusual image in the word "trace": a neologism made from the noun *nativ*,
"path"; literally "he paths and does not path."

This fear of personal annihilation, of leaving no trace, is voiced abruptly
by someone near the speaker, perhaps another soldier experiencing the same
anguish: "My friend, we shall fall." And the poet's reply to the sudden voice
and to himself is the poem's conclusion, both tragic and exultant. Only in
death—the first gesture, a touching of the palms (9) was not sufficient—will
this earth in her entirety, like a flooding wave or an encompassing mother—
come to one's arms.

Sounds from Nearby

צְלִילִם מִקָּרוֹב

קָנִיתִי לִבְנִי פַּעֲמוֹן קָטָן.
בְּנִי, אִטֵּר־יַד־יְמִינוֹ,
נָטַל בְּיָדוֹ אֶת הַפַּעֲמוֹן הַקָּטָן
וְצִלְצֵל בִּשְׂמֹאלוֹ.

פַּעֲמוֹנִים יֶשְׁנָם בְּכָל הָעוֹלָם.
צְפַרְדְּעִים מְקַרְקְרוֹת, לֹא לַטֶּרֶף.
כְּשֶׁבְּנִי מְצַלְצֵל בַּפַּעֲמוֹן הַקָּטָן,
נֶאֱנָחִים אַמְנוֹן־וְתָמָר עִם עֶרֶב.

וּבַלַּיְלָה רָאִיתִי יַעַר מוּזָר -
מַה יָּפוּ עֵינָיו הַנְּבֻכוֹת שֶׁל הָאַיִל!
וּמְצַלְצֵל מְצַלְצֵל פַּעֲמוֹן עַל צַוָּאר -
וְדוֹלְקוֹת אַחֲרָיו גְּדֵרוֹת־תַּיִל.

וְכָל הַכְּתָלִים אֲטוּמִים. וְהַבָּתִּים אִלְּמִים כְּמוֹ סֵפֶר.
אוּלַי שׁוֹמֵעַ הַיָּם הַכָּחֹל
אֵיךְ נוֹבֵט בָּעֲרָבָה הָאֹפֶר.

אַל תִּבְכֶּה, בְּנִי, גַּא הָיָה הָאַיִל.
צַלְצֵל בִּימִינְךָ בַּפַּעֲמוֹן הַקָּטָן -
אַתְּךְ אֲנִי, עַד לֵיל.

The first section of "Night March," from which our first Kovner poem was taken, ends upon the verge of a military attack. At this point the dramatic tension is interrupted for a slow, song-like lyric entitled "Sounds from Nearby."

Characteristically, this poem is not tightly linked to the other sections. Perhaps it recalls a short visit home between nights of combat, perhaps it echoes the reference in the poem that precedes it to the soldiers as "children of my life." Like "Opening," it has a mirage-like quality in which memories of the past clash with or fuse with the present moment.

(1) *I bought my son a little bell.* (2) *My son, left-handed [lit. whose right hand is bound]* (3) *Took the little bell in his hand* (4) *And rang with his left.*

(5) *There are bells all over the world.* (6) *Frogs croak, not for prey.* (7) *When my son rings the little bell,* (8) *Amnon and Tamar sigh as evening falls.*

The helplessness of the child deprived of the use of his right hand (2, *itér yad yeminó*, Judges 3:15) is expressed in the simplest of words. Nature echoes his innocent joy—in the voices of frogs and in the sighing of Amnon and Tamar, the biblical lovers who gave their names to the pansy.

But the naïve negation of "not for prey" (6) has already set the scene for the intrusion of another landscape—swamps, forests, partisans—of other fateful bells of which the father now tells his son:

(9) *And at night I saw a strange forest*—(10) *How beautiful were the bewildered eyes of the ram!* (11) *And a bell on the neck is ringing, ringing*—(12) *And the barbed-wire fences chase (burn) after him [the ram].*

(13) *And all the walls are opaque. And the houses are mute as a book.* (14) *Perhaps the blue sea can hear* (15) *How the ashes sprout in the desert.*

(16) *Don't cry, my son, the ram was proud.* (17) *Ring the little bell with your* RIGHT *(hand)*—(18) *I am with you, till night (falls).*

In that "strange forest" there was a hunt for prey—a Chagallian ram, the sacrificial ram of the Abraham-Isaac episode, was being pursued by fire (12) amidst indifference and treason—the indifference of a deaf world and the betrayal of words and "books," of humanist ideals (13). Note that the Hebrew word used for "chase" in line 12, in referring to the barbed-wire fences, also means "burning (*dolkót*) after him."

The two worlds—that of the burning ghetto and partisans' forests, and that of the Israeli desert in which the poem is set—now fuse into one. "Perhaps the blue sea can hear . . ."—only in this place where the desert stops at the edge of the water can the ashes of that burning sprout; moreover, the desert cannot come to life again without them.

Though helpless and doomed, the ram was not without dignity—so the soldier-father reassures his son. "I am with you, till night falls," he adds, for he cannot promise to remain longer; night is the time of combat (the next poem in the section is entitled "Battle"). But here, in the different war on the soil of their native land, the child will be ringing the bell with his right hand—the traditional symbol of power ("thy right hand hath holden me up"—Psalms 18:35; "thy right hand is full of righteousness"—Psalms 48:10; etc., etc.).

"Sounds from Nearby" is straightforward, lilting, story-like. Its simple words, elementary images, and almost helpless rhymes—*téref-érev* (6–8), *áyil-táyil-láyil* (10–12–16–18), *séfer-éfer* (13–15), etc.—contrast powerfully with the dense texture and multiple allusions of our first Kovner poem. But like all of this poet's verse, this poem is extremely difficult to approach and to discuss in isolation. Basic motifs and images—the burning ghetto; the ram who represents both the slaughtered "flock" and the proud revolt; the act of battle and death seen in erotic terms; the soldiers looked upon as babies ("faces, faces in a thousand cradles")—recur and are elaborated throughout Kovner's work, and their full impact can be grasped only in this context.

8 THE ROLE OF LANGUAGE IN CHAGALL'S EARLY PAINTINGS

In this essay, I shall explore the functions of natural language as a "secondary medium" in visual art, as it appears in the polyphonic work of Marc Chagall. Language is here part of the private "fictional world" that Chagall constructed in his paintings in counterpoint to the languages of the avant-garde. It conveys some of the images and perceptions of a local culture and carries the "thick knowledge" of a periphery that Chagall brought to the centers of modernist art. I shall focus primarily on the role of Yiddish language and literature, which have the deepest roots in his conscious world.

1 THE SEMIOTICS OF CHAGALL'S MODERNISM

Innovations in modern art and science claimed general validity and were accepted in the general canon, yet the context of their discovery was narrowly local and depended on a specific combination of national, linguistic, social, and personal forces and circumstances. The opposition between "Western European" and other cultures, as emphasized in recent criticism, may divert our attention from the fact that European culture itself has been time and again formed by an awareness of the differences among national cultures and their reciprocal oppositions, interactions, and influences.

The most prominent outsiders nestled within the European world were the Jews in their traditional, religious society. In the heart of Europe—in recent centuries, primarily Eastern and Central Europe—they maintained a religion that stood in opposition to the dominant Christianity and a culture based on the teaching and interpretation of an ever growing library of texts. Though influenced by the folklore and beliefs of their neighbors, and often multilingual (using Slavic, German, and other languages), they maintained tightly knit communities with their own social and educational network and an internal multilingualism in three languages of their own: Hebrew, Aramaic, and Yiddish. In Eastern Europe, and especially in the "Pale of Settlement" of the Russian Empire, where until 1917 over five million Jews were kept in a huge geographical ghetto (comprising most of Poland, Ukraine, Byelorussia, and Lithuania), the Jewish masses were concentrated in small towns (called *shtetls*). Two-thirds of the population of a typical *shtetl* was Jewish (67% in Chagall's family town of Lyozno), and *shtetl* life was dominated physically by a towering Church and politically by a Russian administration. It was a more or less self-contained island amid a sea of Christian villages. In the larger towns, Jews constituted half the population (52.4% in Chagall's Vitebsk), and in several big cities, about one third. It was a polka-dotted map, a powerless Jewish empire within an empire, unified by a voluntary cultural network—from the spread of authoritative books and Hasidic sects to modern ideological parties, educational systems, literature, and newspapers.

It was in this context that the Modern Jewish Revolution erupted at the end of the nineteenth and beginning of the twentieth century: a veritable explosion of modernity within one or two generations, entailing both a massive transformation of millions of Jews, and their influx into the centers of European and American culture. Jews eagerly joined the "general" modern culture in manners both extrinsic and intrinsic; while many took up the languages and entered the cultural institutions of the extant European nations, others created a European-type secular culture of their own in Hebrew and Yiddish, accepting European genres and modes of discourse and infusing them with elements transformed from the Jewish tradition. Unlike writers, however, who had to choose either an intrinsic or an extrinsic language (either I.B. Singer or Franz Kafka), painters could simultaneously participate in both.

Chagall (1887–1985) was a typical child of this Modern Jewish Revolution. He was the first of many siblings, born to religious, Yiddish-speaking parents of limited education in Vitebsk, the capital of a province or *gubernia* (in today's Byelorussia), in the Russian Pale of Settlement. He moved rapidly from Vitebsk to St. Petersburg, Paris, Berlin, Moscow, and again France, the U.S.A., and France; he lived through three Russian revolutions, two World Wars, the Holocaust, and the rebirth of Israel; he embraced modern secular Yiddish literature, the Russian language, the achievements of the Russian and French avant-gardes, as well as the tradition of earlier Christian painting. The impact of his unusual art in France and Germany was evident from the beginning: Guillaume Apollinaire, Blaise Cendrars, and Kurt Schwitters wrote poems about him before World War I, when Chagall was still in his twenties; in 1914 Herwardt Walden organized a one-man Chagall show in Berlin that strongly influenced the German Expressionists; and in later years there were major Chagall exhibits in New York, Paris, and London. Werner Haftman, a historian of twentieth-century art, has written, "We think of Chagall as the painter-poet of the twentieth century. He shares this distinction only with Paul Klee."[1]

Chagall was influenced by most of the contemporary art trends of his time. In his paintings we can find quasi-geometric articulations of forms derived from Analytic Cubism; Orphism's predilection for circles in space; a fauve-inspired exuberance for colors that overflow the boundaries of objects; the precise chromatic shapes of Suprematism; the dynamic movement and strong diagonal gestures of Futurism; pre-Expressionist deformations of human faces and figures; a dreamlike arrangement of objects in represented space, anticipating surrealism; and even minute and multiple decorative ornaments typical of the Russian *Mir Iskusstva* ("World of Art") movement from the beginning of the century. In many of his paintings, several seemingly disparate components fuse into a functional unity, often in an asymmetrical, uneasy, but ultimately justified balance, perhaps most typically in his brilliant *Introduction to the Yiddish Theater* in Moscow (1920).[2] Each painting is masterfully constructed with a dynamic interplay of several centers of gravity: in some areas of the canvas, geometrical forms are independent and conspicuous, while in others representational figures are dominant, creating a thematic and situational polyphony; in between, unrelated animals and vignettes inhabit some secondary space. The tensions between those heterogeneous forces endowed his work with its peculiar power. Often Chagall

1   Werner Haftman, *Marc Chagall* (New York: Harry N. Abrams, 1973), 7.
2   See my book *Marc Chagall and the Lost Jewish World: On the Nature of His Art and Iconography* (New York: Rizzoli International, 2006).

suggests depth, perspective, and theme, yet disrupts the continuities of space, time, and perspective. Individual figures are presented in disproportion and deformation, removed from realistic continuity, functionality, or causality, and left floating in a two-and-a-half-dimensional space. Thus the connections (or discontinuities) between his figures and objects has been perceived as enigmatic, surreal, or poetic.

Chagall rarely painted from nature. The typical Chagallian representational vocabulary is made up of modular units repeated time and again in various transformations and combinations overlapping or interrupting each other. Such units were derived from heterogeneous sources: the traditional Eastern European Jewish world with its parareligious folklore, Russian provincial life, emblems of Paris, his beloved wife Bella, his array of animals, and so on. What unifies all those elements is not coherent, logical, or representational continuity, but Chagall's own constructed biography, a world that a viewer must know to understand his paintings. Indeed, Chagall himself supplied such a text, *Mein Leben*, known in English as *My Life*.

Chagall, in other words, created his own fictional world, derived from the multicultural domains encountered in the course of his life, yet combined and unified by the accidents of his biography. Fictional worlds are typical of literary works,[3] and Chagall has often been accused of being a "literary" painter. Yet in literature, a discrete fictional world with separate characters may be created in each novel, while all his life Chagall seems to have evoked one and the same fictional world, dwelling in his "naïve" or "poetic" imagination. The represented domains themselves appear in grotesque or ironic distortions, enabling a retrospective look homeward that is nostalgic, yet not, until late in his career, sentimental. Over time, the repeated representations transform them into a private language of art, acting in counterpoint with formal devices drawn from the prevalent languages of modernism. This was well understood by Chagall's friend in Paris, the poet Cendrars. In his poem about Chagall, he wrote:

Suddenly he paints
He takes a church and paints with a church
He takes a cow and paints with a cow

---

3   See Tomas Pavel, *Fictional Worlds* (Harvard University Press, 1986) and my "Fictionality and Fields of Reference," *Poetics Today* 5 (1984): 227–51.

With a sardine
With heads, hands, knives
He paints with a bull's pizzle
He paints with all the four passions of a little Jewish city
With all the heightened sexuality of provincial Russia.[4]

Chagall rarely added new elements to his basic vocabulary, yet when his own fictional world was exhausted (partly by repetition, and partly by its disappearance into the past), he resorted to the fictional worlds of literature, illustrating Gogol, Abraham Lyesin, La Fontaine, or the Bible. In his own fictional world, however, figures become more and more stenographic, emblematic, and sentimental; exuberant colors take over, the tension between the painterly and the representational forces disappears, and he loses his edge. Chagall becomes predominantly a colorist.

In sum, Chagall responded to modernism in painting by employing cubist, surrealist, Suprematist, and fauvist principles and techniques, but restrained their dominance with the counterweight of his fictional, symbolically representational world. Thus, on the one hand, realism was subverted and deformed, while, on the other hand, formalism was harnessed to poetic and social representation. A similar tension between those two forces has given life and eclectic—or polyphonic—originality to Latin American modern painting and fiction. Indeed, this complex and rich style may be seen as eclectic in a negative sense only from the point of view of an ideal of purity, or one might say, the poverty of purity. Chagall may not have invented his individual stylistic features, but he did invent the treatment of human figures, the gravity and social (dis)continuity, the multicentered composition, and the language of his modular fictional world.

Understanding the semiotics of Chagall's art enables us to see the importance of his cultural background not just for the biography of the painter as a person, but for the understanding of his paintings. If a substantial part of his language of art is drawn from a fictional world, the components of this world are essential to reading his art. Chagall never intended to be an exclusively "Jewish" artist, but an artist in the European and modernist sense of the word. The lost world of Eastern European Jewish folk life was part

---

4   Blaise Cendrars, "Portrait" (October 1913), in *Selected Writings of Blaise Cendrars*, ed. Walter Albert (New York: New Directions, 1966).

of the material with which he molded his paintings; it reflected the earliest layers of his consciousness and provided the concrete and unique substance of his fictional world and surreal moods. From this base, he reached out to modern Yiddish literature, themes from contemporary Jewish history, and the "universal" Bible. Just as Faulkner's or Joyce's origins do not make them provincial, exclusively southern or Irish writers respectively, but provide the rich specificity in which their universal art is embedded, the social locus of their fictional worlds, so does Chagall's Jewish background. Though Chagall's use of cultural connotations that are rooted in Jewish literature and folklore has often been discussed in recent criticism, treatment of it has been marred by misunderstandings and ignorance, for even fine scholars do not know to what extent that world and its language have disappeared into history.

2   NATURAL LANGUAGE IN MODERN ART

As is well known, the effect of a painting is dependent not just on the immediate impression produced by its own painterly language, but also on natural language, narrative knowledge, and the semiotics of culture. Some of these elements are indicated in the painting itself, while others are part of its wider context. A painting is created in a cultural, and yet at the same time private, chamber of resonance: and when that chamber of resonance is no longer common to our whole culture, we have to reconstruct the particular chamber of each artist in order to "read" his work.

The role of natural language in the reading of painting can take on several different forms:

(1) Language describing the ideology or poetics of art. The dependence of paintings on their declarative poetics became crucial in the various trends of modernism; we have to read the manifestos and theoretical writings of the painters and their peers, or the theories constructed from these texts, to be guided in our mode of "reading" the actual art objects.

(2) Language describing the nature of the represented world. In Chagall, our understanding is guided by the knowledge of his own constructed biography and those domains of Eastern European life he evokes.

(3) Language as a secondary medium or a subtext attached to specific paintings or their details. Marcel Duchamp's *The Bride Stripped Bare By Her Bachelors, Even* makes little sense without the specific texts he jotted down

for this work.[5] It is clearly a two-tiered work of art, where the primary medium is painting and the secondary is a specific written text, including its variants, crossed-out versions, and accompanying drawings. Though these are less moving, and operate only behind the scenes, they guide the signification of the visual units and inform the entire work of art. In Chagall, subtexts of this kind are provided by idioms, proverbs, dead metaphors, and literary images of Yiddish language and literature. His private fictional world draws on collective stereotypes, and Yiddish culture represents that collective consciousness.

(4) Language incorporated in the paintings themselves. In many modern paintings, pieces of words and texts appear, often deformed or extracted from their normal context and everyday purposes. These fulfill many functions: they represent the textual nature of modern culture in general, the plethora of words surrounding us; they signal the crossing of the boundaries of visual art and language art, painting and textuality; they represent two-dimensional surfaces, along with wallpaper, thus motivating the foregrounding of the two-dimensional canvas; and they serve well in collages, representing the daily, journalistic, practical, or political world, as tram tickets do in Kurt Schwitters' work. They may also serve specific thematic functions in each concrete case, either referring to another object on the canvas, providing a title for the painting as a whole, teasing its topics with contradictory meanings, or alluding to another text and its denotations.

Chagall was an early practitioner of language use in paintings, and a variegated and prolific one. Since his late teens, Chagall tried to assimilate the Russian language and culture, and later the French. Yet he lived in a Yiddish-speaking world at least until the age of twenty-eight (1887–1915), and then again in Moscow in 1920–22, and in New York in 1941–48. He also communicated and corresponded in Yiddish with Yiddish writers throughout his life and wrote poems, essays, and speeches in Yiddish. From an early age, he absorbed its imagery in his conscious and subconscious mind, absorbing with it the foundations of his fictional world. He read the classics of Yiddish literature, and in Yiddish he read the Bible. These cultural sources combined in his work with his subsequently acquired Russian and French languages and painterly models, yet his linguistic base was in popular Jewish culture.

5   See *The Bride Stripped Bare By Her Bachelors, Even: A Typographical Version by Richard Hamilton* (New York: Jaap Rietman Inc., 1960).

3   YIDDISH IDIOMS AND STEREOTYPES

Many seemingly unreal scenes and gestures in Chagall's paintings can be ex-plained by the use of Yiddish idioms and proverbs,[6] as well as by archetypes developed in modern Yiddish literature. In his memoirs, written in 1922–23 and first published in Yiddish in 1925, Chagall writes that his mother told him "just now" (she died in 1916) about her father, who had disappeared years be-fore on holiday. They searched for him everywhere, and "it turned out that in the nice weather he climbed on the roof, sat on the chimney [sic!], and ate *tsimes* [Jewish sweet carrot stew]." Chagall adds: "Not a bad picture." Cha-gall domesticated the fantastic situations of his paintings in events that pre-sumably happened in his own life. Some critics have taken him seriously and thereby made him into a realist, defusing the surrealist effects of his work. Yet Chagall himself knew perfectly well that his grandfather in the story had en-acted "not a bad picture"—the picture is primary—and added: "And perhaps I dreamt it all" (i.e., the event, the *tsimes*, and mother's story, too).[7] Chagall made a drawing of his grandfather's story that was published in the album *Mein Leben* by Paul Cassirer in Berlin (fig. 1). In a later lithograph, moreover, he embedded this drawing in a frame being painted by young Chagall in a clown's uniform, with his head half inside the white drawing, half outside, in the blue frame (fig. 2).[8] Most important, Chagall had already placed a man on the edge of a roof (prototype of the "fiddler on the roof") many years earlier, in *The Dead Man* (fig. 3). For Chagall, his grandfather's story demonstrates the strain of positive craziness and creative freedom that ran in the family. All three works, moreover, present a realization of the Yiddish idiom *meshugener, arop fun dakh!* (you're crazy, get off the roof!)—a phrase that is said to some-one who is not on a roof at all but who "climbed high" only metaphorically,

6   This issue was known in Chagall reception from the beginning, especially in Yiddish criti-cism: see Chone Shmeruk, "Marc Chagall and the Moscow Yiddish Chamber Theater" (in Yiddish), *Di Goldene keyt* 137 (1994). Chagall himself wrote in his Yiddish autobiography, "I turn around and see my painting where people are 'outside of themselves.'" Ziva Amishai-Maisels ("Chagall's Jewish In-Jokes," *Journal of Jewish Art* 5 [1978]: 76–93) raised the issue in a systematic manner; there are, however, many mistakes and omissions in her reading of the Yiddish and unacceptable allegorizations. It is also not clear why the central images of a culture should be called "in-jokes."

7   Marc Chagall, *My Life* (New York: Orion Press, 1960), 13. Another version appears in Marc Chagall, "eygens: autobiografye" (From my own world: Autobiography), *tsukunft* 30 (1925): 160.

8   This image appears in Julien Cain, *The Lithographs of Chagall*, vol. 1 (Monte Carlo: André Sauret, 1960), 27.

someone who is not clinically insane but pursues an unrealistic, unattainable, or absurd idea.

An idiom is a fixed cluster of words, some or all of which have lost their independent meanings, while the whole means something more and often very different from the sum of its components.[9] Like a dead metaphor, an idiom incorporates a frozen figurative situation or its derivative (e.g., only a crazy man would sit on a sharp-edged roof; hence, if you think or say such-and-such, you must be crazy; get off the roof!). When we use an idiom, we may even visualize or contemplate its figural aspects or imagery, though they have no ontological status in the real world; but when we think of its general meaning, we do so with reference to a given situation. In contrast, a realization of an idiom in literature or painting inverts this relationship: what was a mere expression in language becomes a real object or event in the presented world (a man actually sits on a roof). The image now denotes, while the idiomatic meaning (he's crazy) has become merely a potential connotation. Figurative language is replaced by immediate objects. But when placed in the presented "reality," such objects or events are often out of place, creating an unrealistic, grotesque, or poetic fictional world, as in Kafka's famous metaphor of a person becoming an insect. Literature and art of this sort are not metaphorical; they transfer metaphorically from the level of style to the fictional world itself, and by so doing, make it "irrational," "surrealistic," "fantastic."

To return to the crazy man on the roof: in Yiddish the world for crazy, *meshugener*, is often used as a positive epithet, a warm appellation with affectionate connotations of idiosyncrasy, unpredictability, and creativity. This polysemy (which includes a tension between craziness and creativity) is based on the biblical *meshuga ish ha-ruah* (crazy is the man of spirit, i.e., the inspired person, the prophet; "The prophet is a fool, the spiritual man is mad." [Hos. 9:7]) and on the proximity of *shigóen* (craziness) and *góen* (genius), in Yiddish (Hebrew-derived). Genius is even phonetically embedded in craziness (in every *shigóen* lies a *góen*), supporting the popular belief that genes of craziness and of genius run in the same family. And other idiomatic expressions further complicate the painting's allusions: If somebody tells you a lie or an absurd and unbelievable story, you may retort in Yiddish, *a ku iz gefloygn ibern dakh* ("a cow flew over the roof," meaning, "Sure!" "Get real!"); or in

---

9   An excellent study of the theory of idioms, including many Yiddish examples, is Uriel Weinreich's "Problems in the Analysis of Idioms," in his *On Semantics* (Philadelphia: University of Pennsylvania Press, 1980), 208–264.

full: *a ku iz gefloygn ibern dakh un geleygt an ey* ("a cow flew over the roof and laid an egg").[10] All three works, in other words, include a gesture that subverts the realist continuity and social functionality of a world that is, nonetheless, very "real" in the painter's memory.

The famous painting *Over Vitebsk* (fig. 4) features a Jew hovering above the buildings and churches of the city. He is the embodiment of the fantastic *luftmentshen* (people of the air), created in Yiddish literature by Mendele Moykher Sforim and Sholem-Aleichem: they are people who have no income from productive work and live "on air" as well as "in the air," with no ground under their feet, unlike a healthy nation rooted in its own soil. This expression became a key image of self-criticism of the Jewish diaspora existence in most Jewish ideologies, from Zionist to Socialist, as well as by Western Jews in Berlin or New York vis-à-vis their Eastern brethren. Kafka described them as a special race of miraculously surviving "soaring dogs" (in his story "Investigations of a Dog"). It is no accident that Chagall's hovering Jew carries the attributes of a traditional, religious, old Jew, with his beard, hat, and typical black garb; there was no iconography to represent the Jewishness of Chagall's young, secular generation. The image itself is a realization of an idiom: *er geyt iber di hayzer* (literally: he walks over the houses) which simply means in Yiddish, he is a beggar.[11] It is often used as a euphemism, to describe somebody's profession or state of affairs. *Iber* (literally: over) here means to walk from house to house, from door to door (as in the English expression, "to go over some papers"); but literally, the word means over something, higher than or above; whence the image of a man walking above Vitebsk. In Chagall's painting, the worn-out spatial metaphor of "over" was returned to its original literary sense and visual image.

Yet this is only the beginning of an interpretation; other literary and cultural images are grafted onto the idiom. The so-called "Grandfather of

10   A classical collection of Yiddish proverbs offers an additional, semi-rhymed variant: *a ku iz ibern dahk gefloygn / hot dem shvantz tsebrokhn* (a cow flew over the roof / and broke her prick) (Ignaz Bernstein, *yudishe shprikhverter un redensarten* [Warsaw 1908], 233). Many cows sit on roofs in Chagall's paintings.

11   John Hollander tells me that Meyer Schapiro lectured on this idiom in *Over Vitebsk*. Amishai-Maisels, discussing this painting ("Chagall's Jewish In-Jokes," 89) obviously doesn't know the idiom and the literary cluster attached to it, but quotes another expression, *geyt ibern dorf* (literally: walks over the village) which she translates as "to pass through a town"—but this is not an idiom but a sentence; and Vitebsk, the capital of a *gubernia*, was hardly a village (there is a world of difference between a Christian village and a Jewish town!).

Yiddish literature" Mendele Moykher Sforim (Mendele the Book Seller, pseudonym of Sh. Abramovitsh, 1937–1917; abbreviated Méndele), wrote one of the seminal books of modern Jewish self-understanding, *The Short Travels of Benjamin III.* A Jewish Don Quixote, Benjamin the Third, guided by fantastic books and numerous Hebrew quotations, departs with his companion, Senderl the Woman, from their backward *shtetl* to find a way to Eretz-Israel. A grotesque clash between imagination and reality ensues: they mistake a swamp for a great sea; they cannot even communicate with their Slavic neighbors; eventually they are caught and conscripted into the Russian army, only to be released as good-for-nothings. The world is topsy-turvy, reality doesn't match the quoted texts, and the Zionist dream is a flop. In his mock introduction, the narrator tells us that every person has his guardian angel:

> The angels hit even all kinds of beggars, pushing them: grow, beggars, paupers, poverty-stricken, born, arrived, open, concealed, sprout like grass, like nettles! Go, Jewish children, go—over the houses! . . .[12]

On the road, when Benjamin realizes that they fled their hometown without taking any food, the practical Senderl the Woman retorts,

> What do you mean, Benjamin, to eat? Do you intend to carry a kitchen with us? What for? Are there no inns, no houses on the road? . . . And if there are houses, we can, at one and the same time, go over the houses. For what are all other Jews doing? Today some go to others' houses, and tomorrow, those will go to yet others' houses. It's a Jewish thing, just a grace. . . .[13]

The symbol of this voyage is the ubiquitous *tórbe* (sack), and the similar *pekl* or *pékale* (nomad's pack). It is not just a beggar's sack he carries on his back, but a mishmash of various and sundry food, peddler's merchandise, books to guide him on the road, and whatnot. It is a symbol of the "unproductive" existence of the Jews, their beggars' predicament, their essentially parasitic and "unreal" peddler life, combined with the image of the "Wandering Jew" going into exile. Mendele coined the phrase *kol Isroel—eyn tórbe* (all [the children of] Israel—are one sack), i.e., the quintessence of Jewish existence is the *tórbe*: you are a beggar, a *shnorer* and a nomad, whether you are poor or "rich." Yet

12   Mendele Moykher Sforim, *kitzer masoes binyomin ha-shlisht* (Vilna: Widow and Brothers Romm, 1878), 4.

13   *Ibid.*, 27.

whereas Mendele foregrounded degrading poverty and lack of productive
work, Chagall stressed the connotations of Exile and Jewish destiny that were
also potentially a part of the whole image.[14]

The "Eternal Jew" or "Wandering Jew," a traditional image of Christian,
often anti-Semitic literature, was adopted by modern Yiddish literature as a
symbol of self-understanding (see David Pinsky's play "The Wandering Jew,"
performed in Hebrew by *HaBima* in Moscow). He is a mythical figure, larger
than life, condemned to exile, yet eternal. Bella Chagall used to sing the popular song "A Goles Marsh" (A March of Exile) by the American Yiddish poet
Morris Rosenfeld (1861–1923), which begins thus:

> With the wanderer's staff in hand,
> With no home and with no land,
> No friend or savior on the way,
> No tomorrow, no today,
> Chased, not suffered in our plight,
> Ne'er a day where spent a night,
> Always pain will knock, knock, knock,
> Always walk, walk, walk,
> Always stride, stride, stride,
> While your strength can still abide.[15]

Chagall's painting has the legendary image, but without the pity. Indeed, this
was a key image throughout Chagall's life and work. On 28 July 1948, before

---

14   The expressions "Going into exile" (*geyn in goles*) and "conducting exile" (*praven goles*) are
also used for a man who leaves his town and family to repent for his sins, or goes to places
of study, or leaves to seek his fortune, sleeping in prayer houses on the road, with no place
to rest. For a powerful example, see I.B. Singer's novel *Yoshe Kalb*.

15   Translated by Benjamin and Barbara Harshav. The original reads:

> Mit dem vandershtab in hant,
> On a heym un on a land;
> On a goyel, on a fraynd,
> On a morgn, on a haynt,
> Nit geduldet nor geyogt,
> Vu genekhtikt nit getogt,
> Imer vey, vey, vey,
> Imer gey, gey, gey,
> Imer shpan, shpan, shpan,
> Kol zman koyakh iz faran.

Morris Rosenfeld, "A Goles Marsh," in *Shriftn*, vol. 1 (New York: A.M. Evalenko, 1908), 100.

leaving New York for France, he writes in a private letter to his friend, the Yiddish novelist Y. Opatoshu,

> How are you dear Opatoshu. Ever closer to our voyage to the abysses—perhaps
> of Europe. I feel like going as you feel like dancing. You are toiling now and I am
> toiling on the *peklakh*[16] together with the little, thin, *young Virginia, who must
> also taste a bit of what it means to be a Jew with the sack on his back.* [Chagall's
> common-law wife Virginia Haggard was a Christian. Emphasis added.][17]

This was neither exile from America nor a tragic trip to Europe, where major exhibitions and fame awaited him, but simply a stereotype, a central symbol of Chagall's self-perception as a homeless Jew.

Here realization of an idiom is a direct bridge that links the painting with a whole cultural conceptual world. Without that cultural cluster—in our case, the movement above the houses, the religious garb, the stick and sack—the defiance of gravity may have a different meaning altogether. The painting *Over the Town* (fig. 5), ostensibly similar to *Over Vitebsk* (fig. 4), does not include the element of walking, indispensable for the idiom, or any other attributes of the Eternal Jew; instead it features two lovers flying weightlessly above Vitebsk. In the mural entitled *Music*, the towering figure of a Jewish fiddler looms above the little houses and church—evoking not the Eternal Jew but the soaring power of music that is not bound to mundane reality. In some of Chagall's soaring characters, the idiom loses its relevance; in others, we observe realizations of various expressions, not exclusively Yiddish, that lift people or objects above the force of gravity.[18] Chagall, as soon as he discovered the principle, turned it into an unmotivated device that signals the irrationality of his fictional world, using it almost anywhere. Furthermore, it is a device for making familiar objects strange, as well as an imprint of Chagall's authority over the painting. Thus the fantastic, absurd, or poetic world in the painting, even though it may be derived from Yiddish idioms and literature, is perceived both as a departure from reality and as its most authentic expression. Chagall himself, for example, said that Lenin stood Russia on its head

---

16   "Packages," the symbol of a Jewish wanderer.

17   Chagall's letters to Opatoshu, in the YIVO Jewish Research Institute archives, New York.

18   The "elevated mood," "ecstasy," or "trance" of love lifts the lovers off the ground; a fast
     moving carriage is said to be "flying by" (*farbaygefloygn*); *er flit in di himlen* (he is soaring in
     the heavens) means elation or fantasy and delusion; *zayn kop flit in himl* (his head is flying
     in the sky) implies unsubstantiated fantasy.

like figures in a Chagall painting (and depicted him standing on his head in the painting *Revolution*).

4   YIDDISH LITERATURE

A major influence on Chagall's perception of the Jewish world was Sholem-Aleichem, ostensibly a good-natured humorist, who exposed the irrationalities and absurdities of Jewish life and—through it—life in general. For Sholem-Aleichem, irrationality lies both in the dangerous unworldliness of Jewish existence and in the endearing quality of the true folk person, who sees the abyss yet does not want to see it, glossing over it with a smile. Chagall adopted this stance in his depiction of reality in his early paintings.

Yiddish literature also influenced Chagall thematically. Mendele's *Seyfer Habeheymes* (The Book of livestock) can be quoted at length in this connection: cows, horses, goats, and especially the touching story of a calf, are all echoed in Chagall's world. Mendele's introduction says:

> As I got to know my animals better, as I saw that they were like humans, flesh and blood, like people with all their senses, with feelings, and as I seriously observed their situation, their miserable life, how they are in Exile, suffering from the small humans in the world—the feeling of pity drew me toward them . . . *and their language*, as strange as it seems, is often more intelligible than the over clever, artificial, bookish language that was intentionally invented to screw your brain and remove the slightest thing from any logic. [Emphasis in original.][19]

Chagall had little connection with animals in real life, yet he constructed them as parts of his culturally stereotypical but private fictional world, elements of a universe he had imbibed from his childhood reading. Animals for him could represent the warmth and endearing quality of a living being, symbolize the inarticulate impact of nonverbal communication, or epitomize the ideal of humans living in close contact with nature, an ideal that many Jewish contemporaries saw as specifically Christian because of the patent contrast between the *shtetl* and surrounding Christian villages, and consequently an ideal that came to play a major role in the Modern Jewish Revolution, with its emphasis on a return to the land, to nature.

---

19   Mendele Moykher Sforim, *seyfer ha-beheymes* (The Book of livestock) in *Ale Shriften*, vol. 2, bk. 1 (New York: Hebrew Publishing Company, 1910), 75.

Another theme that Chagall derives from Mendele is connected with childhood. "The children of Kesalon (Fooltown) are old Jews in every respect: in their clothes, the sadness, the worry, the fear, the caution registered on their faces, except that they are little, have no beard, and do not procreate. . . . . They are] Children without a childhood."[20] This image appears in *The Holy Family* (1910), which places a Christian theme within a Jewish family setting. The child is depicted with a beard, because he, too, has been born "an old Jew." Though not as gloomy as Mendele's, Chagall's vision reflected a melancholy existential perception.

We also find many traces of Sholem-Aleichem's children's stories in Chagall's worldview. "The Enchanted Tailor" is a story about a poor tailor who has bought a milk goat in a distant town, but who is surprised to discover, while staying overnight in an inn, that his milk goat is repeatedly conjured away from him and exchanged for a billy goat. The tailor and his goat appear in *Rain* (fig. 6) and other paintings; and the goat is ubiquitous in Chagall's work, especially since it is proverbially the most elementary bread-earner in Jewish poverty. No less ubiquitous is the image of the violin, which also is derived from Sholem-Aleichem's short story, "The Violin." In this work, the child recounts, "The desire to play the violin grew together with me." The violin, we know, was the most widespread prestigious instrument of music in traditional Jewish society:

> A violin, you understand, is an instrument older than all instruments. The first violinist in the world was Tuval-Kain, or Methuselah, I don't remember precisely. . . . The second violinist was King David. And there was a third one, Paganini was his name, also a Jew; all the best violinists in the world were Jews.[21]

Chagall himself dreamt in his childhood about becoming a violinist (before he transformed that dream into the "non-Jewish" art of painting). The animal and the violin—both nonverbal communicators—merged in his imagination, and there is a close empathy between the painter and all these characters.

The big grandfather clock is also a conspicuous figure in Chagall's world, recalling Sholem-Aleichem's story "The Clock," which begins thus: "The clock rang thirteen . . ." and continues somewhat later, "I swear, it's a crime that a

---

20 Mendele Moykher Sforim, "be-seter ra'am," in *kol kitvey mendele mokher sefarim* (Collected writings of Mendele Mokher Sefarim in Hebrew) (Tel Aviv: Dvir, 1950), 379.

21 Sholem-Aleichem, "The Violin," in *Stories for Jewish Children*, vol. 1 (New York: Sholem Aleichem Folksfand, 1918), 42.

clock is not a living thing, a mute tongue, speechless: he would have had to tell and tell! . . ." In the story, the clock dominates the life of the town: the father tries to prevent it from ringing thirteen, and hangs more and more weights on it, until the clock collapses with an unbelievable noise, and everyone mourns it as a dead person. The boy internalizes the experience:

> The whole night afterward, clocks crowded my head. I imagined: our old clock lies on the floor, wearing a white shroud. I thought the clock was alive, but, instead of the pendulum, a long tongue, the tongue of a human being, swings back and forth, and the clock does not ring but sighs, and each sigh takes away a piece of my health. . . . And on the face, where I am used to see a twelve I suddenly see thirteen, truly thirteen—believe me![22]

The dominating clock appears, with its enigmatic, blurred face, swinging diagonally, along with a flying fish and a fiddle (alliterative in Yiddish: *fish, fidl, fligl* [wing]) and a pair of lovers on a riverbank, in Chagall's *Time is a River Without Banks* (fig. 7). Of course, there are two banks to the river, we see indications of a town on both, and we are reminded of Chagall's early encounters with Bella on the bank of the Dvina river, as described in Bella's memoirs.[23]

In this painting, too, Jewish proverbs may be at work again. There is a Hebrew expression, widely used in Yiddish: *yam ha-talmud*, "the sea of the Talmud," or better, "the sea of learning," which indicates an inexhaustible, endless body of knowledge. You can swim in it—a related idiom, describing a learned person and astute scholar, is "he swims in the sea of learning"—but you cannot reach or see the other shore. Several additional proverbs are related to it: (1) the rhymed couplet: *der yam on a breg, di toyre on an ek* (the sea has no shore, learning no end); (2) *di toyre hot nit keyn breg* (literally: learning has no shore).[24] Indeed, *breg* (shore, riverbank) and *ek* (end) rhyme in Yiddish and are interchangeable; the dictionaries translate the word *breg* (shore) also as *ek* (end). Thus, "a river with no shore" actually means "with no end," and, in our context, "timeless." Yet Chagall revives the primary meaning of *breg* and thus paints two shores. Hence, the paradox of the pictorial and verbal aspects of the picture: the river has no shore, yet in order to be a river in a paint-

22   *Ibid.*, 63, 75.

23   Bella Chagall, *brenendike likht* (Burning candles) (New York: Book League of the Jewish Fraternal Order, 1945), passim. It was suggested that the idea came from Ovid; but Ovid has only "time is a river," an idea from Greek philosophy, without the decisive clause that creates the paradox: "a river with no banks."

24   Bernstein, *yudishe shprikhverter un redensarten*, 130–290.

ing, it must have two shores. The young love scene is placed in the shadow of this paradox; the tune is played by Chagall-fish, the artist-fiddler; and the rest is in the hands of color.

5   JEWISH ART AND JESUS CHRIST

Chagall was not an ideologue; and though at some points in his life he was close to programmatic Jewish art circles, he never joined them. Through the years, he maintained contacts with both Jewish cultural circles and French intellectuals. Even in his most "chauvinistic" statement, "Leaves from my Notebook," published in Moscow in a Yiddish journal in 1922, he states, "Beginning with the Renaissance, national arts began to decline. Boundaries are blurred. Artists come—individuals, citizens of this or that state, born here or there (blessed be my Vitebsk)—and one would need a good registration or even a passport specialist (for the Jewish desk) to be able to 'nationalize' all the artists."[25] He is proud of what the "little nation" of Jews has achieved: it gave the world Christ and Christianity, Marx and Socialism, and it will "show the world some art." But he refers to Art in general, measured by international standards, rather than "Jewish art." Indeed, there was no identity crisis here since in the minds of young intellectuals on both sides of the Modern Jewish Revolution, general culture and Jewish culture coexisted in one consciousness.

Because Christianity was central to the European cultural tradition, it attracted many Jews in the modern period: Edmund Husserl, Gustav Mahler, Alfred Doeblin, Roman Jakobson, and many others converted to Christianity. Chagall was not one of them, since he was deeply connected with a Jewish folk sensibility; but culturally, the Christian world was a tangible reality in his work and life. His friends in the interwar period, Raïssa and Jacques Maritain, actively propagated conversion of the Jews. Raïssa, herself a Russian Jew who converted to Catholicism, also wrote a book about Chagall.[26] Hence the many fusions and confusions of Jewish, Russian, and Christian elements in Chagall's paintings; they interact, coalesce, and represent each other, just as other modular individuals—man and animal, or man and woman—do. He presents the sacrifice of Isaac in the form of a Michelangelo *Pietà*, or he portrays the Holy Family with a bearded, "old," little Jewish child; he paints

25   See the English translation in Benjamin Harshav, ed., *Marc Chagall on Art and Culture.*
26   Raïssa Maritain, *Marc Chagall* (New York: Edition de la Maison française, 1943).

himself as a Christ child along with his parents in the famous *Golgotha*. Some Jewish critics were puzzled, even outraged by the use of Christian motifs in the works of a Jewish artist like Scholem Asch or Chagall. But Christian art was the mainstream of the European art tradition and was part of Chagall's intellectual world: as Buddha and Zen Buddhism may appear in the writings of a Christian writer, so did Martin Buber discuss Buddhism along with Hasidism in his writings; and such, too, was the openness of modern Jewish literature in Hebrew and Yiddish.[27]

A special case is the figure of Jesus Christ. His image was part of the modern gallery of Jewish literature. Dr. Yosef Klausner, a native of Russia, editor of the flagship of Jewish literature in Europe, *Ha-Shiloah*, and the first professor of Hebrew Literature at the Hebrew University in Jerusalem (between 1925 and 1949), devoted many years to the study of Jesus of Nazareth and his time. Similarly, Uri-Tsvi Grinberg, the Expressionist poet who wrote in Yiddish and Hebrew and who edited the avant-garde Yiddish journal *Albatros*, used the figure of Jesus prominently in his work. There can be no doubt that Chagall knew *Albatros*, for it was a major organ of the *Khalyastre* (Happy Gang), a group of Yiddish Expressionist poets, who also published the journals *Khalyastre* and *Literarishe revi*[28] in Paris, with many illustrations by Chagall.

Grinberg had been a frontline soldier during World War I, had deserted, and lived in hiding. After experiencing a pogrom in his hometown of Lemberg (Lvov), he became an ardent Zionist who firmly believed (already in 1924, in Berlin) that the earth was burning under the feet of the Jews in Europe, and that one day they would be gassed. In 1924 he left for Palestine, where he became a prominent Hebrew poet and extreme nationalist. In 1922 he wrote a Yiddish "concrete" poem in the form of a cross, which was entitled "Uri-Tsvi Before the Cross / INRI" (INRI printed in large Latin letters; fig. 8).[29] Chagall painted a similar image, *The White Crucifixion* (fig. 9), with the same letters I.N.R.I. above the cross, and below, he added an Aramaic version of the text in Hebrew letters, "Jesus of Nazareth King of the Jews." In "Uri-Tvsi Before the Cross" and in the long poem "In the Kingdom of the Cross," Grinberg addresses Jesus as

27   See, for example, the themes and sources of Buddhism, Christianity, psychoanalysis, the Russian Revolution, American politics, and so on, in *American Yiddish Poetry: A Bilingual Anthology*, ed. Benjamin and Barbara Harshav (Berkeley: University of California Press, 1986).

28   Edited by Peretz Markish and Oyzer Varshavski respectively: they translated Chagall's autobiography from Russian into Yiddish in 1924–25, when all of them lived in Paris.

29   Uri-Tsvi Grinberg, "Uri-Tsvi Before the Cross / INRI," *Albatros: Journal for the New Expression of Poets and Artist* 2 (November 1922): 3.

"our brother," symbol of Jewish suffering, hanging on crosses all over Europe for two thousand years. I will quote a few lines pertinent to Chagall:

> At the churches
> Hangs my brother
> Crucified
> Frozen
> From his covered member
> Girls get pregnant. . . .
> Why am I one of the suffering caravan, not hanging next to you on a village pillar at a crossroad, sun drying me, night weighing on me? . . .
> Brother Jesus, a Jewish skin-and-bones shrinks (two thousand years after you. Old!) . . .
> Brother Jesus. You had two thousand years of calm on the cross. Around you, *no longer world*. . . . At your feet: a heap of cut-off Jewheads [allusion to the pogroms]. Torn *talises* [Jewish prayer shawls]. Pierced parchments. Blood-stained white sheets . . . Ancient Jewpain. Golgotha, brother, you don't see. Golgotha is here: all around. Pilate lives. And in Rome they sing psalms in the churches . . .
> The Jews! The Jews!
> When poisoned gas enters the temples
> *And icons suddenly scream in Yiddish* . . .
> On the wound-ridden body a torn *talis*—the body
> Feels good in a Jewish *talis*—Oh, good in a *talis*:
> The wind cannot blow sand on the dripping wounds. . . .
> Oh-Ho, I am king in a wound-and-blood *talis*! [Emphasis added.][30]

Such was the Jewish context of Chagall's *The White Crucifixion*, which included Jesus wearing a *talis*, as well as the context of similar images in later paintings responding to the Holocaust. Of course, unlike Grinberg, Chagall did not paint it with an Expressionist scream.

Just as Chagall borrowed images from Yiddish literature, so did his painting evoke responses from inside Jewish culture. Here is a comment about the painting entitled *Flayed Ox* (fig. 10):

> Look closely at the red, flayed calf, hanging as a crucifix over the whole city. As the true crucified, the father of all the crucified in the world, since the evil of a

---

30 Uri-Tsvi Grinberg, "In the Kingdom of the Cross," in *Collected Yiddish Works, Vol. II: 1922–1958* (Jerusalem: The Magnes Press, 1979), 394, 431, 433, 459, 460.

living creature wielded its power over a living creature. See how the red of its blood screams, see the brutal cut in its body split in two, see the purity of its face licking from the bowl—

Does another crucified like this exist among all the crucifieds?

Weren't we all stunned, trembling in our childhood, when we saw the neighbor butcher slaughter our beloved calf? Isn't Fayerberg's "The Calf"[31] authentically Jewish for all time? And is there a more authentic feeling of pity for the lot of the powerless? And a stronger scream of rage at the brutality of the heartless? And isn't Chagall here like Fayerberg? . . .

Look closely and see the zenith of human Evil, emanating from an idyll that is clear purity and beatitude.[32]

This was written in Yiddish after the Holocaust by the President of Israel Zalman Shazar, a Hebrew scholar and former Israeli Minister of Culture, who was born in Byelorussia two years after Chagall. Given their shared cultural background, the calf may be more appropriate than the ox in the painting's title.

Naturally, Chagall had ideological hesitations about crossing religious boundaries in his paintings. As a young man of twenty, before leaving for St. Petersburg to study art, he went with his mother to Lubavitsh to see the head of the Chabad Hasidic sect and ask for his advice; characteristically for that time, the Rebbe told him he must judge for himself. And half a century later, Chagall wrote to the first Israeli President Chaim Weitzmann, invoking the traditional authority of the Rebbe, and asked for advice from "the highest Jewish authority" about whether to accept a commission for a Christian church. According to Chagall, who felt apologetic towards his Jewish friends, Weitzmann, too, answered that Chagall must decide for himself. And he did.

6   TEXTS AND QUOTATIONS IN PAINTINGS

In Chagall's art, writing plays a conspicuous role. To be sure, words or parts of words were used by Picasso and his followers in France and in Russia (for example, Kazimir Malevich). Chagall, however, often uses long texts, and the textual engagement of his paintings is usually complex. This was plainly a function of Chagall's origins and interests in Jewish culture, which had been a profoundly textual culture. The Jews had no cathedrals filled with art objects

---

31   Story written by M.Z. Fayerberg in Hebrew in 1897 and published in 1899.
32   Zalman Shazar, *Di Goldene keyt* 60 (1967): 33.

(even though synagogue art—limited as it is—was extolled in Chagall's generation). Their "otherness" was fully embodied in their "other" letters, their writing in the "opposite" direction, and their "other" and essentially private library. In Chagall's works, texts fulfill a global function, representing the culture of his fictional world.

The quoted words also fill numerous specific functions, often simultaneously. They serve as synecdoches, a part of objects in the represented world (for example, inscriptions in a cemetery); they issue multimedia signals, suggesting nonvisual aspects of the represented frame of reference (referring, for example, to the song "Bridegroom's Voice, Bride's Voice" with the image of the Dancer in the theater mural *Dance*); they offer titles for some of the other material in the painting; they present allusions that bring in additional frames of reference that are otherwise indiscernible in the painting proper (biblical quotes and references to biblical events); they serve as a metalanguage that shows the artist's interference in his presented world (such as the tiny names of his family members inserted in longhand in *Introduction to the Yiddish Theater*; and they fulfill a design function within the composition of the painting.

Chagall often writes a text and subsequently erases part of it, leaving the full content as his own private knowledge—a mystifying gesture that appears on other levels of his paintings as well. Further, he deforms words and texts, just as he does other represented objects, perhaps because he originally had in mind two different audiences but increasingly lost the audience that could read the Hebrew and Yiddish inscriptions. In spite of his acculturation and his shift to speaking Russian or French, most of the texts in his paintings are in Hebrew letters, whether the language be Hebrew or Yiddish. Russian rarely appears as an independent text, but as an object within a represented reality: a sign on a store, a newspaper headline (*War!*), or a quotation from a revolutionary slogan in the early Soviet years (such as Lenin's slogan *War on the Palaces!*).[33] Although most of Chagall's long texts are biblical quotations or quotations of Hebrew inscriptions, they are always set within the world of Yiddish; there is no independent Hebrew text or sentence composed by him in his oeuvre.[34]

33   See the half-effaced slogan in *Peace to Huts–War on Palaces* (1918) in *Marc Chagall: The Russian Years, 1906–1922*, ed. Christoph Vitali (Frankfurt: Schirn Kunsthalle, 1991), image 134.

34   For the illustrations to the Bible that Chagall made in 1930–31, he used the brilliant Yiddish translation of the Bible by the American Yiddish poet Yehoash (sent to him by his friend Y. Opatoshu from New York) and the images of the patriarchs are perceived in Eastern European Jewish terms. Chagall had no Hebrew beyond Bar-Mitzvah, and in his Yiddish correspondence throughout the years, he makes elementary mistakes in the Hebrew words.

One example of Hebrew text appears in *The Cemetery Gate* (fig. 11), apparently a realistic painting from nature made in his "Vitebsk period." The colors, however, are not realistic at all. The upper part is treated in a cubist manner, while the lower half, almost photographic, offers an unrealistic textual collage. On each of the two pillars of the gate is a long indecipherable text, such as may be found on a tombstone, precisely written out and then obscured, as if worn away with time; at the heads of both pillars, in large letters, are Hebrew dates, equivalent to 1812–1890. These cannot indicate the opening and closing dates of a real cemetery (certainly not of an ancient cemetery, as Vitebsk had), but must refer to a person's life. Chagall has apparently transferred them from an individual gravestone. Most likely, Chagall, when in Vitebsk, discovered the gravestone of his paternal grandfather, whom he admired for his learning, and was happy to place his date of death, 1890, on a Star of David set upon the peak of his imaginary gate. We know that the grandfather from Lyozno, who had a house in Vitebsk, had died when Chagall was a child, whereupon the family sold his house "in the sands" and moved to a neighborhood in Vitebsk proper. If the dates indeed refer to this grandfather, Marc was three years old when David Chagall died.

The text on the top triangle is from Ezekiel's vision in the Valley of Dry Bones, and here it may speak as much of the resurrection of his grandfather as it does of the resurrection of the Jews, according to a Zionist interpretation. The absent context is: "Then He [God] said unto me, Son of man, these bones are the whole house of Israel: behold, they say, our bones are dried, and our hope is lost:[35] we are cut off for our parts" (Ez. 37:11). The text on the gate reads, from midverse (Ez. 37:12): "Behold, I will open your grave[s] [and cause] you [to come up] out of your graves, my people / And bring you onto the land [of Israel] [here verse 13 is missing and some text is obfuscated] [and shall put] my spirit in you, and ye shall live."[36] However, the first two clauses are placed in the reverse direction, as in Russian: the first half on the left side, then switching to the right. There is only one change in the biblical text and it is significant: on the horizontal plank, instead of אדמת ישראל = *admat Israel* (the soil of Israel), he wrote ארץ = *eretz* (the

---

35   The Zionist hymn "Ha-Tikva" begins with a verse protesting these words: "Our hope is not yet lost."

36   Authorized King James Version.

Land), as the Zionists affectionately referred to Palestine.[37] Furthermore, he misspelled *eretz* ארץ , as if it were Yiddish (ערץ, beginning with an *ayin* ע instead of an *alef* א), indicating the spoken language. Finally, one may see in the soaring blue sky the Zionist colors.

The Jew in Bright Red (fig. 12) depicts a weary, ancient Jew with a fiery red beard, clad in black, who sits with his back to a red house. Half-rising, his figure suggests that he is about to leave the cluster of *shtetl* houses immediately behind him, while still looming beyond the house we see a massive yellow halo, like a globe or a sinking sun, covered with a biblical text. The text opens with *lekh-lekha:* "Now the Lord had said unto Abram, Get thee out of thy country and from thy kindred, and from thy father's house, unto a land that I will show thee" (Gen. 12:1). In the original, this chapter promises a "Zionist" vision of going to the Holy Land and becoming a great nation. In folk semiotics, however, and in the Yiddish language, the expression *lekh-lekho* (get thee out) symbolizes the expulsion of the Jews. This section of the Bible is called *parshes lekh-lekho* (the chapter or episode of banishment); and it acquired a metaphorical meaning: "Now it is time for the Chapter of Banishment" means not the weekly reading, but its contemporary implementations. Indeed, "Lekh-Lekho" is the title of the last chapter of Sholem-Aleichem's *Tevye the Milkman*, referring to the expulsion of the Jews from all Russian villages in 1892. But in this painting, no doubt, it refers to the expulsion of a million and a half Jews who had to leave their homes within twenty-four hours, as ordered by the Russian army in the areas near the German front in 1914. Related to the painting, there is a drawing in gouache, india ink, and pencil on paper, titled *Remembrance* (fig. 13). Though the Guggenheim Museum catalogue marks the date as "ca. 1918," the drawing has an inscription in Chagall's handwriting: "Erinnerung 1914" (on top of an earlier pencil mark "Chagall 1914"). No doubt the inscription was made when Chagall was in Berlin in 1922 or 1923 (for German is rare in Chagall's texts), and the date 1914 refers to the expulsion (and perhaps the date of his original plan for this painting). This is amply confirmed by the painting's subject, which shows a banished Jew who takes his mother's home with him, on his back.

37 Chagall's Zionist leanings were covered up during the Revolutionary times, and revived during the thirties and forties. In the murals for the Soviet Yiddish theater he paints "Carmel," wine from Eretz-Israel, a Zionist gesture. It is plausible that *The Cemetery Gate* refers to the Balfour Declaration of 2 November 1917, promising a Jewish homeland in Palestine. The painting was postdated "1917" and certainly does not refer to the October Revolution.

A related drawing is the so-called *Walking Village* (fig. 14) which depicts a whimsical superimposition of a series of houses on a body with human legs, reclining backwards. In fact, this was an illustration in a collaborative work, a book-length poetic cycle entitled *Troyer* (Grief) by the young Yiddish poet David Hofshteyn (published in Kiev in 1922), with "cover and illustrations by M. Chagall." It is an avant-garde poem, written in response to the pogroms in Ukraine in 1919, that explores the paradox and absurdity of the twin birth of Jewish tragedy and world renewal, with a hyperbolic tone, modernist imagery, avant-garde graphics, and futuristic rhythms. The last poem of the cycle reflects the poet's visit to the recently devastated towns. Destruction and emptiness are covered with the lucid air of autumn, and the poet concludes, "What do I need the lucidity, the clarity / that leaks into the cracks of ruins?"[38] In Chagall's *Walking Village*, a tiny figure pops out of a window with an accusing finger and hurls Hofshteyn's memorable iambic pentameter line into the empty world: *vos darf ikh zi di loyterkayt di klore* (What do I need the lucidity, the clear, transparent lucidity?), while the reader and the text supply the next line and the full context. In the original drawing itself, we see something like male genitals between two big legs (this was subsequently erased in the Soviet printing), evidently a popular conception of the psychoanalytical version of the irrationality of this world. The drawing piles on a series of empty, blank houses (ironically, like Suprematist white squares and triangles), with only one sign of life: smoke in the last house. Human legs create a portmanteau image: the body of houses may be seen as a human body leaning unnaturally backwards, smoking a pipe. It may also be the reverse: a town walking.

The received title of this drawing, *Walking Village*, is rather misleading. In translating the term *shtetl* people often confused two very different administrative concepts, "village" and "town": in Russia, villages were settlements of Christian peasants who worked the land, places where Jews did not live; while Jewish towns generally had little to do with farming. Since *shtetl* (small town) is a diminutive of *shtot* (city) in Yiddish, it would be natural (though misleading) for Chagall, a newcomer in France in 1910, to derive "village" from "ville." But in the context of the poem it is safe to assume that the title is *The Town Is Walking*, which is a Yiddish idiom (*di shtot geyt*) meaning "the whole town

38   David Hofshteyn, *Troyer* (Kiev: kultur-lige, 1922). The couplet was translated in Franz Meyer's Chagall biography as "What do I need her for / the sincerity, the purity?" which does not convey the real meaning of this text. Franz Meyer, *Marc Chagall: Life and Work* (New York: Harry N. Abrams, 1963), 742.

goes"; all the Jews are leaving their hometown, fleeing from pogroms into exile. Indeed, the book opens with a carter and his wagon leaving home (or carrying it away?), depicted on top of a child's head, where we read the inscription, in a child's longhand: "To all those slaughtered before their time" (fig. 15).[39]

7   TYPEFACES AND SPELLING: A MULTICULTURAL PLAY

Accounting for all the language elements in Chagall's paintings would require an annotated edition that deciphers all the texts and allusions and explains their different cultural levels. Apart from the referential gestures exemplified above, Chagall was a sophisticated user of the language material itself. He treated language as he treated other representational elements in his fictional world and other formal elements on his canvas: deformation and polyphony of voices were his guiding principles, allusion and whimsical twists his constant devices.

Chagall used Hebrew, Yiddish, and Russian texts, but often confounded their respective spellings and direction of writing in a multicultural manner. As we know, Hebrew is basically spelled with consonants, while Yiddish evolved a European-type spelling system, including all vowels. Hebrew words within Yiddish, however, use the Hebrew consonantal spelling, to separate the Holy Tongue from the mundane language. After the Communist Revolution, the Hebrew (or "clerical") spelling of Yiddish words was abolished and all words acquired vowel letters. Thus in *Mein Leben* the inscription on his mother's tombstone reads שגל = *ShGL* (capitals represent the actual letters; *Sh* is one letter in Hebrew) while in the same book his father's tombstone reads שאאגל = *ShAGAL*, with all vowels filled in.[40] His mother died in 1916 and his father after the Revolution, in 1921. The artist adopted the Soviet spelling and used it throughout his life for his own name and in private correspondence. But in his paintings he played with the differences and their cultural connotations. On several occasions, he signed his paintings in consonants only: משה סגל = *MShH SGL* (pronounced: *Moyshe Segal*), invoking the Jewish art pedigree of an eighteenth-century synagogue painter Chaim Segal. In the painting *Rain* (fig. 6), a Russian word is even spelled in consonants: ЛВК = *LVK* (for *lavka*,

---

39 And not, as the usual translation goes: "To those who departed before their time."

40 The images are reprinted in *My Life*, facing pages 10 and 146. *ShGL* is a variant of *SGL* (Segal), a Hebrew acronym, hence spelled with consonants only.

"store" in Russian), perhaps to indicate Jewish ownership. On the other hand, in the midst of a holy text in *The Jew in Green* (1914), we find a Yiddish insert, *der slutsker magid* (the preacher from Slutzk). "Preacher" is a Hebrew term for a religious profession, normally spelled מגיד = *mgid*; by inserting the vowel *a*, Chagall indicates that the preaching was done in Yiddish.

The interactions between Hebrew and Cyrillic letters often hinged on the direction: Hebrew and Yiddish read right to left, while Russian goes from left to right. Sometimes he changed the direction of a Hebrew text, as we saw in *The Cemetery Gate*. In one case he even changed the order of the two tablets of the Ten Commandments, indicating his double-directed culture. He signed a painting *MARC* לאגאש = *MARC [LAGASh]* (here, the Yiddish letters are represented in square brackets, as they read in their normal Yiddish order, but when read in reverse they sound *ShAGAL*). On the stage design of a train, in Sholem-Aleichem's "Agents," he wrote III פאר רייכער לק = *FAR REYKHER[ers] LK III* (for smokers [lk III]); when read in the reverse direction, it says: III cl[ass], mixing Yiddish with Russian.

An interesting case appears in the mural *Introduction to the Yiddish Theater*, which depicts Efros, the literary director of the theater, bringing Chagall to the stage director Granovski. In a preliminary study for this painting, the Yiddish inscription above the figures, reads יקסװװאנארג לאגאש עפראם = *IKSVVONARG LAGASh EFROS*. Efros, a Hebrew name traditionally spelled אפרת = *APRT* receives an "outrageous" Soviet spelling, *EFROS*. The other two names are inverted; if read in the Russian direction, they read "Shagal Granovski.[41] This is similar to the reversible rhymes (*perevertni*) in Russian Futurism, but it also expresses the multicultural symbiosis of Chagall's generation. In the actual painting, moreover, Chagall deletes a letter in both his and Efros's names and inserts miniature drawings of a literary critic and a painter instead, thus achieving a double-media denotation. Further, in writing in the director's name, he changes ס = *S* into ט = *T*, and repeats the first syllable twice: *IKTIKTVNARG*. When read in reverse, we get *GRANV* (only half of the Yiddish *VV* is left; the rest is redundant), but when read from left to right we get *IKT IKT*, the Russian acronym of Granovski's theater as spelled in Yiddish: "Ievreysky Kamerny Teatr" ("Jewish Chamber Theater"). This is a double characterization that combines the name of the director and his the-

---

41   From the Biblical vocalization it is clear that he pronounced his own name "Lagash," while "Granovski" he read left to right.

ater, also underlining the fact that the director of the Yiddish theater spoke not Yiddish, but Russian.

Similar close attention to cultural details can be seen in the use of type-faces in Chagall's paintings. In the Ashkenazi religious tradition, which he knew from his childhood, Hebrew letters appeared in several socially deter-mined categories of typefaces: (1) The so-called square letters (mostly based on straight lines or round backbones but with the thickness elaborated in cur-vaceous forms and ornaments) were obligatory in handwritten Torah Scrolls and in printings of the Bible, having an aura of "holy text." In the Bible, the letters were accompanied by markers of vocalization and syntactic-musical reading accents, in the form of tiny dots, dashes, and other markers below, above, and inside letters. (2) Moderate square letters were used as normal typefaces in printed Hebrew and Yiddish, usually printed without the vocal-ization markers. Typically, in engravings on a tombstone, the curvaceous em-bellishments could be moderate, as imitated by Chagall in *The Cemetery Gate* or as later developed by him in casual floating biblical names in his stained-glass windows. (3) *Rashi* letters were used for commentaries printed on the margins of a Bible or Talmud: a commentary must never be confused with the holy text itself. (4) *Vayber-taytsh*, (women's typeface)—a special script between printed and cursive—was used for books for women on religious topics in Yiddish. All Hebrew words within the Yiddish, however, are printed in Hebrew square letters, and placed in parentheses in mid-sentence, between the feminine words, not to mix the feminine and masculine. (5) *Written let-ters* were used for writing in longhand: for personal correspondence, manu-scripts, and the like. Those had "childish" and "adult" varieties—each letter separate or concatenated respectively.

Chagall used square letters to indicate textual quotations from religious texts, and moderate square letters for other "serious" purposes. He—and the whole secular movement—would rarely use the second-class *Rashi* or the women's scripts. He often used "written" letters for the painter's personal message (e.g., the list of his siblings and parents in *Introduction to the Yiddish Theater*) or to indicate a character's personal statement ("I am an acrobat," "I am frolicking," written on the belts of the clowns standing on their heads).

Yet he also used the following types: (6) Modern printed letters, which were developed in Yiddish and Hebrew secular literature; (7) Geometrical let-ters, which reduce all letter shapes to straight strokes or semicircles, as de-veloped in the modern movement. Such letters were used in Constructivist designs of book covers and in secular Yiddish schools and institutions—for headlines, front pages, invitations, posters, etc., and were often given fancy geometrical forms and three-dimensional bodies.

One example is the cover of the Soviet Yiddish literary journal שטראָם = *ShTROM* ("stream" or "torrent," connoting both the torrential stream of the Revolution and the slogan of "going with the stream," accepting it). The title is drawn on a diagonal bias, a favorite device of Chagall. The first letter *Sh* is fully geometrical, but inverts the traditional manner: in "square" letters, the base is thick and the three diagonal strokes are thin; while here the base is just a line, whereas the right side is thick. The body of the side stroke and the heads of the two others are of a precise, quadrangular form, rather than the traditional curving sides and heads. The geometrical bodies are used as a background for "construction" themes. The second letter, *T*, has a geometricized imitation of the traditional rounded upper part. The third and fourth letters (*R, O*) are modern, simplified, and stylized imitations of square letters whimsically Chagallized. The fifth letter, *closing M* (used only at the end of a word) is again geometrically "square" in its sides and in its overall closure—yet the parallel lines move slightly apart, making dynamic the whole. The rectangle head has a symbolic dollop on top. Thus Chagall uses his "demonstrative eclecticism" repeatedly to evoke juxtapositions and surprises inside each letter and between the letters. The allusions to the distinct typefaces and their cultural connotations are not lost on the reader.

Furthermore, the sides of the letters can be used as backgrounds for Chagallian little figures and shaded spaces. In the rectangular base of two of the geometrical "printed" letters, "written" letters announce in Soviet spelling, "monthly journal."[42] The written letters, however, have an unusual thickness that is rendered sometimes as a white and sometimes as a dark surface. These provide an intimate, casual feeling to the Constructivist *ShTROM*, like a personal letter to the reader; yet the Constructivist part itself has been softened and humanized in the middle (which El Lissitzky, taking Constructivism seriously, would never have done) through the portrait of the head of a high school boy, one of Chagall's emblems indicating general (Russian) education.

A very different cover was made two years later in Paris for the Yiddish Expressionist literary journal כאליאסטרע = *KhALYASTRE (Happy Gang)*. To indicate "the Jews (Yiddish literature) conquer Paris," his atheist friends

42   Literally, "Monthly Notebooks": *khoydesh* (month) is a Hebrew word spelled *HDSh*, now Sovietized; *heftn*, "issues," like the French *cahiers*.

are made to wear emblems of religious garb. The Eiffel Tower and the rect-angular leaning houses of his Paris paintings are here, as are the lines and clusters of tiny dots. The "beautiful" (with his thick, "feminine" lips) Peretz Markish hangs down the top of the Eiffel Tower, holding the title *Khalyastre* (which turns into a building), and the climbing Oyzer Varshavski on the right proudly holds a banner: *Paris.* A boy, Chagall himself, holds out the number of the issue, *2.* The text is in simplified, square letters, mocked and disrupted: the *A* wants to walk away, the second *A* turns its foot backwards and has dots instead of its central diagonal backbone; and in *Paris* the first is a written let-ter, with the others printed, yet rounded and moving in a written direction. By juxtaposing typefaces, subverting and mixing them, Chagall turns them into malleable graphic bodies; he uses their social functionality, ironizes it, and foregrounds its problematic nature.

8   CHAGALL: INTENTIONALITY AND IDENTITY

Throughout his career, Chagall has evoked interest in major centers of art by means of his exotic pictorial world and surreal compositions. Yet the extent to which his work owes its density of meaning to his local culture has not been fully explored. Oversights and mistaken readings of Jewish texts and subtexts are routine in recent criticism of Chagall, even in the work of excellent schol-ars who have contributed greatly to our understanding of his œuvre. A recent book on Chagall in Russia, for example, reproduces an illustration to a Yid-dish children's tale in verse by Der Nister, and subtitles it "The Sleeping Man and the Cockerel"; yet inside the drawing itself there is a Yiddish inscription in large, childish letters: "Little Grandma died"—a reference to the poem, which plainly should have been read.[43] In another book the black hole on (the open-mouthed) grandma's face is interpreted as a beard, producing the title *Man in Bed and Rooster.*[44]

An eminent Chagall specialist claims that in Chagall's milieu they "used Hebrew mainly to talk to rabbis, preachers, and wandering men of God," while in fact no one, including the rabbis and preachers, spoke Hebrew at the time. The same scholar identifies the painting *Feast Day* as taking place on *Purim* instead of the serious *Sukoth*, as the fruit (*ethrog* and *lulav*) in the

43   Alexandr Kamensky, *Chagall: The Russian Years 1907–1922* (New York: Rizzoli, 1989), 245. In addition, the image is printed in reverse and the text appears in mirror script.

44   *Marc Chagall*, ed. Vitali, image 99.

man's hand and his solemn posture indicate; it would be like confusing Halloween with Christmas.[45] Yet another important Chagall scholar discusses two versions of *The Pinch of Snuff* based on a reading that assumes one has an inscription "Life" and the other "Death"; but actually the inscriptions (on the curtain of a Torah Scroll) read הי = *HI* (abbreviation of God's name), not חי = *XI* (alive) and סת = *ST* (Torah Scroll) not מת = *MT* (dead).[46] Even specialists on Jewish art make similar mistakes. Hebrew and Yiddish cultures parted company at the turn of the century, and living in Jerusalem does not guarantee a deep knowledge of the Yiddish world. As the Hebrew saying goes, "This is a discipline [a teaching] and it requires study."

Ziva Amishai-Maisels, who has written several detailed Chagall studies, has developed what amounts to a conspiracy theory, in which Chagall appears as a great manipulator who inscribed his personal grudges (against Malevich, Lissitzky, Granovski, the Christians, the Jews) as crossword puzzles in his paintings. In her "In-Jokes" paper she claims that Chagall "purposely [sic!] used Yiddish idioms and other Jewish sources in his early works in a manner which made them incomprehensible to the Christian world." And in the second version of her interpretation of "Chagall's Murals for the State Jewish Chamber Theater,"[47] she accuses Chagall of duplicity. On the one hand, "by visually translating Yiddish idioms [. . .] which would be understood neither by Russian nor French Christians . . . he could even assail with impunity the Christian religious paintings which influenced him." On the other hand, "he showed his discomfort with Judaism by utilizing modern formal elements which he felt Jews would be less likely to understand." But Chagall hardly needed to show discomfort with Judaism: his Jewish milieu and viewers were secular atheists who also admired the formal innovations of modern art. Nor is the use of Yiddish idioms an intentionally anti-Christian act. No evidence in Chagall's writings or private correspondence supports such a view.

Such claims are based on an essentialist ideology of racial and religious "identity," which runs counter to the cosmopolitan, ambivalent, and polyphonic consciousness of secular Jews in the twentieth century. Maisels's references to Chagall's "identity-pendulum" and "the constant oscillations in

---

45   Werner Haftman, *Marc Chagall* (New York: Harry N. Abrams, 1973), 20.

46   Susan Compton, *Chagall* (London: Royal Academy of Arts, 1985), 177.

47   Ziva Amishai-Maisels, "Chagall's Murals for the State Jewish Chamber Theater," in *Chagall: Dreams and Drama*, ed. Ruth Apter-Gabriel (Jerusalem: The Israel Museum, 1993), 21–39.

Chagall's [national] self-image"[48] are based on the assumption of univalent ethnic identities (either Jewish or French), and yet even her periodization of Chagall's identity cannot be sustained. When, in her view, Chagall allegedly "returned to full assimilation within the French world in 1923–35,"[49] he, at the same time, made some forty illustrations to three volumes of Lyesin's Yiddish poetry,[50] illustrated the Bible from a Yiddish translation, corresponded with Yiddish writers, published Yiddish poetry, and appealed to the YIVO (*yidisher visnshaftlekher institut* [Yiddish Scientific Institute]) in Vilna in 1929 to erect an international museum of Jewish art. At the same time, he complained that Jews did not appreciate or commission art, and he himself did little work directly treating Jewish topics. In theoretical terms, moreover, the artist's private pronouncements are not necessarily identical with the complexity of his art; Freud, Kafka, or Einstein were more concerned with their Jewishness in private correspondence than in their creative work.

Was Chagall a "Jewish artist"? Or was he a Russian, French, or modern artist? Is Salman Rushdie an Indian, Iranian, Muslim, or British artist? Is Gauguin a Tahitian painter? Imposing a contemporary need for exclusive racial identity on Chagall only brings him back to the ghetto he strove to escape, and inadvertently excludes him from the more universal canon of major modern artists. Today, we know much more about the role of culture in art, and can understand that most creative work is done at an intersection of several cultural strains. All Third World cultures exhibit this daily. But identifying blood with form does not help. The importance of cultural density and its interaction with formal problems requires our knowledge of all cultural sources. An essentialist definition of an artist is unnecessarily reductive and largely counterproductive; only a perspectival cluster of several constructs will do justice to a body of art as complex and multivalent as that of Chagall.

The tensions between local culture and the new languages or arts were fruitful for many artists of the period. Thus a recent major exhibition of Joan Miró featured him as a "Catalan painter" and stressed "his need to become what he often called an "international Catalan."[51] Jewish language and litera-

48   Ziva Amishai-Maisels, "Chagall's Jewish In-Jokes," 76–77.

49   Ziva Amishai-Maisels, "Chagall's Murals for the Jewish Theater" in *Marc Chagall*, ed. Vitali, 107–27. This is an earlier version of the essay that appears in Chagall, ed. Apter-Gabriel.

50   Abraham Walt (Abraham Lyesin), *lider un poemen* (1888–1938) (Poems and long poems (1888–1938), 3 vols. (New York: Forverts Association, 1938).

51   Carolyn Lanchner, *Joan Miró* (New York: The Museum of Modern Art, 1993), 19.

ture represent the earliest linguistic layers of Chagall's consciousness and are an essential part of his private fictional world. It is no accident that the oral subtexts are primarily in the "oral" language, Yiddish, and the written texts are in the "Holy Tongue," Hebrew. Russian and French literary subtexts were added in his illustrations when emanating from specific books, such as the exquisite Russian provincial world of Gogol's *Dead Souls*. And all those were perceived through painterly conceptions of the European avant-garde and interacted with their stylistic tendencies: at first, Russian Neo-Primitivism, the Russian reception of the Fauves, and the "World of Art" decorative style, then cubism and Suprematism. In its sources, Chagall's art represents cultural and stylistic eclecticism. Yet eclecticism was a salient hallmark of many modernist artists. Since the invention of cubism by Braque and Picasso, most artists felt impelled to negotiate new combinations between cubist and other elements. Indeed, the history of culture is a history of eclectic combinations and recombinations. There is no reason to privilege a "pure" style over an "eclectic" style, or, as we may call it, a polyphonic style; nor should Malevich (though historically important and easily definable) be ranked above the richer and more imaginative Chagall.

Figure 1.   Marc Chagall, from *Mein Leben*, 20, Radierungen (1923).

Figure 2. Marc Chagall, *Our House in My Village* (ca. 1948).

Figure 3. Marc Chagall, *The Dead Men* (1908), 68 cm x 86 cm. Musée National d'Art Moderne, Centre Georges Pompidou, Paris.

Figure 4. Marc Chagall, *Over Vitebsk* (1915–20), 67 cm x 92.7 cm. Museum of Modern Art, New York.

Figure 5. Marc Chagall, *Over the Town* (1917–18), 153 cm x 209 cm. Tretyakov Gallery, Moscow.

Figure 6. Marc Chagall, *Rain* (1911), 88.7 cm x 108 cm. The Peggy Guggenheim Collection, Venice.

Figure 7.   Marc Chagall, *Time Is a River Without Banks* (1930, 1936), 100 cm x 82 cm. Museum of Modern Art, New York.

Figure 8.　Uri-Tsvi Grinberg, "Uri-Tsvi Before the Cross / INRI" (1922).

Figure 9. Marc Chagall, *The White Crucifixion* (1938), 152.5 cm x 137 cm. Art Institute of Chicago.

Figure 10.   Marc Chagall, *Flayed Ox* (1947), 99 cm x 80 cm. Private collection, Paris.

Figure 11.   Marc Chagall, *The Cemetery Gate* (1917), 86 cm x 67 cm. Private collection, Basel.

Figure 12.   Marc Chagall, *The Jew in Bright Red* (1914–15), 100 cm x 80.5 cm.
Russian Museum, Leningrad.

Figure 13.   Marc Chagall, *Remembrance* (ca. 1918), 31.7 cm x 22.3 cm. Solomon R. Guggenheim Museum, New York.

Figure 14.   Marc Chagall, *Walking Village* (1920), 32.6 cm x 29 cm. Musée National d'Art Moderne, Centre Georges Pompidou, Paris.

Figure 15.   Marc Chagall, illustration from *Troyer* (1922).

9 A. SUTZKEVER

Life and Poetry[1]

POETRY AND ITS CONTEXTS

Abraham Sutzkever is one of the finest poets of the twentieth century. To be sure, he is not a philosophical poet; there was no sophisticated philosophy in Jewish culture. Nor is he a descriptive poet; the language of Modernism was opposed to description, and the fictional worlds of Sutzkever's poetry are presented through evocation and allusion rather than direct statement. But the language of his poetry—the profound sound orchestration and the metaphorical and mythopoeic imagery—is as dense, unmediated, and suggestive as that in the poetry of Mandelstam or Rilke. And his responses to historical reality are often as sharp as in many poems by Bertolt Brecht. The paradoxical amalgam of these two extremes of twentieth-century poetry— self-focused poetic language and ideological *engagement*—is successful in Sutzkever's work because both are presented through the events of the poet's own biography. As he himself observed dryly, in a retrospective poem written at the age of seventy-five:

Inside me, a twig of sounds sways toward me, as before.
Inside me, rivers of blood are not a metaphor.

("Inside Me")

1   Introduction to A. Sutzkever, *Selected Poetry and Prose*, translated by Barbara and Benjamin Harshav, University of California Press, 1991.

The twig of sounds is as tangible as the rivers of blood, both are swaying in-side him as a budding branch in the spring; there is no ambivalence, but one, entwined, double source of poetic energy.

Three magic circles enclose Sutzkever's poetry, making it difficult for the contemporary American reader to see his greatness: (1) the all but obscured, rich, literary Yiddish language; (2) the misleadingly private Jewish Holocaust; and (3) his terrifying and exhilarating biography. I shall try briefly to evoke all three.

Sutzkever came to Yiddish literature in a moment of populist excitement with the earthy, idiomatic, folksy, often coarse, spoken Yiddish language, ide-alized in literature at the turn of the century by the satirical realist Mendele and the tragicomic imitator Sholem Aleichem, and reborn in the Expression-ist poetry and fiction of the 1920's and in the social realism of the thirties. In this context, he strove to create exquisite aesthetic objects, as refined as music, as colorful and unreal as Expressionist nature painting, as rich and precise as the language of the Vilna Yiddish Scientific Institute. Sutzkever is an incom-parable virtuoso of meter, rhyme, strophic forms, and ever-changing dynamic rhythmical patterns, forms that may seem obsolete to the contemporary Eng-lish ear, but are nevertheless essential to much of Russian or German modern poetry. His is a "Neo-Classical Modernism," which combines the emphasis on well-designed strophic forms with a Modernist metaphorical poetic language and "unreal," mythopoeic fictional worlds.

Mallarmé said that a poet is not one who invents new words but one who invents new places for words. Sutzkever both invented words and found new places for them, new word-and-sound combinations. But the unmistakable precision and freshness of Sutzkever's Yiddish verse require a reader who would both know the rich, multilingual, and multilayered context of "juicy" Yiddish and could, at the same time, savor the effects of Modernist poetry, its images and neologisms. This great poet is only great as a poet can be: in the context of his own language. This is especially true for Modernist poetry, intensely invested in language innovation, rhythm, and sound orchestration.

The Holocaust seems to erect a barrier between Jewish writers and many non-Jewish readers, as if it were a private business of the Jews. But actually, in Sutzkever's poetry, it can be read as a focused close-up, a parable of the unbe-lievable times of this century, of human nature and dignity, of the inexplica-ble puzzles of existence and the palpable reality of extinction, and—through all this—of the beauty of observation, consciousness, and language.

The Holocaust dyes all of Sutzkever's writings but by no means does it absorb him entirely. From his very beginnings, the poet was marked by a curiosity about nature, a wish to merge with the vis-à-vis, as only a truly narcissist poet may have. His eye and ear for the colors and sounds of the icy blue roads of his childhood Siberia, the forests and swamps engraved by glaciers in the Lithuanian north, and the sand dunes and craters of the Israeli Negev, never let go.

Sutzkever wrote obsessively throughout the darkest times, hiding in a chimney or fighting in the swamps. Yet, his Holocaust theme gained depth with time, precisely because he was able to confront it from the base of another alternative of Jewish existence, the state of Israel. Sutzkever is also one of the innovative poets of Israel, of its nature and revival. Writing in Yiddish rather than Hebrew, he perceives the Israeli landscape as an intimate outsider, through the discourse of biblical scenes from his childhood imagination. A similar historical perspective marks his perception of the Holocaust, indeed of the totality of annihilation of a millennium-old European Jewry, as symbolized in the demise of its northern capital, Vilna, the "Jerusalem of Lithuania." In his world, the Holocaust is part of personal memory, steeped in those two years of hell, but it is never cut off from the larger view of Jewish past and future, as it is with some "Jewish" assimilated writers. The omnipresent, explicit or tacit, coexistence in his poetry of the alternative domains of Jewish history—Vilna, the Bible, Israel, the Destruction, and rebirth—places each theme in a multiple perspective. They seem to be mirrored in one another. And then, all are reflected again in the other, intimate mirroring between his lyrical I and his imaginary "Twin Brother" (see the poem by this name), his slaughtered self over there and his unbelievably surviving writing self here and now.

JERUSALEM OF LITHUANIA

The myths and meanings of Jewish culture and beliefs are not embodied in godlike persons but are anchored in space. The moral and narrative story of the Bible focuses on the relationship between a people and their God, as dramatized in the recurrent loss of and return to their promised land. The prophets predict and mourn the downfall of Jerusalem, the "Faithful City" that became like a "whore." And the most family-oriented holiday, the Passover Seder, produces a narrative performance symbolizing the myth of exile and return to the land as the very essence of Jewish existence. It concludes with the wish to be "Next year in Jerusalem." Jerusalem became the spatial metonymy for the ethical, cultural, and spiritual being of the people and their link to an abstract, all-encompassing God. By calling a city in Northeastern Europe, "Jerusalem of Lithuania," they assigned to it the symbolic locus, the spatial base for a transformed Diaspora culture and consciousness.

Jews appeared in central Europe at the beginning of the Christian Era. Others moved up from the Byzantine Empire to Eastern Europe and apparently spoke Slavic languages. We do not know when individual Jews migrated to or through Lithuania but their settlements there are documented from the fourteenth century on. In the sixteenth century, an influx of Jews from Germany enlarged the Jewish population and spread the Yiddish language.

Lithuania, the last pagan country in Europe, was a Grand Duchy ruling over a vast area of forests, rivers, and swamps, stretching from Prussia to the periphery of Moscow and from the Baltic almost to the Black Sea, including what are today Lithuania proper, all of Byelorus, southern Latvia, parts of Russia and Poland, and Ukraine (later ceded to Poland). In 1322, Grand Duke Gediminas (in Polish, Giedymin) built his new capital Vilnius (in Polish, Wilno) on the banks of the river Vilya. In 1386, Giedymin's grandson married the Queen of Poland and merged the two dynasties. Lithuania accepted Christianity and eventually entered into a formal union with Poland in 1569. Lithuanian gentry and intellectuals assimilated to Polish culture and a Polish-language university was founded in Vilna in 1803. The great Polish Romantic poet Adam Mickiewicz and the Nobel Prize Laureate Czeslaw Milosz, both "Lithuanians" by origin, were connected with the city and the area (see Milosz's memoirs *Native Realm*). Vilna became both a Polish and a Jewish cultural center.

The Jews of Poland and Lithuania created an autonomous state within a state. The "Council of the State of Lithuania" was a kind of Jewish autonomous parliament. The four "Principal Cities" of Jewish Lithuania, Vilna among them, had jurisdiction over dozens of smaller towns, and those, in turn, ruled over Jews scattered in many villages. They dominated the entire Jewish population, imposed religious rules, and collected taxes for the Jewish communities and for the king. A network of social, cultural, and religious institutions—schools, synagogues, printing houses, books, professional synagogues or unions, hospitals, and philanthropies—covered all aspects of life (except for power and territory). The Jews were the only ethnic group in Europe not divided into official classes, or castes. The social and linguistic gaps between Byelorussian peasants, Polish magnates, and the German- or Polish-speaking citizens, and between all of them and Western Europe, did not exist among the Jews. They belonged to one extraterritorial network, speaking and writing their private two languages—the Holy Tongue of the texts and Yiddish for daily life. It was a network reinforced by a private universe of discourse with an intensive code of beliefs, behavior, and texts, dominated by the totality of a separate religion. Hence it was natural for the Jews to move between those tightly closed classes and nationalities—from the countryside to the small towns, to the cities, and overseas, and vice versa—facilitating trade and spreading crafts and artifacts. It was a network with no boundaries and the ties of Vilna to all corners of the empire as well as to Western European communities were manifold.

Vilna became a famous center of learning, first rabbinical, then secular. "Lithuanian" rabbis and teachers spread throughout the Jewish world. In the eighteenth century, this central role was symbolized by the towering figure of the Vilna Gaon ("genius") (1720–1797). He dominated all of Lithuania and stopped the spread of the Hassidic movement in the name of the "Misnagdim," who based their Jewishness on learning. Religious academies ("Yeshivas") were founded in small Lithuanian towns, such as Volozhin, Mir, Slobodka, and Navaredok. In 1795, after the second partition of Poland, Vilna was incorporated into Russia. When only two rabbinical seminars were allowed in all of Russia, one was established in Vilna and later became a teacher's seminar. Of the two Jewish printing houses permitted in the Empire, one was in Vilna, the famous house of Rom, which executed the formidable task of printing the whole Babylonian Talmud in mosaic patterns as well as hundreds of books and pamphlets in Hebrew and Yiddish.

We must remember that the population numbers throughout the period were small. It is estimated that in 1650, about 350,000 Jews lived in all of Eastern Europe. In 1765, 3,887 Jews were counted in Vilna proper. At the outbreak of World War II, in 1939, only 60,000 Jews lived in the city (in a general population of 200,000). With the refugees coming in from Poland at the beginning of the war, their numbers rose to 80,000. To the contemporary reader, this may seem a small city. But the point is that the structure of the population was different from what we know in modern urban societies. Jewish Vilna was small, but the area it dominated was immense. It was, as it were, the "shopping center" and learning campus of a huge hinterland, which in the twentieth century reached several million. People would come from surrounding towns and villages to trade or study and return to their hometowns or move to the West, and still be proud of their "Vilna" origins. The parents of the Vilna Gaon; the Haskalah historian of Vilna, Rashi Fin; the founders of the YIVO (Yiddish Scientific Institute), Max Weinreich and Zelig Kalmanovich; the Yiddish poet Sutzkever and the Hebrew poet Abba Kovner; and the Polish poets Mickiewicz and Milosz were not born in Vilna itself, though their names are linked with that cultural center. Jerusalem of Lithuania was the symbolic focus and aristocratic pride of a vast, extraterritorial Jewish empire.

Ironically, it is the Jews who preserved the boundaries of the Grand Duchy of Lithuania, which was six times the size of the present-day Lithuanian state (though they did not speak Lithuanian, which never was the common language of that empire). *Líte* (pronounced *Leé-tah*), as the area is called in Yiddish, and its Jews, the *Litvaks*, are marked by a separate Yiddish dialect, cooking traditions, typical mentality, and the passion for learning. In the mid-nineteenth century, *Líte* became the center of modern Hebrew literature: works of fiction and poetry, historical scholarship, and translations of world literature were written and published in Hebrew. And in the twentieth century it became a center of Yiddish education, publishing, and scholarship.

The Jewish secular movement in the nineteenth and twentieth centuries revolted against the traditional orthodox society and tried to create a Jewish culture and society molded upon European models. But it, too, adapted the glory of Vilna—"the city of the Vilna Gaon"—as a center of learning and culture. The modern Jewish myth of "Jerusalem of Lithuania" took over the vacant seat of the long-abandoned Lithuanian capital and combined it with the biblical discourse of Jerusalem, which, like Vilna, had "hills all around her." In 1897, the Jewish Socialist party of Russia and Lithuania, the "Bund," which became a major supporter of Yiddish culture, was founded here. In the twentieth century, the city became a microcosm reflecting all the Jewish ideologies and cultural trends of the time. Between the two World Wars, the city belonged to Poland (1920–1939). At that time, there were in Vilna: a Hebrew, a Yiddish, and a Polish-Hebrew teachers' college, each supplying teachers for the vast hinterland of Eastern Europe and for Eretz Israel; secular schools in Yiddish, in Ashkenazi Hebrew, and in Sephardi Hebrew; religious schools in traditional Yiddish for teaching Hebrew texts, or in Polish for "modern" Jews observing the Sabbath; Yiddish theater; several Yiddish newspapers; major publishers; Yiddish journals for linguistics, economics, and children's journals; the Union of Female Glovemakers and other trade unions; health organizations; youth movements; and political parties of all shades. In the privately endowed Strashun Library, young and old, gymnasium students and scholars, read the Talmud along with the writings of Herzl, Moyshe-Leyb Halpern, and Karl Marx. Young Jews went to the Polish University, to universities in Western Europe, or snuck across the nearby border to the Communist paradise. All those cultural and political options lived in constant dialogue with each other; they conducted a multidirectional argument on one stage. It was the epitome of a new Jewish secular culture as a galaxy of interrelated and competing possibilities.

Like Prague, located between the empires—between Russia and Poland and close to the cultural and trading roots with Germany—Vilna remained a strong Jewish center, where both intellectuals and the masses spoke Yiddish. At the same time, the links with the outside world were open: Vilna émigrés lived in South Africa and America; one could encounter Vilna students and tailors in Paris, Liège, and Berlin; there were intimate cultural ties with Eretz Israel and all major Jewish centers in the world; and Sigmund Freud was a member of the YIVO Board.

Vilna was proud of its literary tradition. Zalman Reyzen, a prolific translator and author, who single-handedly wrote an eight-volume *Lexicon of Yiddish Literature*, published and edited the daily newspaper *Vilner Tog*, in which he promoted Yiddish literature and published budding writers, including the first poems of Abraham Sutzkever. (Reyzen perished in a Soviet prison.) Russian, Polish, German, and world literature were read and translated. The Jews were powerless, poverty was rampant, but Culture was everything. And above all, "Jerusalem of Lithuania" was a symbol of the Second Jerusalem, the Jewish national and cultural life that subsisted in Europe for a millennium. This is the atmosphere in which Sutzkever grew up.

CHILDHOOD IN SIBERIA

Abraham Sutzkever was born in 1913 in Smorgoń, then a middle-sized industrial city southwest of Vilna. In 1915, during World War I, the Russian high command expelled a million and a half Jews from their hometowns, as potential "spies" for the Germans. All Jews of Smorgoń were ordered to leave within twenty-four hours and the city was plundered and burned. Today the Holocaust has overshadowed the events of World War I, but then too a large

Jewish population was uprooted from places where they had lived for centuries. The two Vilna Holocaust poets, Sutzkever (in Yiddish) and Abba Kovner (in Hebrew), were among them; exile was their childhood experience.

On the roads, the Sutzkevers met a rich merchant, who helped them move to his town, Omsk, a central city of western Siberia on the Irtysh River, far from the Jewish Pale of Settlement. Sutzkever lived there until he was seven years old. In Omsk, his father died of heart failure at the age of thirty; typhus and civil war ravaged the city; but the enchanted world of Siberia, as perceived in a child's imagination, became the first fictional space of his poetry. Siberia, the symbol of Russian oppression and exile, the haunting name itself, became inverted in his classical poem "Siberia" (which attracted Marc Chagall to illustrate it from his own childhood imagination). The beauty of the white expanse, the power of the ice breaking on the Irtysh, the music of father's violin, all merged in images of the palpable, lasting nature of the nonmaterial world: "wonder-woods sway wide on windowpanes," "snow-sounds falling on my head" when father played his violin—and a wolf peeping in the window "to sniff the music's flesh."

In Sutzkever's poetic mythology, the world of his Siberian childhood is unattainable, beyond the boundaries of normal reality, hence eternally beautiful as evoked in imagination and poetry. A key image of the poem is the snowman, left behind in the Siberian winter: enclosed "in a hut of sounds," it can never melt. The snowman is a monument to his childhood, but the poet himself is a "snowman in a cloak of skin," an unreal, imaginary being, and the sounds of his masterful strophes will remain a monument to him. The poetic topos of human images preserved in a sculpture (as in poems by Pushkin or Keats), which are endowed with eternal life precisely because they are dead, frozen in the spring, and remain forever young—this poetic paradox is enhanced here in a manifold additional unreality. In Sutzkever's poem, the spring is a winter, and only winter can keep the young snowman intact; the sculpture is made not of bronze or ceramics, but of melting snow, and only freezing time can keep it alive. It is not a sculpture present to the eyes of a meditating poet but placed in a distant space, present only in memory. And, in its unmelted form, it lives only in the magic sounds of poetry. And today, a new dimension is added: to most readers, the sounds of Sutzkever's Yiddish words themselves are as inaccessible as the Siberian snowman.

All this is relevant because the same pattern, formed in Sutzkever's childhood imagination, became a key to his post-Holocaust poetry. The poet's belief in the *real* existence of the nonexistent—or their *subsistence* (as Bertrand Russell would say) in some distant, unattainable world—is transformed later into Sutzkever's evocation of the no-longer-existent Vilna from the landscapes of Israel. The dead who disappeared in the Holocaust must be alive in some realm because they are vividly present in imagination and recalled in poetry. The power of a child's fantasy becomes the poetic myth of the mature Sutzkever.

Among his Siberian recollections, he tells that once, when the Tsar and his family were killed in the Urals (not far from Omsk), a soldier brought a huge stolen diamond that had belonged to the Tsar and sold it to the watchmaker Berger. Berger was afraid to keep it in town and brought it to Herz Sutzkever who hid it in his house. The father, ill and frail, showed the treasure, the mysterious emperor's diamond, glimmering blue in the rays of the sunset, to his beloved youngest son, Abrasha. This rare intimacy with father and the magic light emanating from the diamond, amid the shadows of the dark hut, made an indelible impression on Sutzkever and became the "glimmering essence" of his later poetry (see, for example, the poem "What Did You Expect to See, Prying"). His father died and was buried in the Jewish cemetery in Omsk. At the funeral, Abrasha felt a tremendous urge to leap into the grave, to join his father, but a dove appeared and pulled the child's eyes to the sky. The disbelief in the finality of his father's death and the miraculous snow-white dove saving his life are again magnified and mirrored in Sutzkever's Holocaust poetry.

YOUTH IN VILNA

In 1920, when the Russian Civil War had subsided, Reine Sutzkever returned with her three children and settled in Vilna, where they lived for twenty years in a small hut in the suburb of Snipishok. Her oldest brother (of ten siblings) had revolted against their father and left for America, where he did well. His quarterly checks supported Reine and her children.

All her life, Sutzkever's mother mourned her dead husband and never remarried. Through her, Abrasha adored his father's memory and his maternal grandfather. This grandfather was a rabbi in a small town, who devoted his life to writing a "sharp" book on a Talmudic topic in the Lithuanian tradition, and was nicknamed the "Gaon [genius] of Mikhalishok" (the book was published posthumously in Vilna in 1909). The poet's older brother went to study in France and migrated as a pioneer to Eretz Israel. His older sister, a beauty with long black braids, was admired as a genius, skipped three classes in school, and wrote poetry in Russian. When she died of "brain fever" (meningitis) at the age of thirteen, Abrasha fled home and wrote in the sand: "eternal." Again, the inexplicable death of a godlike, sick person was entwined with a sense of beauty and poetry and the child's imagination of eternal life.

Abrasha apparently internalized the images of the artists: his father, his poet sister, a girl dancer he met, and himself as a poetic child. By writing poetry he was fulfilling their dream and revitalizing their existence. In poetry he found something that will overcome death. He truly believed that only through poetry would he survive the Holocaust—hence it had to be a different kind of poetry, endowed with magical power to change reality, a poetry, as he often wrote, that both God and the dead would like to read. Of course, this is a romantic perception, reinforced by the romantic and symbolist poetry he read; but it also has deep roots in his own biography. Furthermore, a basic paradox underlies this perception: Yiddish poetry at the time was secular in its very being, but his mother conveyed an intense religiosity that transcended her own life (composed of widowhood, poverty, exile, and Holocaust). This may be the source of the poet's early attraction to a nonnormative, self-centered religiosity, as a base for his poetic mythology. First, he embraced a Spinozaist pantheism and, later, he resorted to a poetic pantheon for the dead, a denial of "realism" as a way to assert the subsistence of the annihilated world in some cosmic space.

Abrasha was a sickly child, suffered from headaches, and was unable to study in school. At first, he had a private rabbi (religious teacher), then he attended a religious school in his neighborhood and later a Polish-Hebrew high school. Sutzkever met Freydke, his life's companion and wife, when she was twelve and he was fifteen. Since the age of fourteen, Freydke worked in the bibliography section of YIVO, the Yiddish Scientific Institute, and knew a lot of Yiddish poetry by heart, especially the work of Moyshe-Leyb Halpern. Sutzkever began writing poetry at the age of thirteen, first in Hebrew, then in Yiddish. But he never attended a Yiddish school or had any idea that Yiddish poetry had been written before him. Now he elected a course of self-education, spending long days in the Strashun Library. At the age of sixteen, feeling enormous rage "against himself, his poems, and the world," he burned all his poems, against the protestations of his mother and Freydke. It was a traumatic and purifying event, marking a new stage of "religious" awe before the magic and power of poetry and a new commitment to serve it with no compromise. Sutzkever was influenced by the great Yiddish linguist and director of the YIVO, Dr. Max Weinreich, and by other scholars, including the literary historian Zelig Kalmanovich and the linguist Noah Prilutski. He studied Yiddish in depth, enriched and purified his language, wrote poetry in Old Yiddish, which he learned at the YIVO, and began to translate the medieval Yiddish romance *Bove Bukh*, written in Venice in 1508, in precise *ottava rima* stanzas, by Eliyahu Bakhur (or Elye Bokher).

As a youth, Sutzkever joined the Vilna Yiddish scouts' organization, "Di Bin" (The Bee), and was sworn in by Max Weinreich on the Buffalo Mountains outside Vilna, "faithfully to guard secular Yiddish culture." The Bee promoted love of nature ("all the birds spoke Yiddish," as nature teacher and cultural critic A. Golomb said, and Yiddish terminology for flowers and trees was avidly coined and learned). Both nature and literature were symbols of human dignity and an antidote to the confined life of the traditional Jewish "ghetto" (a mere symbolic designation, since there was no actual ghetto in Medieval Vilna). In that rarified Vilna atmosphere, it was just one or two interwar generations that promoted the ideal of a Jewish secular culture at peace with its past, embracing Jewish history on the one hand and lower-class folklore on the other, as parts of its integral heritage. There was an aristocratic conception of the purity of language and elitist literature, of Yiddish as part of world literature, measuring its achievements by the highest criteria.

As in other Jewish youth movements of that period, boys and girls of the Bee went on memorable excursions and summer camps in the beautiful Vilna area—an unusual pastime for Jews—sang around bonfires and discussed literature. The young poet developed a pantheistic admiration of Nature, as a mirror for the self-assertion of the individual, the free wanderer among forests and mountains, and for the rich life of his psyche. In the Bee, Abrasha struck up an intense friendship with Miki Chernikhov, the precocious son of a famous Vilna lawyer. At Chernikhov's home, the family read aloud all of Pushkin's epic poem "Evgeny Onegin," written in a melodious and flexible iambic tetrameter. Miki (later a survivor of the Soviet camps and subsequently American Professor Michal Astur) introduced Abrasha to the best Russian Symbolist poets, and read and translated Edgar Allen Poe for him. Abrasha knew Yiddish better than any other language, but he imbibed the musical forms of poetry in the European tradition. He read Polish Romantic poets, steeped himself in the difficult poetry of Cyprian Norwid, and attended lectures by Professor Manfred Krydl, a famous Polish literary theoretician and critic, at the Vilna Polish university.

Through his neighbor and older friend Leyzer Wolf, a wildly original, grotesque Yiddish poet, he joined the group of writers and painters known as "Young Vilna." But Sutzkever was a loner and the leftist-oriented group looked askance at his poetry, lacking "social" (that is, political and leftist) commitment. At the same time, he was recognized and published by A. Leyeles in *In Zikh*, the journal of the New York Introspectivists, and his first book was published by the Yiddish Writers' Union in Warsaw. He befriended Jewish painters and was influenced by the ideals of art in Modernist painting.

World War II broke out. Sutzkever married Freydke. In September 1939, Poland was divided between Germany and the Soviet Union. The Russians entered Vilna, arrested many Jewish leaders of all political trends (including the attorney Chernikhov, who, once having defended Communists in fascist Poland, now disappeared in their jails), and turned the city over to independent Lithuania, which renamed it Vilnius. In May 1940, Lithuania too was swallowed up by the Soviets. Sutzkever's book, *Valdiks* ("From the Forest"), one of the masterworks of Yiddish poetry, was printed in tiny Lithuania, in a crevice of space and time: between the two totalitarian empires, Germany and Russia, and between the German-Polish war of 1939 and the world war of 1941. It is the most exquisite crystal of the Yiddish language and, perhaps, the last Yiddish book printed in Europe before the Holocaust.

HOLOCAUST

On June 22, 1941, the Germans attacked the Soviet Union and two days later they occupied Vilna. Over 100,000 Jews of Vilna and the provinces were liquidated in the suburb of Ponar. *Ponar* became the terrifying symbol of the annihilation of Jerusalem of Lithuania and the Jewish nation in Europe. Only some 20,000 Jews remained, crammed into a ghetto of seven small streets, repeatedly persecuted and decimated by Germans and Lithuanians, and finally liquidated in September 1943.

From the first days of Nazi occupation, Jewish men were snatched up in the streets and dragged off to the horrifying Lukishki prison or to Ponar, from which they never returned. At best, they were taken to forced labor. Abrasha hid in his mother's hut in Snipishok. For six weeks he lay in a crawl space under a little roof below their window, where he bored a hole in the tin roof and feverishly wrote his poems. When his disappearance roused suspicion, Freydke came at night to take him out, but he could not walk. Later, he joined

Jewish worker brigades or hid in various places. On September 5, 1941, he was taken by the Lithuanians to be shot. He and the Vilna Rov, Rabbi Gustman, were forced to dig their own graves in the Sheshkiner Hills. It was a beautiful September day. The Lithuanians stood behind him and cocked their rifles. And then Sutzkever had a poetic experience: "When they ordered us to put our hands over our eyes, I understood that they were going to shoot us. And I remember, as if it were now: when I put my fingers on my eyes, I saw birds fluttering. . . . I never saw birds flying so slowly, I had a great aesthetic joy in seeing the slow-slow motion of their wings between my fingers." The Lithuanians shot over their heads and took them to the newly established ghetto.

In the ghetto he eventually found both his mother and Freydke. He succeeded in transferring his mother from the "second ghetto" (soon liquidated) to the first. During the *"Aktsia"* (round-up of Jews) of the "yellow permits," he fled the ghetto and found refuge in the cellar of a Polish peasant woman. His mother hid in a *"malina"* (a hiding place), but when Sutzkever returned to the ghetto she was gone. The *malina* had been discovered and all its inhabitants were taken away. In the beginning of 1942, Freydke bore a son in the ghetto hospital, but giving birth to Jewish children was forbidden and the Germans poisoned him (see the poem "To my Wife"). Writing poetry, or simply, as he puts it, "living poetically," saved his life in the ghetto: "It is a spirit that enters you and it is stronger than all the bullets." As Sutzkever explains: "There was a madman in Vilna, he walked into a synagogue and saw a painter standing on top of a ladder and painting the ceiling. So he said to him, 'hold onto the brush because I'm taking away the ladder.' That's how I was: I held onto the brush and held myself, did not fall down. That was the remarkable thing."

Soon, Sutzkever joined a group of intellectuals and young people who went to work every day in the building of the YIVO, outside the ghetto, in the so-called Rosenberg Stab (officially, *Einsatzstab, Reichsleiter Rosenberg*). This institution, organized by Dr. Pohl, Director of the Frankfurt museum for the study of eastern nations, prepared resources for the "Science of Jewry without Jews" (*Wissenschaft des Judentums ohne Juden*). Here, in the library and archives of the former Yiddish Scientific Institute, the Germans assembled books from the valuable Strashun Library and other plundered libraries and synagogues of Vilna. Under the supervision of German "scholars" of Judaism (who knew neither Yiddish nor Hebrew), the ghetto brigade had to sort out the books and designate materials for shipment to Germany or to a paper factory. Risking their lives, Sutzkever and his friends smuggled hundreds of rare books and manuscripts into the ghetto, often under the pretext of "heating paper," and put them in the library or buried them. Many of those materials were eventually brought by Sutzkever to Moscow or uncovered in Vilna after the liberation and from there were smuggled to New York and Jerusalem. Many valuable books and manuscripts were shipped by the Nazis to Germany, recovered after the war, and brought to the YIVO branch in New York.

The YIVO also served as a base for contacts with the non-Jewish city. Here, Sutzkever and his friend, the poet Kaczerginski, got the first machine gun for the FPO, the United Partisan Organization, which they smuggled into the ghetto. In the ghetto itself, during a lull between one *Aktsia* and another, an intense, illegal cultural life was conducted, as if continuing the prewar multi-directional activities of Vilna: a school was established, a hospital, a library, a theater, social and philanthropic organizations, Hebrew and Yiddish literary events, music concerts, painting, and a youth club. Sutzkever taught Yiddish poetry and organized an exhibit in the Ghetto devoted to the American Yiddish poet, Yehoash, whom he admired for the musicality of his verse and his love of nature. For his long poem, "The Grave Child," Sutzkever received in 1942 the literary prize of the Ghetto Writers' Union.

Sutzkever, Freydke, Shmerke Kaczerginski, Ruzhka Korchak, Michael Kovner, and other YIVO workers were members of the FPO. I shall not repeat here the well-known story of the failed Vilna ghetto uprising and the heroism of its fighters who went through sewers to the forests, where they joined the Soviet partisan army fighting the Nazis. Sutzkever, Freydke, and Shmerke Kaczerginski left the ghetto on September 12, 1943, with a group of partisans led by the legendary Zelda, who made dozens of forays from the forests to Vilna, to save surviving Jews. They walked for a hundred kilometers between hostile villages and German army units until they reached the same areas around Lake Narocz where he and Freydke had gone on nature-loving excursion before the war.

IN THE FOREST

It was not a simple matter for city youth (especially the intellectual, idealistic youngsters who made up most of the underground movement) to live in the forests and swamps, through rain, snow, and starvation. The Gentile population of the countryside was hostile and denounced any hiding Jew or Jewish group they discovered to the Germans. The Polish rightist underground,

Armia Krajowa, was busy slaughtering Jews in the forests. The only force they could join was the Soviet partisan movement, which became strong only at a later stage. But here, too, anti-Semitism was rampant.

Sutzkever's group was directed to the Byelorussian partisan Brigade headed by Markov, operating in the primeval forests and swamps around Lake Narocz. Only young Jews from the ghetto, capable of fighting and bringing weapons with them, were allowed into the forest—they had to leave their families behind, to be slaughtered in the ghetto. But in the forest, some five hundred Jews were mustered before Markov, including the fighting unit "Vengeance." The Jewish unit was dismantled, their weapons taken away, and most young people were taken out of fighting units and assigned to service units, while hundreds, including most of the women, were left in the forest to their own devices. Many were killed by the Germans. On Yom Kippur, over thirty thousand German soldiers surrounded the forest and began combing it. Markov and his fighting units fled, leaving the weak behind. Sutzkever's group was ordered to carry the wounded with them. Through deep, impenetrable swamps, they spread branches on the mire and crossed to a dry island. Even here, German spies arrived, but the Sutzkevers hid among bushes, deep in the freezing water, and survived. When the brigade returned, Sutzkever and Kaczerginski were summoned by Markov and assigned to write its history.

Suddenly, a cable came from Moscow announcing that a plane would be sent to rescue Sutzkever from the German occupied territory. Back in the ghetto, Sutzkever had sent a sheaf of poems, including the long poem "Kol Nidre," with some partisans to the forest. From there, the poem was sent on to Moscow, where it made an enormous impression. For the first time in the Soviet Union, this poem by an incognito ghetto writer showed the full horror of the Final Solution. Ilya Ehrenburg, then a highly influential writer whose columns in *Pravda* were read on the front, compared it to a Greek tragedy. Justas Paleckis, President of the Lithuanian government-in-exile in Moscow, had known Sutzkever before the war. Paleckis, a leftist poet, had spent years in Lithuanian jails with Jewish Communists, from whom he learned Yiddish and Hassidic songs. In 1940, when a Soviet Lithuanian capital was established in Vilnius, Paleckis had translated some of Sutzkever's poetry into Lithuanian. Now he remembered the poet and saved him.

Markov provided guards and a horse-drawn sleigh to take Sutzkever and Freydke to an airstrip in another partisan region, ninety kilometers away. The journey through German territory was filled with dangers; one of the partisan guards was an anti-Semite and tried to shoot them. Eventually the Sutzkev-ers were left alone to cross a railroad. The Germans had cut down trees on both sides of the railroad to prevent partisans from blowing up trains, and the whole strip was mined and heavily guarded by the Germans. Dismembered wolf carcasses, human bodies, and limbs littered the field. As the poet recalls, he stepped among the mines to the rhythm of a poem, with Freydke in his foot-steps, and was saved, in spite of German fire from the distance. Later he wrote that writing poetry is like walking on such a mine field—you never know where you will step next (see the poem, "A Winter Night"). When they finally reached the other partisan brigade, a small plane landed on the ice-covered lake. Sutz-kever sat in its opening, with Freydke tied to his knees, and two wounded par-tisans were stuck in the rear. The plane veered through the heavy fire of the German front, diving suddenly, and eventually emerging on the Soviet side.

RESURRECTION

In March 1944, the Sutzkevers reached Moscow. Ehrenburg wrote an article in *Pravda* about Sutzkever, "The Victory of a Human Being." For the first time, *Pravda* wrote openly about the Holocaust and about Jews participating in the war against Nazi Germany. Sutzkever received letters from all corners of the Soviet Union, including some from old friends, like Miki Chernikhov, who was still interned in a camp. Vilna was liberated in July and Sutzkever returned to his "slaughtered city." Surviving Jewish partisans from the forests took part in liberating the city, including the Hebrew poet Abba Kovner and the Yiddish poet Shmerke Kaczerginski. Together they dug up remaining cul-tural treasures saved from the Germans and built a Jewish Museum, which was closed and confiscated by the NKVD some three years later.

As the poet tells it, "I felt that I must be the witness of all those events, that I was destined to be the witness. I entered a spectacle someone staged, I thought I played a role in it. Who staged the spectacle, I don't know. Who needed it? What for? In those years of destruction, I always felt I was a witness to an immense earthly and cosmic play. I felt a divine sense of messianic mis-sion, those were the most elevated moments of my life." As we see, the mythi-cal conception of his poetry permeated the poet's perception of his own life; poetic imagery and poetic discourse entered his daily discourse, too. And now that this messianic perception was realized, Sutzkever was chosen to appear at the Nuremberg trial as a witness to the destruction of the Jewish people.

In 1947, via Vilna, Lodz, and Paris, Sutzkever and Freydke came as illegal immigrants to Eretz Israel, the land of his mother's dreams. The pioneering, secular culture that built the young society of Israel was based on a miraculous revival of the Hebrew language. Like Yiddish, modern Hebrew mastered all areas of modern life and society and all genres of European culture. However, the scars of the "war of languages" between Hebrew and Yiddish for dominance in secular Jewish culture were still fresh in the Hebrew Palestine. Nevertheless, Sutzkever succeeded in raising the sentiments of Zionists from Eastern Europe (such as the scholar and President of Israel, Zalman Shazar). The Hebrew Trade Union Federation "Histadrut" provided the means for the establishment of a high-level cultural and literary quarterly in Yiddish, *Di goldene keyt* ("The Golden Chain"), which Sutzkever has edited from 1948 to this day. One hundred forty-two issues, of about 250 pages each, have appeared, bringing together the scattered remnant Yiddish writers from Europe, North and South America, Israel, and the Soviet Union. A new haven for the last generation of Yiddish literature destroyed in Europe was found, gathered in the Holy Land.

Sutzkever has appeared at international poetry festivals, has been translated into many languages, and has received dozens of literary prizes, including the Israel Prize, bestowed by the state on persons of unusual achievement. Yet, the destruction of his people in Europe and the demise of his language permeate his words, along with the sense of the futility of words.

10 NOTE ON THE SYSTEMS OF HEBREW VERSIFICATION[1]

Bible to Present

Verse and rhyme, used in serious poetry as well as in a variety of other kinds of writing (historical chronicles, book dedications, gravestone inscriptions, community annals), were an omnipresent feature of Hebrew culture in all periods and in all centers of the Jewish dispersion. Marked by strong tendencies of formalism and conservatism, the forms of Hebrew verse have nevertheless changed radically as Hebrew culture interacted with Greek rhetoric, Arabic secular literature, Italian Renaissance poetry, German eighteenth-century verse, Russian Romanticism and Futurism, Yiddish folklore, and English modernism. Almost all possible systems of rhythm and rhyme had been active in Hebrew literature in one period or another. Given a language with a stubborn core of vocabulary, morphology, spelling, imagery and basic mythology, the differences in formal systems were largely responsible for the great divergences in the nature and poetics of Hebrew poetry in its major historical centers.

One must bear in mind that a Hebrew poet—in Rome, in Mainz, in Yemen, in Vilna, in St. Petersburg, in New York, or in Henderson, North Carolina—was always placed at an intersection of at least three traditions: (a) the modes of Hebrew writing perpetuated in his own community; (b) the

---

1 Published in *The Penguin Book of Hebrew Verse*, edited by T. Carmi, 1981. For a larger presentation of this history, see under "Prosody, Hebrew," *Encyclopedia Judaica*. Readers with no Hebrew may skip the Hebrew examples.

distinctly different poetic forms developed in his own language, Hebrew, in other cultural centers, either of his own time or in the past; (c) the poetic norms predominant in the language of the country in which he lived, the language which he read and spoke daily. A shift of orientation from one to another of these poetic systems was often responsible for the changes evolving in the forms or in the very nature of Hebrew verse.

Since in most historical periods the adherence to prevalent poetic norms was a rather strict one, it is possible to outline a number of major 'areas,' or systems of genres and forms, which governed certain geographical and historical domains. The following simplified survey will present some typical features of the most important areas in the history of Hebrew poetic forms.

THE BIBLE

[The rhythms of Biblical poetry are rather complicated. The following remarks are here only as a general orientation.]

Biblical poetry, and perhaps biblical literature as a whole, provides a most flexible system of expressive forms. The basic principle is parallelism. A poetic unit consists of two or three versets (or 'cola') displaying traits of equivalence in their rhythmical make-up, their syntax, and their semantics, as well as in many concomitant features, such as the number of syllables in parallel words, sound-repetition, and morphology. In most cases, however, there is neither a permanent nor a fixed parallelism of whole versets. Of the three kinds of parallelism (rhythm, syntax, semantics), usually at least two will be applied. But we never know in advance which exactly, whether it will be complete or partial, word-for-word or verset-for-one-word; whether it will be based on synonymy, equivalence or opposition, in a direct or in a chiastic order. In any given pair of versets, there is a mutual reinforcement of the overlapping patterns of parallelism—of meaning, syntax, and stress—all of which are based on the same unit: the major word, which alone carries the phrasal stress and the lexical meaning. Since each verset consists of a small and tightly compressed group of words—usually two or three—the effect is conspicuous and strong. (In translation those are not words but rather word groups, as in the English Bible.) Two or three of any kind make up a basic unit, that is, a rhythmical unit that cannot be divided in sub-units.

The system of this type of rhythm may be described as *semantic-syntactic-accentual free parallelism*. It is based on a cluster of shifting principles, the

most prominent one being the semantic-rhetorical, the most obviously con-
strained one being the rhythmical. In later periods, the rhythm of this poetry
was taken to be basically accentual. Indeed, in biblical poetry the number of
stresses per verset, though free, is clearly restricted—usually 2, 3, (or 4), and
quite often equal or similar in both versets of a pair (e.g., 3 + 2, the so-called
'dirge meter'). The number of unstressed syllables between adjacent stresses
was perceived from the point of view of later and more rigorous meters as
entirely free. Yet, it was sometimes very much regulated as well: in one syntactical clause, two adjacent stresses were precluded, and if a word was too
long it had a secondary stress, thus providing usually 1 or 2 unstressed syllables between adjacent stresses. As a result, scholars have often perceived syllabic regularity in biblical versets; yet this is purely accidental. No systematic
rhyme is to be found in the Bible, but there is a very pervasive usage of sound
patterns, alliteration, sporadic end-rhyme, puns, acrostics and formulas, either embellishing or reinforcing the major principles of parallelism.

Here is an example of a poem of a rather ordered type:

וְתִשְׁמַע הָאָרֶץ אִמְרֵי־פִי.	הַאֲזִינוּ הַשָּׁמַיִם וַאֲדַבֵּרָה
תִּזַּל כַּטַּל אִמְרָתִי,	יַעֲרֹף כַּמָּטָר לִקְחִי
וְכִרְבִיבִים עֲלֵי־עֵשֶׂב.	כִּשְׂעִירִם עֲלֵי־דֶשֶׁא

(1) Give ear, O ye heavens, and I will speak;

(2) And hear, O earth, the words of my mouth.

(3) My doctrine shall drop as the rain,

(4) My speech shall distil as the dew,

(5) As the small rain upon the tender herb,

(6) And as the showers upon the grass.

(Deuteronomy 32:1–2; the Authorized Version)

There are 3 + 3 stresses in each of the first two pairs of versets, and 2 + 2
stresses in the last pair (though here the first words are long and could have
been pronounced as having a secondary stress, making the lines equivalent to
the previous ones).

The first two versets are almost entirely parallel. But the words הַאֲזִינוּ
('give ear') and וְתִשְׁמע (literally 'and she will hear') are synonymous in
meaning and not in morphology. 'I will speak' and 'the words of my mouth'
are neither synonymous nor syntactically equivalent, but their meanings are
parallel. The last pair is not an independent sentence, but each of its versets

is parallel to the second word of the previous pair and is governed by the previous verb.

There is variation in the equivalent words: 'heavens' and 'earth' are parallel by opposition; 'rain' and 'dew' both express fruition by water, but there is a gradual shift: one is strong and the other subtle, rather like two poles of one scale.

There is also a concatenation of the three pairs: versets 3 and 4 unfold the theme of the first pair (the unnamed object of the verb in 1 becomes the subject of phrases 3 and 4); versets 5 and 6 parallel the second word in 3 and 4. This almost perfect parallelism (changing in the following parts of the same poem) is variegated here too; thus the connotations of the words referring to water in the last four versets are chiastically ordered: the water is strong (3) - weak (4) - weak (5) - strong (6).

Many poetic texts in the Bible are, however, less symmetrical. The same principles are applied, though with greater freedom and flexibility, as one may observe in the opening of Isaiah 1. There is usually a greater variety in the number of versets in a group, as well as a second level of organization in which several groups of versets are combined in one long sentence. Symmetry, predominant in the previous example, is amply used by the prophets, but is usually engulfed in the wider flow of the argument. Thus, the formulaic opening of Isaiah 1:2, which is rather close to our previous example:

Hear, O heavens	and give ear, O earth:	for the Lord hath spoken
כִּי יהוה דִּבֵּר	וְהַאֲזִינִי אֶרֶץ	שִׁמְעוּ שָׁמַיִם

consists not of two but of three parts, the first two paralleling each other rigorously and the third remaining 'free,' with the resultant structure *aab*. A thorough analysis of the whole passage will show a complex network of equivalence relationships in which every word participates in one way or another, and which is reinforced by the pervading imagery and prophetic tone.

THE POST-BIBLICAL PERIOD

During the first centuries after the close of the Bible, various rhythmical forms were developed, with no single established rigorous system. Parallelism of phrases, reinforced by rhetorical figures, is discernible everywhere. It seems, however, that several kinds of more regular rhythms evolved during that period. The basic tendency was to regularize the biblical accentual tradition, primarily into a 4-stress pattern. There were, however, three distinctly different interpretations of this basic rhythm:

(a) A constant number of words per verset, e.g., four words as in some of the *Hekhalot* hymns and in a number of short Talmudic epigrams or poetic passages (e.g., גזע ישישים); or three words as in the *akeda* איתן למד דעת.

(b) A regular number of major stresses, whereby one stress often subordinated two words. Thus the *avoda* by Yose ben Yose lends itself to a reading in a regular pattern, as accepted by most scholars, of 4 + 4 (or 2 + 2/2 + 2) major stresses:

אַזְכִּיר גְּבוּרוֹת אֱלוֹהַ / נֶאְדָּרִי בַּכֹּחַ // יָחִיד וְאֵין עוֹד, / אֶפֶס וְאֵין שֵׁנִי.

The rules for imposing one stress on two words are rhythmical rather than syntactic. The length of the poem and the very possibility of reading it in this manner support such a reading.

(c) A 4-stress pattern is imposed on the line. Though there are often less than four words, the long words get two stresses each. This system is clearly opposed to the one mentioned in type (b). It creates a kind of alternating meter, which can be seen while a modern metrical scheme is applied.

בָּאֲרָזִים נָפְלָה שַׁלְהֶבֶת -
מַה יַּעֲשׂוּ אֲזוֹבֵי־הַקִּיר?
לִוְיָתָן בְּחַכָּה הוֹעֲלָה -
מַה יַּעֲשׂוּ דְּגֵי־הָרְקָק?

By imposing two stresses on 3-syllabic words as in modern poetry (and disregarding some half-syllables) we get something similar to a modern 4-trochee line. Applying similar principles (the details of which cannot be given here) we find that this meter is predominant throughout the writings of Ben Sirah. It creates a regularity in the number of syllables not unlike the one found in Syriac poetry. It was, however, by no means a rigid syllabic order in the sense of latter-day systems.

THE *PIYUT*

In Palestine under Byzantine rule, somewhere between the second and the sixth century, an entirely new kind of formal poetry developed, namely *piyut* (from the Greek *poyetan*), which served for liturgical purposes. In this tradition, highly formalized poetic cycles (*kerovot, yotserot*) were composed for the

Sabbaths and holidays. Basically these were complex cycles of strophic poems with rigid norms for a variety of formal devices assigned separately to each part of the cycle. Most of the poems were stringed on an acrostic of the 22 letters of the Hebrew alphabet (sometimes incomplete or containing the name of the poet).

The major forms developed in this poetry were: a strictly observed strophic structure; a permanent rhythm based on a fixed number of words in each line; and obligatory rhyme. At first, rhyme was everywhere and of all kinds—at the beginning of lines, at the end of lines, or throughout a line (like Old English and Germanic alliteration). Rhyme was based on repetition of either morphological endings or of words of the same root, or of semantic properties (e.g., all lines ending with names of rivers); or pairs of oppositions. See, for example, some of the rhymes in Yannai's כלו עינינו : [Loving One—enemy] אוֹהֵב - אוֹיֵב, [is loved—hated] אָהוּב - שָׂנוּי, [from within—from without] מִבַּיִת - מִחוּץ, [below—above] בְּמַטָּה - בְּמַעְלָה. Thus, the kinds of rhyme exhausted all aspects of the word. Some rhymes involved the whole word re-curring in all lines of a strophe or a poem. The basic and predominant inno-vation, however, was end-rhyme based on sound parallelism. It was a highly complex rhyme involving most of the sounds of the rhyming words. There were two complementary requirements: (1) in each rhyming word two out of the three consonants of the Hebrew root had to participate in the rhyme (with the vowels between them varying); (2) the last syllable of each rhyming word had to be identical as well. Each rhyme was repeated at the end of all the lines of a strophe, i.e. 4, 5, 8 or 9 times. For example, SHiRaTI - kaSHaRTI - SHoRaRTI - SHeRiRuTI; in this case SH and R are the rhyming root conso-nants, and TI the rhyming last syllable.

This rhyme, based on a discontinuous group of sounds yet including the entire last syllable, may be called 'discontinuous-terminal.'

Thus a meter based on the number of words generated a rhyming system based on the sound patterns covering the whole word. Such a system, of course, was very demanding for the poet and it was only made possible due to the highly 'difficult' style of the poetry of Eleazar ben Kallir (? sixth century) and his followers (especially in Italy in the tenth century) based on almost unlim-ited word innovations, allusions, and ellipses. With the transition to a simpler style, the difficult requirements of rhyme had to be dropped and only the last syllable repeated in all lines of a strophe remained as an absolute norm of He-brew medieval rhyme. This process was completed by the eleventh century.

The rhyming system of the Hebrew *piyut* was the earliest known massive, systematic and obligatory use of rhyme in poetry, and it is very plausible that through the Christian Syriac church employing Aramaic (a cognate language to Hebrew), and via Latin liturgy, the principle of rhyme was transferred to European poetry.

The basic forms of the Palestinian *piyut* were carried through Italy to the whole of medieval central and eastern Europe (Ashkenaz), where they dominated the creation of liturgical poetry until modern times (notably in the genre of the *seliha*—'supplication,' which favored 5-word lines in 4-line strophes, rhyming *aaaa bbbb cccc*).

HEBREW QUANTITATIVE POETRY IN SPAIN

The Hebrew poetry that flourished in Spain from the tenth to the fifteenth century was based on the Arabic system of poetics adapted to the Hebrew language. In secular poetry, the meter was quantitative, i.e. there was an orderly pattern of long and short syllables throughout a line repeated in all the lines of a poem (similar to the system used in classical Greek poetry). Under Arabic influence the Hebrew language here emphasized a difference between 'short' vowels (*shva*, *hataf*, and the conjunction *u*) and the regular vowels, considered as 'long.' This distinction disregarded the stress which was the major rhythmical factor in biblical poetry. The typical secular poem was a long poem (*qasida*) consisting of a chain of lines, each composed of two metrically equivalent versets (the *delet*, 'door,' and *soger*, 'lock'). Each poem had only one rhyme repeated throughout its dozens of lines as a string of beads (the metaphor used by the theoreticians; the Hebrew word for 'rhyme' means literally 'bead').

It should be noted that the schemes of such quantitative meters were of two types: the regular type, in which a short syllable alternates with a fixed number of long ones throughout the line except at the end of each *delet* and *soger*, where the feet may be shortened. For example, the most widespread meter was (from left to right):

$$\smile - - - / \smile - - - / \smile - - // \smile - - - / \smile - - - / \smile - -$$

and the alternating type, such as Judah Halevi's Zionide, where two basic feet alternate:

$$- - \smile - / - \smile - / - - \smile - / - \smile - //$$
$$- - \smile - / - \smile - / - - \smile - / - -$$

There was also a kind of free meter, with an irregular order of short and long syllables, which was, however, fixed in a permanent scheme and repeated in all the lines of a poem, as in many of the girdle poems (see below).

The Hebrew poets also employed a meter of 'long' syllables, avoiding the short ones altogether (*mishkal hatenu'ot*). On the other hand, they developed a syllabic meter, based on a regular number of syllables per line (6 or 8), which allowed the free use of short vowels but disregarded them as syllables.

At the same time, however, Hebrew poets in Spain favored a new form that had been developed in Spanish-Arabic poetry and was possibly based on Romance strophic songs. This was the so-called *muwashshah* or girdle poem, comprising two kinds of strophes: (1) each basic strophe had its own rhyme (or rhyme pattern), but was alternated with (2) girdles, strophes of a separate form (and meter) repeating one rhyme (or rhyme pattern) throughout the whole poem. The last girdle usually employed colloquial Arabic or colloquial Romance, thus indicating the melody to be used for the poem.

The girdle poem combined the effects of the string which unified the whole poem in a refrain-like manner with the love for variation in rhyming typical of European poetry as well as of the earlier Hebrew *piyut*. Thus a poem by Ibn Ghiyyat rhymes in the following manner (capitals represent the permanent, girdle rhymes; lower case letters—the changing rhymes of the basic strophes): AA/BA cd/cd/cd AA/BA ef/ef/ef AA/BA.

Elsewhere, in the Byzantine Empire and after it in the Balkans, the Ottoman Empire, northern Africa and other countries, Hebrew poetry showed strong influences on the one hand of the Spanish center and on the other of the traditional *piyut*, one based on a rigorous syllable counting and the other, on the contrary, on a fixed number of words per line. There were also influences of Turkish strophic forms, especially in songs. Rhyme was obligatory throughout, with very few exceptions.

ITALY AND OTHER COUNTRIES

Italy was located at the center of the Jewish world of the Middle Ages. Influences from all directions, from all Hebrew centers, were exerted on the writings of Hebrew poets there, with Italian poetry as a major influence. Rhymed and strophic Hebrew poetry written in Byzantine southern Italy in the ninth century in the vein of the Palestinian *piyut* appeared far earlier than rhymed poetry in Latin or Italian. The tradition of the *piyut* was predominant here until the fourteenth century. When Immanuel of Rome (c. 1261–after 1328) set out to write sonnets, much in the fashion of his Italian contemporaries, he found a language for secular poetry only in the Hebrew verse of Spain. As a result he transferred from Spain not only the poetic language and imagery but the quantitative metrical system as well, writing perfect ('Italian') sonnets in quantitative ('Arabic') meters. Sonnets, *ottava rima*, *terza rima*, and other Italian strophic forms combined with the language and meter of Arabic Spain for several centuries.

Little by little, Hebrew poetry in Italy lost its requirement for quantitative meters and became purely syllabic, much as Italian poetry was. In this case, however, unlike the Hebrew syllabic meter of Spain, all short vowels were counted as syllables. In fact, though the number of words with feminine endings is very small in Hebrew, these became the predominant rhyming form, activating rather artificial and archaic words in rhyming positions, all under the influence of Italian poetry. This syllabic system was adopted by the new movement of secular poetry known as the *Haskalah* (Enlightenment), which developed in Germany in the late eighteenth century and moved to Austria and Russia in the nineteenth century, and which laid the foundation of modern Hebrew literature.

ACCENTUAL-SYLLABIC METERS IN THE MODERN PERIOD

While accentual-syllabic (or tonic-syllabic) meter has dominated European poetry for several centuries now, it was accepted only recently, in about 1890, as the main form for Hebrew poetry. The first major poet consistently to use this metrical system, strongly influenced by Russian versification, was Bialik. In Hebrew, as in English, German and Russian poetry, it is based on a regular pattern of stressed and unstressed syllables. The Hebrew language, however, unlike English, has a vast number of long words of three or more syllables each. Thus rhythmical variation is achieved by skipping some of the metrical stresses rather than by stressing weak positions. For example, Iago's opening words in Act 1, Scene 2 of Shakespeare's *Othello* are, in English:

Though in the trade of war I have slain men,
Yet do I hold it very stuff o' the conscience
to do no contriv'd murder: I lack iniquity . . .

and in Alterman's Hebrew translation:

אָמְנָם בַּעֲבוֹדַת־הַמִּלְחָמָה

שָׁפַכְתִּי דְּמֵי־אָדָם, אַךְ לִבְּבִי

סוֹלֵד מֵרֶצַח־בְּמֵזִיד. אֲהָהּ...

Iambic pentameter is used in both versions but the rhythm is quite different. The following diagram divides the actual graphic words of each language by bars and uses a dash for each possible stress:

English

| – | ⌣ | ⌣ | – | ⌣ | – | – | – | – | – |

| – | – | – | – | – | – | ⌣ | – | ⌣ | – ⌣ |

| ⌣ | – | – | ⌣ – | – ⌣ | ⌣ | – | ⌣ – ⌣ ⌣ |

Hebrew (from left to right)

| ⌣ – | ⌣ ⌣ ⌣ – | ⌣ ⌣ ⌣ – |

| ⌣ – ⌣ | – | ⌣ – | ⌣ | ⌣ ⌣ – |

| ⌣ – | ⌣ – ⌣ | ⌣ ⌣ – | ⌣ – |

Whereas the first line in English has ten words, in Hebrew it has only three, and whereas in English it is possible to stress seven of these, in Hebrew only three stresses are allowed. Such an irregular line as the third in Shakespeare's original is not permitted in Hebrew metrical verse, which complies with the rules of the very rigorous Russian tradition. Its great variety is achieved by skipping stresses in various places and changing the divisions between words from line to line.

The example given here is in the Israeli (or Sephardic) pronunciation, now dominant in Israel. The emergence, however, of accentual-syllabic meters in Hebrew poetry, with Bialik and Tchernikhovsky in the last decade of the nineteenth century, was in a different dialect, that of the Ashkenazi pronunciation developed in medieval Europe. The basic rule of that pronunciation is that whenever possible, stress should fall on the penultimate syllable. When the penultimate syllable is a half-syllable, the stress recedes to the third from the end; only monosyllable words are ultimately stressed.

The shift from the Ashkenazi to the Israeli pronunciation caused an extremely painful crisis in Hebrew poetry, especially since the poetic values of

Hebrew poetry in its modern phase were placed heavily on meter and sound in the best Russian tradition. Though for centuries European Jews had prayed and studied Hebrew from early childhood in one of several Ashkenazi dialects, the pioneers in the Land of Israel since the beginning of the twentieth century have spoken Sephardic. In Hebrew poetry, however, the Sephardic (or 'Israeli') dialect became dominant only in the late 1920s. The stress on the last syllables of most words sounded harsh and 'masculine' to the poets of the previous generation, who preferred 'melodious' poetry with feminine rhymes. Indeed, it was to them a new language and they wrote rather artificial poems in the spoken dialect. Some poets tried to translate their own poetry from Hebrew into new Hebrew, involving themselves in a reshuffling of sound-meaning relationships that rarely succeed.

MODES OF MODERNISM

The dangers of a mechanical and overpronounced meter in a language with a strong ultimate stress were met by breaking away from the rigors of symmetry. The freeing of rhythm in Hebrew poetry took two major directions. Under Russian influence, a verse-form was developed, employing a metrical scheme with a large number of deviations, as if hovering between anapests and iambs. This poetry, influenced by the poetics of Akhmatova, Blok, Yesenin and Mayakovsky, relied heavily on sound effects and rich rhyming. Though the norm for Hebrew rhyme accepted one stressed syllable at the end of a line (as is common in English), poets in the Shlonsky tradition excelled in highly complex and very rich and innovative rhymes, based on a discontinuous set of sounds going from the end of a line far back into its middle. For example, Alterman uses rhymes such as:

KSuMÁ HI - KoS HaMÁIm; LeKH uSHMÁ - haHaSHMÁL; SiPuNÉKHA - kaSe PaNÉKHA.

Again Hebrew poetry, as in the *piyut* of Yannai and Kallir, moulded its rhymes not on the last syllable but on the whole word, based on the nature of the Hebrew word, which has only consonants as part of its lexical core and vowels belong merely to the morphological system. This rhyming principle, founded on the nature of the Hebrew language, created a tension between richness of sound on the one hand and discord on the other, in the best tradition of Mayakovsky and Pasternak. As the rhyming sounds are discontinuous, and require identity of the stressed vowels but not necessarily of the final sounds, it may be called 'discontinuous-accentual' rhyme.

A different trend was the free verse based on a paucity of rhymes and a strong deviation from any metrical background, playing essentially on variation of phrases, long and short lines, and in general on local rhythmical effects or on the rhythms of prose. The first wave of this development appeared in the 1920s (notably with David Vogel) under the impact of German Expressionism. A second wave developed in the late 1950s and 1960s with the transition from a Russian-oriented metrical poetry to a poetry based on understatement and imagery, primarily under the influence of English modernism.

RHYME: A SURVEY

Rhyme was dominant in Hebrew poetry at least from the sixth to the twentieth century. In the eighteenth century, under European influence, unrhymed poetic drama and epic poetry appeared, and in the early twentieth century Tchernikhovsky's unrhymed idylls and some of Bialik's quasi-biblical unrhymed poems. In the second decade of the twentieth century, with the impact of Expressionism, the predilection for systematic rhyming in lyrical poetry disappeared. This trend has strengthened in the last generation.

Though often highly inventive under the constraints of rhyme, poets were never free to select the rhyming principles. In the rhymed *piyut* (and only in some genres) one could either repeat the same word throughout or find as many rhyming words as lines in a strophe (4, 5, 8 or 9), according to the requirements of the discontinuous-terminal rhyme of the 'difficult' Kallirian tradition.

At a later stage of the *piyut*, the requirement for rhyming two root-consonants was dropped and only the last syllable remained mandatory in rhyme, including however the preceding consonant (*consonne d'appui*) but disregarding stress. E.g., kaROV-la'aROV, shéLEG-medaLÉG (though in other languages OV, EG is perfectly sufficient). This terminal rhyme became the obligatory Hebrew rhyme in Spain and elsewhere throughout the medieval period. As stress was disregarded in the meter, so it played no role in rhyme. Only in Italy did rhyme become stress-bound, involving all sounds from the stressed vowel onwards, with a distinction between feminine rhyme (shÉLEG-pÉLEG) and masculine rhyme (medalÉG-orÉG). This, basically, has remained the rhyme of modern Hebrew poetry in accentual-syllabic meters to this day.

In modernism, however, especially under Russian influence, a rich rhyme was developed, inexact in its final syllable, discontinuous in its set of sounds, covering the whole word again (as in the *piyut*) or even several words, but stress-bound, as the meter depends primarily on stress (as in Alterman's examples above).

The four major rhyming possibilities shown in Table I, moving clockwise, were employed in Hebrew poetry throughout its history.

Similar radical changes occurred in rhyme-patterning. The *piyut* developed a very rigorous system of strophic structures. Each strophe, however, allowed for only one rhyme: *aaaa bbbb cccc*. In Spain the major tradition required one rhyme throughout the whole poem (sometimes, 10, 40 or 60 lines). Under the impact of Italian strophic poetry (with some Spanish precursors) alternation of several rhymes in one strophe was introduced: e.g. *abab; aba bcb cdc*. Reinforced by the Russian tradition of masculine-feminine alternation in rhyme, this has remained the predominant rhyme pattern.

SYNOPSIS

Thus Hebrew poetry turned full circle (see Table II). It started in the Bible (I) with a system of phrase parallelism based on several of the major components of the phrase: semantics, syntax, phrasal stress. In the *piyut* (II), a meter of a fixed number of words and a rhyme based on the sound pattern of the whole word was developed. In medieval Spain (III), the system went down to the lower unit of syllable; rhyme was based on the last syllable only. Syllabic meter in Hebrew shifted from a quantitative principle (in Spain) to the number of

Table I: **Systems of Rhyme**

	− continuous	+ continuous
− stress	1. discontinuous-terminal (*piyut*) aReMÁ – hehRíMA – RuMÁ	2. terminal Spain shéLEG – medaLÉG
+ stress	4. discontinuous-accentual (Modernism) SHÉLEg – SHokÉLEt	3. terminal-accentual (modern age) ShÉLEG – pÉLEG/ medalÉG – orÉG

Table II: The Major Systems of Hebrew Verse (in their logical and chronological order)

Length of Line	Free	Fixed	
Basis of Meter	**Phrase**	**Word**	**Syllable**
ANTIQUITY AND MEDIEVAL (From phrase to syllable)	I. *Bible*: free accentual meter / varying semantic-syntactic-rhythmic parallelism in phrase groups	II. *Rhymed Piyut*: word-meter / number of words	III. *Spain*: quantitative meter / number of syllables + order of long/short
	Rhyme: sporadic	rich, discontinuous, based on whole word	based on last syllable
			IV. *Late Italy & Haskalah*: syllabic meter / number of syllables
			Rhyme: stress-bound
			V. *Modern*: accentual-syllabic meter / number of syllables + order of stressed/unstressed
MODERN AGE (From syllable to phrase)	VII. *Modernist*: Free Verse	VI. *Modernist*: accentual 'net' (in the Russian tradition) / number of major stresses + deviating from syllabic order	stress-bound
	changing balance of phrase groups	rich, discontinuous, based on whole word	
	Rhyme: not obligatory		

syllables (in Italy, IV) to an accentual syllable system (in modern poetry, V). Hence the system moved back (at an accelerated speed): at first to a poetry leaning strongly on the number of major stresses in the line (in Russian-influenced Hebrew modernism, VI) and a rhyme covering the whole sound structure of the rhyming words, then to an English-influenced free verse (VII) based on a changing balance of phrase groups. Of course, this schematic cycle is quite abstract and simplified; the subordinated factors always played an additional and often important role. And in recent years a kaleidoscope of forms has existed concurrently, competing with and complementing each other.

The awareness which a Hebrew poet may have of the relativity of systems of versification and rhyming does not help him in choosing whatever he needs for his particular poem. Indeed, biblical verse does seem 'free' from the point of view of the modern reader trained on strictly syllable-counting accentual-syllabic verse. It is, however, impossible to imitate, except for small passages or for specific stylistic purposes, as much as it is impossible for an English dramatist to write Shakespearean iambic pentameters. Each system has evolved major verse forms with very typical combinations of syntactic and semantic, as well as rhythmical features. This combination, once automatized, has as it were 'exhausted' the possibilities of the system. Like their European and American contemporaries, Hebrew poets today either write basically free poetry, leaning heavily on the rhythmical formation of each line and passage, or are in search of a renewed form which would not sound epigonic on one hand and, at the same time, would be able to encompass the rhythms of the new spoken language.

SOURCES OF THE CHAPTERS

Chapter 1. "Theses On the Historical Context of the Modern Jewish Revolution," JSQ [*Jewish Studies Quarterly*] Vol.10 (2003), No. 4, 300–319.

Chapter 3: "The Only Yesterday of *Only Yesterday*," in S. Y. Agnon, *Only Yesterday: A Novel*, translated by Barbara Harshav, Princeton, N.J.: Princeton University Press, 2000, pp. 7–29.

Chapter 4: "American Yiddish Poetry and its Background," in: Benjamin and Barbara Harshav, *American Yiddish Poetry*, Stanford: Stanford University Press, 2008, pp. 1–67.

Chapter 5: "Preface and Introduction," in: Herman Kruk, *The Last Days of the Jerusalem of Lithuania: Chronicles from the Vilna Ghetto and the Camps, 1939–1944*, edited and introduced by Benjamin Harshav; translated by Barbara Harshav, YIVO Institute for Jewish Research/ Yale University Press, 2002.

Chapter 7: "Natan Alterman," pp. 106–119, and "Abba Kovner," pp. 148–151, in S. Burnshaw, T. Carmi, and E. Spicehandler, eds., *The Modern Hebrew Poem Itself*, New York: Holt, Rinehart and Winston, 1965.

Chapter 8: "The Role of Language in Modern Art: On Texts and Subtexts in Chagall's Paintings," *Modernism/Modernity*, Vol. 1, No. 2 (April 1994), 51–87.

Chapter 9: A. Sutzkever, *Selected Poetry and Prose*, translated from the Yiddish by Barbara and Benjamin Harshav, with an Introduction by Benjamin Harshav, Berkeley: University of California Press, 1991.

Chapter 10: "Note on the Systems of Hebrew Versification," in *The Penguin Book of Hebrew Verse*, edited and translated by T. Carmi, Penguin Books, 1981.

Note: The sources are signed either Benjamin Harshav or Benjamin Hrushovski.

.